Epica Book 21
Europe's
Best Advertising

DIRECTOR
Andrew Rawlins

EDITOR
Patrick Taschler

ART DIRECTOR
Patrick Taschler

SYNOPSES
Mark Tungate

EDITORIAL ASSISTANT
Francelina Pacaric

COVER IMAGE
Scott Kleinman
(Getty Images)

PUBLISHER
AVA Publishing S.A.
enquiries@avabooks.ch

DISTRIBUTION
North America
Sterling Publishing Co.
www.sterlingpub.com
All other countries
Thames & Hudson Ltd.
sales@thameshudson.co.uk

PRODUCTION
AVA Book Production Pte Ltd.
production@avabooks.com.sg

Printed in Singapore

Contents

Foreword
by Juan Cabral

When I started working in advertising I thought that ideas where the driving force of the industry. Silly me. Of course I later figured out that it was all about numbers.

But I have to say, that for the last couple of years, I've realized that it's not about numbers anymore. Numbers evolved into something else. Something worse.

The real driving force of the industry is Fear.

Fear is the real client these days. What a shame.

Clients deal with too much pressure. Almost to the point where they can't think for themselves – it's like something else controls their heads. That's why ads are becoming more mediocre at a time when media is blossoming.

So there's more mediocrity around us.

But I have to say, I've been pretty lucky with a few of the clients I've worked with lately. I would go even further and say thanks to them.

For leaving fear outside the meeting room.

For avoiding safety (there is no safety).

And for thinking with their hearts (at least for a brief moment – that takes some guts).

Because it's about winning people's hearts, not their heads.

That's where healthy brands live, in the audience's hearts.

Agencies and clients need to work hard to create bubbles where ideas can be fertile. Where brands can dream – even for a bit. In those sporadic moments I remind myself where the real force of the industry lies.

Juan Cabral,
Creative Director, Partner, Fallon London

Epica d'Or (Film)

Epica d'Or (Press)

Epica d'Or (Outdoor)

Epica d'Or (Interactive)

EPICA D'OR (FILM)	FALLON LONDON	CADBURY'S DAIRY MILK CHOCOLATE "GORILLA"
EPICA D'OR (PRESS)	MARCEL, PARIS	FRANCE 24 "BEYOND THE NEWS" CAMPAIGN
EPICA D'OR (OUTDOOR)	BBDO DÜSSELDORF	PEPSI "DARE FOR MORE" CAMPAIGN
EPICA D'OR (INTERACTIVE)	FARFAR, STOCKHOLM	DIESEL UNDERWEAR "HEIDIES" WEBSITE

FILM WINNERS

FOOD	LOWEFRIENDS, COPENHAGEN	FELIX KETCHUP "TOP DOWN"
CONFECTIONERY & SNACKS	FALLON LONDON	CADBURY'S DAIRY MILK CHOCOLATE "GORILLA"
ALCOHOLIC DRINKS	ABBOTT MEAD VICKERS BBDO, LONDON	GUINNESS "TIPPING POINT"
NON-ALCOHOLIC DRINKS	& CO., COPENHAGEN	CAFE NOIR "RABBIT"
COMMUNICATION SERVICES	DDB OSLO	TELENOR "THE ESSAY"
TRANSPORT & TOURISM	DDB AMSTERDAM	DUTCH RAILWAYS "NEW TIMETABLE"
RETAIL SERVICES	WALKER, ZÜRICH	FLEUROP INTERFLORA "ANNIVERSARY"
FINANCIAL SERVICES	DDB AMSTERDAM	CENTRAAL BEHEER "AMBULANCE"
PUBLIC INTEREST	TBWA/PARIS	AMNESTY INTERNATIONAL "SIGNATURES"
AUDIOVISUAL EQUIPMENT & ACCESSORIES	THE JUPITER DRAWING ROOM, CAPE TOWN	MUSICA DVDs "LITTLE BRITAIN"
HOMES, FURNISHINGS & APPLIANCES	NORDPOL+ HAMBURG	EPURON WIND ENERGY "POWER OF WIND"
HOUSEHOLD MAINTENANCE	HEIMAT, BERLIN	HORNBACH "HAUNTED"
TOILETRIES & HEALTH CARE	JWT, PARIS	WILKINSON QUATTRO TITANIUM "FIGHT FOR KISSES"
CLOTHING & FABRICS	NITRO, LONDON	NIKE RUSSIA "BALLERINA"
FOOTWEAR & PERSONAL ACCESSORIES	GREY&TRACE, BARCELONA	PILOT V LIQUID LIGHT MARKER "HISTORY OF LIGHT"
AUTOMOBILES	CONTRAPUNTO, MADRID	CHRYSLER VOYAGER "IT IS MINE"
AUTOMOTIVE & ACCESSORIES	DDB BERLIN	VOLKSWAGEN SERVICE "CUCKOO CLOCK"
MEDIA	JUNG VON MATT, BERLIN	13TH STREET "SUNDAY ROAST"
RECREATION & LEISURE	DDB LONDON	VOLKSWAGEN/INDEPENDANT CINEMA "TOY STORY"
PROFESSIONAL EQUIPMENT & SERVICES	DDB OSLO	HYDRO "TRAIN"

PRINT WINNERS

FOOD	SHALMOR AVNON AMICHAY/Y&R, TEL AVIV	HEINZ KETCHUP "DINER"
CONFECTIONERY & SNACKS	DUVAL GUILLAUME BRUSSELS	BAZOOKA BUBBLE GUM "AIRBAG"
DAIRY PRODUCTS	PUBLICIS, ZÜRICH	EMMENTALER CHEESE "HOLES"
ALCOHOLIC DRINKS	DDB&CO, ISTANBUL	VILLA DOLUCA WINES "GLASSES" CAMPAIGN
NON-ALCOHOLIC DRINKS	BBDO DÜSSELDORF	PEPSI "DARE FOR MORE" CAMPAIGN
COMMUNICATION SERVICES	KOLLE REBBE WERBEAGENTUR, HAMBURG	GOOGLE EARTH "CHANGING PERSPECTIVES" CAMPAIGN
TRANSPORT & TOURISM	KING, STOCKHOLM	SJ RAILWAYS "ENVIRONMENTAL IMPACT"
RETAIL SERVICES	DDB LONDON	HARVEY NICHOLS "CATFIGHT" CAMPAIGN
FINANCIAL SERVICES	ANR.BBDO, GOTHENBURG/STOCKHOLM	FOLKSAM "HAIRY BABY GIRLS" CAMPAIGN
PUBLIC INTEREST	KOLLE REBBE WERBEAGENTUR, HAMBURG	MISEREOR CHARITY "WAR ORPHANS" CAMPAIGN
AUDIOVISUAL EQUIPMENT & ACCESSORIES	TBWA\VIENNA	NIEDERMEYER "SUPERZOOM"
HOMES, FURNISHINGS & APPLIANCES	DDB OSLO	IKEA "FASHION" CAMPAIGN
HOUSEHOLD MAINTENANCE	TBWA\ESPANA, BARCELONA	SPONTEX "SWIMMING POOL" & "BOAT"
BEAUTY PRODUCTS & SERVICES	YOUNG & RUBICAM, FRANKFURT AM MAIN	GARD HAIR SPRAY "DANDELION"
TOILETRIES & HEALTH CARE	DRAFTFCB KOBZA WERBEAGENTUR, VIENNA	CONDOMI "ULTRA THIN"
CLOTHING & FABRICS	& CO., COPENHAGEN	JBS UNDERWEAR "NAKED MEN" CAMPAIGN
FOOTWEAR & PERSONAL ACCESSORIES	SERVICEPLAN MUNICH/HAMBURG	STABILO BOSS "DETAILS" CAMPAIGN
AUTOMOBILES	CONTRAPUNTO, MADRID	SMART FORTWO "FOREST", "FIELD" & "STONES"
AUTOMOTIVE & ACCESSORIES	1861 UNITED, MILAN	YAMAHA MARINE "AIRPLANE"
MEDIA	MARCEL, PARIS	FRANCE 24 "BEYOND THE NEWS" CAMPAIGN
RECREATION & LEISURE	KNSK WERBEAGENTUR, HAMBURG	HANSAPARK "ARE WE THERE YET?"
INDUSTRIAL & AGRICULTURAL PRODUCTS	SERVICEPLAN MUNICH/HAMBURG	HOFFMANN MINERAL "WORLD OF MINERALS" CAMPAIGN
PROFESSIONAL EQUIPMENT & SERVICES	ADVICO YOUNG & RUBICAM, ZÜRICH	NJP TONSTUDIO "POWER OF SOUND" CAMPAIGN
PRESCRIPTION PRODUCTS	PALING WALTERS, LONDON	CANESTEN HC "BRA" & "PANTS"

TECHNIQUE WINNERS

MEDIA INNOVATION	EURO RSCG DÜSSELDORF	DULCOLAX LAXATIVE "TOILET PAPER ROLL"
CONSUMER DIRECT	LEO BURNETT FRANKFURT	ORTHODONTIST DR. RATHENOW "PACIFIERS"
BUSINESS TO BUSINESS DIRECT	ARNOLD WORLDWIDE, MILAN	ARNOLD GUERILLA "VOODOO KIT"
ADVERTISING PHOTOGRAPHY	TBWA\PARIS	AMNESTY INTERNATIONAL "CHILD SOLDIERS" CAMPAIGN
ILLUSTRATION & GRAPHICS	McCANN ERICKSON LONDON	HEINZ SALAD CREAM "POURABLE SUNSHINE" CAMPAIGN
PUBLICATIONS	BRUKETA & ZINIC, ZAGREB	PODRAVKA ANNUAL REPORT "WELL DONE"
PACKAGING DESIGN	DEPOT WPF BRAND & IDENTITY, MOSCOW	COMILFO CHOCOLATES

INTERACTIVE WINNERS

WEBSITES (DURABLES)	FARFAR, STOCKHOLM	DIESEL UNDERWEAR "HEIDIES"
WEBSITES (NON-DURABLES)	LOWE BRINDFORS, STOCKHOLM	STELLA "LE COURAGE"
WEBSITES (BUSINESS TO BUSINESS)	FARFAR, STOCKHOLM	NOKIA N800 "THE INTERNET WALK"
ONLINE ADS	NETTHINK, MADRID	ADIDAS "IMPOSSIBLE IS NOTHING"
ONLINE FILMS	FAR FROM HOLLYWOOD, COPENHAGEN	DANISH ROAD SAFETY "SPEED BANDITS"
INTEGRATED CAMPAIGNS	FORSMAN & BODENFORS, GOTHENBURG	NEW SWEDISH ENCYCLOPEDIA CAMPAIGN

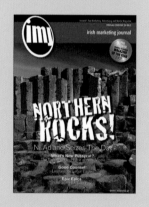

The jury

The Epica jury is made up of journalists from leading advertising magazines in Europe and the EMEA region. A total of 34 publications from 27 countries were represented on the jury in 2007.

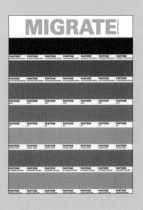

AUSTRIA
Extra Dienst

BELGIUM
Pub

CZECH REPUBLIC
Strategie

DENMARK
Markedsføring

ESTONIA
Best Marketing

FINLAND
Markkinointi & Mainonta

FRANCE
CB News

GERMANY
Lürzer's International Archive
Werben und Verkaufen

GREAT BRITAIN
Creative Review
Marketing Week
The Drum

GREECE
+ Design
Marketing Week

HUNGARY
Kreatív

IRELAND
IMJ

ITALY
NC Nuova Comunicazione
Pubblicitá Italia
Pubblico

THE NETHERLANDS
Marketing Tribune

NORWAY
Kampanje

POLAND
Media & Marketing Polska

PORTUGAL
Briefing

ROMANIA
Campaign

RUSSIA
Advertising Ideas

SERBIA
New Moment

SLOVAKIA
Stratégie

SLOVENIA
MM

SOUTH AFRICA
Migrate

SPAIN
El Publicista

SWEDEN
Resumé

SWITZERLAND
Persönlich
Werbe Woche

TURKEY
Marketing Türkiye

Photos: Resumé/Epica

Annual report

The awards ceremony took place at the Rival Hotel in Stockholm on January 11th, 2008. The event was hosted by Resumé, Sweden's leading advertising magazine.

A total of 732 companies from 47 countries participated in the 2007 Epica awards. Entries increased 3% to 5.642 vs. 5.461 the previous year. For the first time in 2007, four grand prix were attributed.

Fallon London won the film Epica d'Or with their Cadbury's Dairy Milk 'Gorilla' commercial. The film was created and directed by Juan Cabral. This marked the first-ever award for 'Gorilla'; a film that went on to enjoy success in many other international festivals.

The Epica d'Or for press advertising went to Marcel, Paris for their France 24 'Beyond the News' campaign and BBDO Düsseldorf won the outdoor grand prix with their Pepsi 'Dare for More' poster campaign. Epica's first interactive grand prix was won by Farfar, Stockholm for the Diesel underwear 'Heidies' operation.

Germany was the most successful country in 2007, as it was the previous year, with a total of 100 awards, including 14 gold. The UK dropped from 2nd to 3rd position, behind Sweden and just ahead of France. South Africa, present for the first time in 2007, finished 6th overall in the country rankings. It was also a good year for Croatia which won its first Epica gold.

Jung von Matt was the most successful agency with 12 awards from its five German offices, ahead of DDB Amsterdam with 10 prizes. TBWA\Paris, which had lead the rankings since 2004, dropped to third position. DDB Oslo was the only agency to win gold in 3 categories. This helped DDB to top the network rankings with 11 winners from six countries, ahead of BBDO with 6 from four countries.

All the gold, silver and bronze winners are shown in the Epica Book, together with a selection of other short-listed entries.

	Entrants	Entries	Gold	Silver	Bronze
Austria	12	111	2	2	4
Belarus	1	2	-	-	-
Belgium	26	169	1	4	6
Bosnia-Herzegovina	1	3	-	-	-
Bulgaria	7	39	-	-	1
Croatia	7	26	1	-	1
Czech Republic	11	76	-	2	-
Denmark	17	92	4	3	8
Egypt	1	1	-	1	-
Estonia	1	1	-	-	-
Finland	24	165	-	4	4
France	33	431	5	26	14
Georgia	1	1	-	-	-
Germany	94	982	14	54	32
Greece	23	119	-	1	3
Hungary	8	47	-	-	1
Iceland	4	23	-	-	-
Ireland	12	69	-	5	-
Israel	9	76	1	2	3
Italy	38	280	2	6	4
Kingdom of Bahrain	1	2	-	-	-
Kuwait	2	5	-	-	-
Latvia	2	4	-	-	-
Lebanon	7	60	-	-	3
Lithuania	3	15	-	-	-
Luxembourg	0	0	-	-	-
Macedonia	3	9	-	-	-
Mongolia	1	1	-	-	-
Netherlands	35	281	2	19	9
Norway	12	117	3	4	7
Poland	14	56	-	1	4
Portugal	11	72	-	2	5
Romania	25	146	-	3	3
Russia	22	75	1	3	1
Saudi Arabia	1	5	-	-	-
Serbia	5	17	-	1	-
Slovakia	6	37	-	1	1
Slovenia	12	41	-	1	-
South Africa	16	71	1	12	4
Spain	25	210	5	6	4
Sweden	86	685	7	26	22
Switzerland	18	316	3	5	8
Tunisia	1	4	-	-	1
Turkey	19	124	1	1	4
United Arab Emirates	13	115	-	1	2
United Kingdom	50	420	8	25	13
Ukraine	11	39	-	-	1
USA	1	2	-	-	-
Total	732	5642	61	221	173

a GLASS and a HALF FULL PRODUCTION

HE'S BEEN WAITING FOR
THIS MOMENT FOR ALL HIS LIFE.

TONIGHT 22.30. CHANNEL 4.

Getting the love back

by Lewis Blackwell

It has a massive entry on Wikipedia, has been uploaded thousands of times on YouTube and has been viewed, commented on or shared many millions of times over the web. It delights many and annoys a few. It is the spot that won the Epica d'Or for film: Gorilla, for Cadbury's Dairy Milk.

Not every Epica d'Or winner can be seen as paradigm-shifting, or emblematic of an era, but for this film it would not be excessive to make such claims. The way that Gorilla works as an advertising film is clearly of this time, this late web 2.0 era, and could not quite have happened in this way before. It is a powerful, contained spot with an advertising message – traditional in those terms – and yet succeeds because it is also a fantastic piece of entertainment designed to take off and grow organically as word-of-mouth content over the internet.

Did I sense that somebody hasn't seen it?

OK, a quick summary. Open on close-up of a gorilla, notice soundtrack coming in of 'In the Air Tonight', Phil Collins' early 1980s smoochy soft-rock anthem. Gradually, oh-so-slowly pull back to reveal that the gorilla is sitting at a drum kit. His face twitches sensitively, he flexes his shoulders and neck… then sets to with crashing drumsticks in a fearsome display in time with the famous drum break that surges into the song. After nearly 90 seconds cut to a end-title screen that advises this is a Glass and a Half Full Production. That's it. Branding? Product

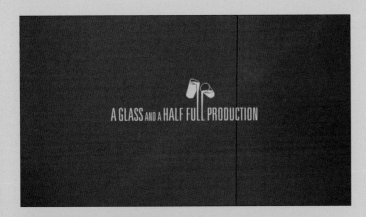

shot? Forget it… unless you spotted that the studio backdrop was a kind of nice purple, a similar colour to the Cadbury's Dairy Milk wrapper.

It's pure fun, a beautiful selling of innocent indulgence – which, of course, is what eating a bar of well-made chocolate is about. But some people, to judge by the numerous blogs, don't like it: they don't think advertising should be this much fun, they think it is pure entertainment, they don't see how a client could have bought it. Over to Chris Willingham, Client Services Director at Fallon London, the agency behind it, to justify this allegedly unjustified creation of joy:

"The client had a situation where the brand was losing share and traction in the marketplace. It was a national institution of a sort, but it was losing its way. We were asked to 'get the love back' and that's where the work began."

For the Fallon and Cadbury's team, the 'big idea' of the campaign is not the specific film but the Glass and a Half Full Production concept: this is built out of the brand promise of 1.5 glasses of real milk in every bar. With this promise embedded in the production-company idea, they realized they had a franchise to please people and the basis for a great campaign.

With this positioning comes a wonderful opportunity for creative thinking. Bring in the big guns, bring in Juan Cabral, the Fallon creative director famously behind Sony Bravia 'Balls'. He proceeded to write and shoot the resulting Gorilla spot, his first film as director, with the support of Blink Productions. While it looks a simple shoot, one gorilla-suited guy in a studio playing the drums, as ever minimalism is often the hardest thing to bring off. That gorilla suit is just about the best you can hire on the planet – brought over from Los Angeles, with no less than three handlers required to operate! That's one inside and two controlling the subtle eye contact and little twitches.

Even before shooting, the agency knew the film would never run much in conventional media. The idea was to achieve reach and penetration through ingenious seeding of the 90-second spot in key programming breaks. Then the frequency would be achieved online. However, they didn't just achieve what they set out to do: instead, the spot has played many millions of times more than they hoped and has reached deeply into a broader range of customers than the 20-29 year olds targeted. No wonder sales have shot up.

There have been rumours that the client didn't originally get the idea and asked for a few extra branding changes. But Willingham refutes this: "We always had a gorilla in mind, playing along to that track. It was brilliantly set out as a treatment by Juan early on and changed very little in being executed."

Top executives at Cadbury have been quoted as saying they weren't sure about how the film would work. They should be commended for having the confidence to stand back and let it run, to embrace and even experiment a little with the potential of a great creative and media idea.

"We say that you have to think digital at all times, offline and online," concludes Willingham. "It's all about interactivity… we ask ourselves: is it stretchy and malleable?"

Yes, it's stretchy and malleable. It's great fun, a great winner and I for one can't wait to see where they take this campaign next. There's not much advertising you can say that of.

Lewis Blackwell is a creative and brand adviser, former SVP Group Creative Director of Getty Images and editor/publisher of Creative Review, and a renowned author and speaker.

13

BEYOND THE NEWS FRANCE 24

DARFUR, BEYOND THE NEWS

THE NEW 24 HR INTERNATIONAL NEWS CHANNEL
LA NOUVELLE CHAINE D'INFORMATION INTERNATIONALE 24H/24
القناة الجديدة 24 ساعة للأخبار الدولية

FRANCE 24

2006 launch ad

In the eye of the news

by Mark Tungate

If the purpose of a news and current affairs channel is to make you think – to open your eyes to matters of which you may not have been aware – shouldn't the channel's advertising do the same thing? That's certainly the case of French agency Marcel's Epica d'Or-winning press campaign for France 24.

The ads are not flashy, jocular or an "instant fix". In fact, at first sight, they are somewhat baffling: giant machines constructed from repeating and interlocking photographs. Look more closely, however, and you'll see that the images are literally connected: as your eye moves from one to another, you soon grasp that they tell the real story behind major issues.

What's the connection between the Twin Towers, George Bush, Saddam, war machines and barrels of oil? And how do Wall Street and the automobile industry affect our ability to reverse climate change? Why are children starving in Third World countries while drug companies spend a fortune researching cures for disease? Each ad lets the reader join the dots. The slogan reveals that France 24 takes us "Beyond the news".

Launched in December 2006, France 24 has always be

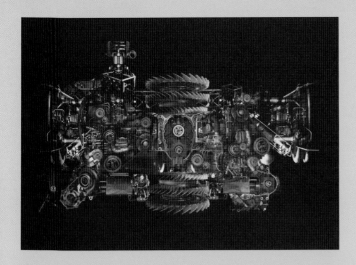

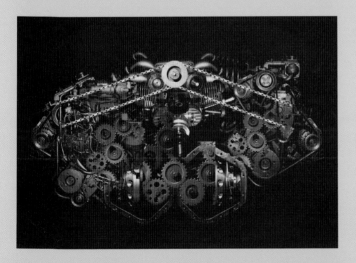

an unusual channel. Broadcasting simultaneously in French, English and Arabic – with Spanish to follow – its goal is to provide a French perspective on international news, as opposed to the Anglo-Saxon vision of CNN and BBC World.

More to the point, it specialises in analysis rather than sensationalism, which is why its launch campaign featured an iceberg: France 24 shows what's hidden below the surface.

"We wanted to build on the idea of the iceberg, but in a more allusive and subtle way," says Frédéric Témin, who with his fellow creative director Anne de Maupeou heads Marcel. "France 24 is not all about scoops, but rather about taking a more considered approach to the news. The campaign expresses this by making the reader do some of the work. There are a number of immediately accessible images that plunge you into the picture, but then you have to take a closer look to understand exactly how they relate to one another."

Anne de Maupeou admits that she and Témin are fans of the long-running British campaign for The Economist, which uses clever word-play to get readers' brains ticking over. She added: "The channel's target audience of educated professionals allows you to take a more intellectual approach. People like being asked to think about advertising occasionally."

Copywriter Eric Jannon and art director Dimitri Guerassimov faced the difficult task of creating a campaign that was challenging – but not too challenging. Guerassimov explains: "The basic idea is that you see the gears of information engaging. But you have to be able to view it at a purely graphic level too, so the machines can't be too dense or ugly."

If the images became too complicated, the reader would give up. The stunning black background and the silvery beauty of the imaginary machines became the bait. "It had to look superb purely as an image in order to pull the reader in for a closer look," says de Maupeou, who confirms that there was "a lot of post-production" before the ideal versions were achieved.

Frédéric Témin adds: "The great thing about today's technology is that you can create beautiful images practically from your living room. This campaign may not have been given the go-ahead so easily by the client if we'd just turned up with a couple of sketches. We were able to make a version that was sufficiently clean and complete to convince him."

The "him" in question was Alain de Pouzilhac, the former adman who is now CEO of France 24. Témin reveals that de Pouzilhac was delighted by the impact of the "iceberg" image that launched the channel. Even though that first image was also created by Marcel, there was pressure on the agency to top it. "When the new campaign came out, we were pleased by the positive reaction in the press and online," says Témin.

15

Discussing the agency's working methods, Témin observes that they do not spend too much time devising complex new theories of advertising, or debating the proliferation of "media platforms". "Those subjects are a bit 20th century. Once you come up with a great central idea, the solution follows naturally. Our mission is not to tell our clients how to run their businesses, but to provide striking creative ideas and images that will raise the profile of their brands."

In other words, Marcel is not out to re-invent the wheel. But it has invented some diabolically cunning news machines...

dare for m■re

Truth or dare?

by Jan Burney

dare for m■re

dare for m■re

Judging from the stunning images of the Epica d'Or Outdoor winning campaign, you might expect its creators to be outdoor types themselves - surfing dudes, maybe, or heli-skiers. In fact, Christopher Neumann, one half of the team behind the Pepsi Dare for More posters, was a "not very sporty" student of comparative literature before joining BBDO in Düsseldorf as a trainee copywriter. He admits to trying hard to indulge in some "active-daily-motion-nearly-a-work-out schedule" before going to sit in front of his PC each day, but extreme sports are clearly not his thing. His partner, art director Michael Plueckhahn, quit handball recently because of lack of time but he plays football twice a week and describes himself as "sporty but not extreme".

Sport has always been a major theme of Pepsi branding, so when the team were given their "short and clear" brief to build a strong, involving outdoor campaign that would fit perfectly with the brand, they quickly decided to investigate these "trendy, timeless sports that everybody is somehow fascinated by". Then they began to explore settings that would feel natural whilst being linked with the Pepsi lifestyle: seeing them, people could say, "It's a pity we're not a freeclimber, surfer or snowboarder - but, hey, we are sporty and we drink Pepsi." "The Pepsi theme is

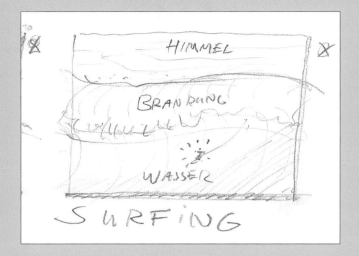

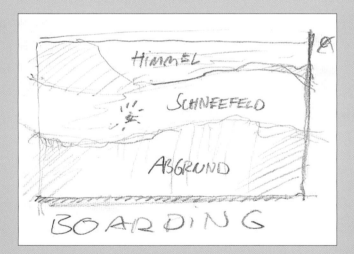

a big boy's fantasy, isn't it?" Plueckhahn confesses. "It's things I've always wanted to do but never managed in real life - so I did them in advertising!"

The things he's talking about are the amazing physical feats demonstrated by the heroic, solitary figures who are only just visible amid the awesome landscapes of the Dare for More posters.

The first is a surfer, alone under a red evening sky and riding a massive white wave as it cascades over the blue sea. Next is a snowboarder, swerving through the white powder of a sheer mountain descent, a tiny figure against a background of red sky and blue cliffs. Last of the trio is a free-climber, hanging precariously from the underside of a vast natural arch of red rock that vaults between the blue mountains below him and the infinity of white sky above.

"How do they do that?" is probably what everyone gasps when confronted by these images, dramatic glimpses of nature amidst the concrete and asphalt of major city locations. Audiences may imagine intrepid location scouts and photographers risking avalanches and frostbite in search of the perfect Pepsi shot. But the reality was more prosaic.

"Actually we were brainstorming," Plueckhahn explains, "and suddenly there was this picture of a man floating in water which, in combination with the white surf and red sand on the beach formed - when seen from above - the Pepsi wave. Once we'd brought it into the perspective you see on the poster, turning the swimmer into a surfer and using a red evening sky as the red of the Pepsi flag, it was only a small step to deciding on the other images."

"The sad art director's truth," he continues, "is that it was all done as post-production. We worked with image banks, searching for the perfect pictures to combine with amazing landscapes." He describes the task of amalgamating countless pictures as a "huge puzzle" but emphasises that, "We had that experienced retoucher, Stefan Kranefeld, who is really an artist.....A shoot would have been much more tricky, full of challenges from locations to weather conditions." He can't conceal a tinge of regret as he adds, "I had to admit that it would be better to do it that way...", but he hopes the resulting images make onlookers feel they can dive into other worlds and experience a mental refreshment, thanks to Pepsi.

Manipulated or not, the posters feature such majestic natural phenomena that it would have been almost shameful to diminish their impact by introducing other elements into the picture. Recognising that the final images epitomised the Pepsi brand with no need of reinforcement, the creative team quickly decided to omit a pack-shot or even a brand name - and fortunately their clients agreed. Plueckhahn and Neumann's combination of wondrous nature with the Pepsi wave succeeded in projecting the idea of the "magical world of Pepsi" without embellishment. There is just one subtle reference in the posters' "Dare for More" strapline, where the brand logo replaces the "o" in "more".

17

Typical audience reactions have been, "Wow!", "Great!" "I want to be there". Unsurprisingly, the client liked both the posters and these reactions to them - enough to commission a follow-up campaign. But Plueckhahn and Neumann can't give away any secrets about its content. Except for one little detail: apparently we can, 100%, "dare for more".

Jan Burney is a writer and consultant for advertising and design.

Heidies in plain sight

by Mark Tungate

When fashion brand Diesel wanted to launch its new 'intimates' range, it clearly couldn't take an orthodox approach: the usual combination of trade fairs, press releases and fashion shows just didn't seem right. After all, the brand had been making waves with its advertising since the 1990s, when it won a string of awards for its work with groundbreaking agencies like Paradiset DDB in Stockholm and Amsterdam's Kesselskramer.

One of things the Diesel team likes best is irony – or even better, parody. So this time it created a tongue-in-cheek reference to reality TV shows like Big Brother. As you know, these typically involve locking a bunch of oddballs in an apartment bristling with sound and video equipment.

To make its wish come true, Diesel returned to Stockholm to work with leading interactive agency Farfar. The resulting campaign was a total Web 2.0 experience with zero conventional media budget – and it still attracted thousands of connections as well as worldwide press coverage.

The pitch was this: a couple of models – both named Heidi – "steal" the new Diesel intimates collection and "kidnap" a sales

guy named Juan. Then they lock themselves in a hotel room equipped with the pre-requisite sound and video equipment. They "hijack" the Diesel.com website in order to broadcast the resulting antics to the world. They are determined to make themselves famous, they explain to camera, and so they are going to hold Juan captive for a week and invite visitors to suggest what they should do with him. All three of them would be dressed in Diesel underwear from start to finish.

Although the set-up was provocative, the results steered clear of anything too raunchy. The Heidies and Juan kept their undies firmly on and their pranks were harmless fun: forcing Juan to do the washing up or dressing him in a pink dinosaur outfit, for instance. There were pillow fights and shootouts with water pistols. Viewer suggestions ranged from the playful request that the girls wear oversize panda masks to a more sophisticated online poll on the ultimate celebrity pet, which resulted in a chihuahua arriving in the room.

Live images from the hotel room were available 24 hours a day. Flash video streaming enabled visitors to choose their own camera angles when following the action: five cameras were streaming video simultaneously, an amazing technical feat. Messages from visitors to the site were displayed on a big screen in the hotel room.

The operation utilised many different aspects of the internet, from online polls to social networking sites. Through Diesel.com, the Heidies would ask visitors what they could do to become more famous. They also took pictures of each other and placed them on Flickr, a photography site. Clips on YouTube generated hoards of fans. Numerous blog postings linked back to the action, and the Heidies' MySpace page attracted messages of good will from new "friends" such as Paris Hilton, Lily Allen and – of course – Heidi Klum.

As news of the two pretty girls and their captive spread like wildfire across the web, visits to Diesel.com went through the roof. By the third day, site traffic had tripled from the usual 29,000 daily visits to more than 100,000 a day. A Diesel spokesperson said: "People told us they had phoned in sick at work so they could stay home and follow what was going on. Messages came flooding in."

In terms of the Diesel brand, store staff reported that customers had been asking for the "Heidies underwear". The five-day experiment ended when Andrea Rosso – the son of Diesel founder Renzo Rosso – appeared at the door of the hotel room to "liberate" Juan. But the room was not quite abandoned, as a final party took place. This time, Juan and his new friends were allowed to wear clothes.

"When it was all over, we got messages begging us to keep the site open," said the Diesel representative. "As far as we're concerned, the operation was 100 per cent successful."

So Diesel and Farfar won the first-ever Interactive Epica d'Or by showing the world how to generate controversy and coverage, as well as selling underware, with no conventional media budget - while the Heidies earned their 15MB of fame.

Mark Tungate is a journalist and writer based in Paris. He is the author of Media Monoliths and Adland - a Global History of Advertising, both published by Kogan Page. He co-hosts a weekly TV programme on advertising and writes the synopses for the Epica Book.

Agency	Lowe Friends, Copenhagen	At the dinner table, a man notices that the label on his bottle of Felix Ketchup appears to be upside down. He mentions this to his wife, who promptly turns the bottle to rest on its flat lid. The "top-down" design enables the ketchup to flow freely, with no long waits. The man squirts some ketchup onto his food. "I think I've found out the construction," he tells his son. "You're a genius, dad," the kid replies. "Yes," the man continues, "but it's really a pity they turned the label upside down." Some people can't deal with evolution.
Creative Director	Hans-Henrik Langevad	
Copywriter	Kim Juul Andersen	
Art Director	Mads Kold	
Production	Studio 24, Stockholm	
Directors	Roy Andersson	
	Stig Åke Nilsson	
Producers	Pernilla Sandström	
	Julie Moelsgaard	
Client	Felix Ketchup, "Top Down"	

HEINZ
1869
HOT
KETCHUP
HEINZ
57 VARIETIES

Food **21**

Agency	Shalmor Avnon Amichay/Y&R, Tel Aviv
Creative Directors	Gideon Amichay
	Tzur Golan
Copywriter	Yariv Twig
Art Director	Yariv Twig
Photographers	Yoram Aschheim
	Melanit Turgeman
Client	Heinz Hot Ketchup

Agency	BTS United , Oslo
Creative Director	Thorbjørn Naug
Copywriter	Petter Andersen
Art Director	Lars Holt
Production	Komet film
Producer	Jens Lien
Client	Gilde, "Football"

Some little kids are playing football. When one of them falls and grazes his knee, he's retired to the bench – where he's handed a Glide hotdog as consolation. One of his team-mates notices this and is soon squirming on the ground in mock agony. He also gets to sit on the bench munching a hotdog. Ten minutes later, the entire team is faking injuries. The opposing side has nobody to play against. Glide makes the tastiest sausages.

Agency	DDB London
Creative Director	Adam Tucker
Copywriters	Joanna Wenley
	Grant Parker
Art Directors	Grant Parker
	Joanna Wenley
Production	Rogue Films, London
Director	Sam Cadman
Producers	Alice Rowbotham
	Natalie Powell
Client	Nimble Bread, "Builder"

Working on a construction site, a builder can't help noticing that the waistband of his jeans seems to have loosened. He's forced to constantly hitch them up. They fall down at the most inappropriate moments, with hilarious consequences. What on earth is going on? Finally, in the kitchen at home, the man sees that his wife has been making his sandwiches using Nimble, "the low-calorie bread that tastes so good, you'll never guess". No wonder he has a new slim-line waist.

Agency	Advico Young & Rubicam, Zurich
Creative Director	Urs Schrepfer
Copywriter	Martin Stulz
Art Director	Christian Bobst
Production	Cobblestone Filmproduktion
Director	Robert Nylund
Producers	Tanja Uselmann
	Daniela Berther
Client	Citterio, "Electric Fan"

A man lays out some super-thin Citterio ham on a plate and puts it on the dinner table. When he turns away, his cute dog leaps up onto a seat to sniff at the plate. At that very moment – improbably enough – the electric fan blows the entire contents of the plate out of the window like autumn leaves. The man turns back and sees the dog staring at the empty plate. The dog looks guilty. The man looks irritated. Citterio: very thinly sliced ham.

Agency	Young & Rubicam, Frankfurt
Creative Directors	Uwe Marquardt
	Christian Daul
Copywriter	Kai-Oliver Sass
Art Director	Natalia Richel
Client	Oryza Rice

WITHOUT

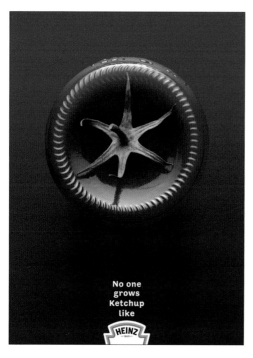

No one
grows
Ketchup
like
HEINZ

No one grows Ketchup like Heinz.

Agency	Leo Burnett, Paris	**Agency**	McCann Erickson, London
Creative Director	Stephan Ferens	**Creative Directors**	Brian Fraser
Copywriter	Eric Esculier		Simon Learman
Art Director	Eric Esculier	**Copywriters**	Robert Brown
Client	Heinz Ketchup		Tim Swan
			Miguel Soares
		Art Director	Gary Marjoram
		Photographer	Kevin Summers
		Client	Heinz Ketchup

Heinz mayonnaise. Now in squeeze bottle.

Agency	Impact/BBDO, Jeddah	Agency	Leo Burnett Brussels
Creative Director	Ahmad Beck	Creative Directors	Jean-Paul Lefebvre
Copywriter	Ahmad Beck		Michel De Lauw
Art Director	Ahmad Beck	Copywriter	Vincent Daenen
Photographer	Steve Kosman	Art Director	Guido Goffeau
Client	Goody Hot Sauce	Photographer	Philippe Lermusiaux
		Client	Heinz Mayonnaise

Agency	Saatchi & Saatchi Russia, Moscow	A TV wildlife documentary shows a bear unsuccessfully trying to catch leaping salmon. We hear uproarious laughter. Then we see another bear: but this one is sitting on a sofa watching the TV, chortling away at the documentary while he contentedly devours Vici crab sticks. When he hears the front door slam, the bear is forced to leap out of the sofa and reassume his position as a bearskin rug on the floor. But he still can't resist a quiet chuckle. If you love seafood, you'll love Vici.
Creative Director	Stuart Robinson	
Copywriter	Stuart Robinson	
Art Director	Stuart Robinson	
Production	RGB Vilnius	
Director	Richardas Matacius	
Producers	Tomas Kondratavicius	
	Dmitry Lashkin	
Client	Vici Crab Sticks, "Laughing Bear"	

Agency	CLM BBDO, Paris
Creative Directors	Gilles Fichteberg
	Jean-Francois Sacco
Copywriter	Laurent Laporte
Art Director	Sophian Bouadjera
Illustrator	Sophian Bouadjera
Client	Suzi Wan

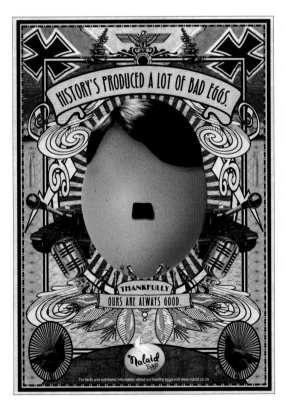

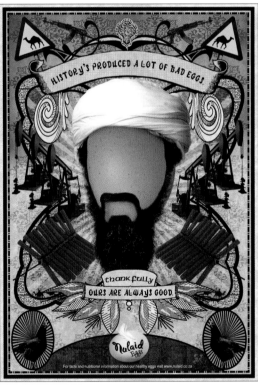

Agency	Percept Gulf, Dubai	Agency	The Jupiter Drawing Room,
Creative Director	Prashant Sankhe		Johannesburg
Copywriter	Wayne Fernandes	Creative Directors	Graham Warsop
Art Director	Tushar Mahajan		Michael Blore
Client	Nando's Restaurants		Tom Cullinan
		Copywriter	Aviv Weil
		Art Director	Shane Forbes
		Illustrator	Shane Forbes
		Client	Nulaid Eggs

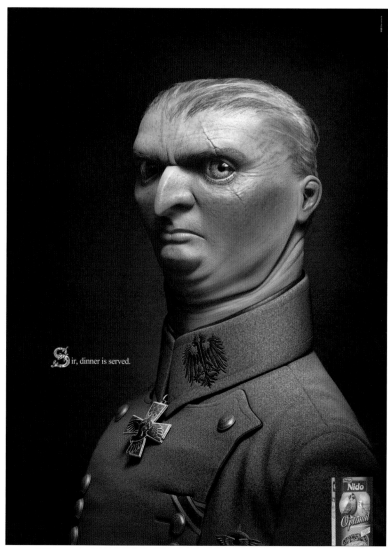

28 Food

Agency	Euro RSCG, Prague	**Agency**	DDB Spain, Madrid
Creative Director	Dejan Stajnberger	**Creative Directors**	Turi Tollesson
Copywriter	Nucharat Nunthananonchai		Richard Browse
Art Directors	Nawarat Teerapresart	**Copywriter**	Isabel Martinez
	Lenka Kovarikova	**Art Director**	Agnes Aran
Photographer	Zoltan Matuska	**Illustrator**	Peter Fendrick
Client	Lemon Leaf Restaurants	**Client**	Nido Birdfood

Agency	McCann Erickson, Munich	**Agency**	TBWA\Vienna
Creative Director	Erich Reuter	**Creative Directors**	Robert Wohlgemuth
Copywriter	Michael Utta		Gerd Turetschek
Art Director	Amelie Sedlmayr		Elli Hummer
Client	Happy Dog Dogfood	**Copywriter**	Karin Schalko
		Art Directors	Jeff Stenzenberger
			Christian Pfeifer
		Photographer	Andreas Franke
		Illustrator	Fanni Kovacs
		Client	Pedigree Dogfood

Agency	McCann Erickson Romania, Bucharest	Agency	Callegari Berville Grey, Paris
Creative Directors	Adrian Botan	Creative Director	Andrea Stillacci
	Alexandru Dumitrescu	Copywriter	Yannick Savioz
	Craita Coman	Art Director	Jérôme Gonfond
Copywriter	Olivia Basag	Photographer	Ilario, Magali
Art Director	Ionut Ludosanu	Client	Findus Frozen Fish
Client	Maggi Soups		

Fries lightly, not oily.

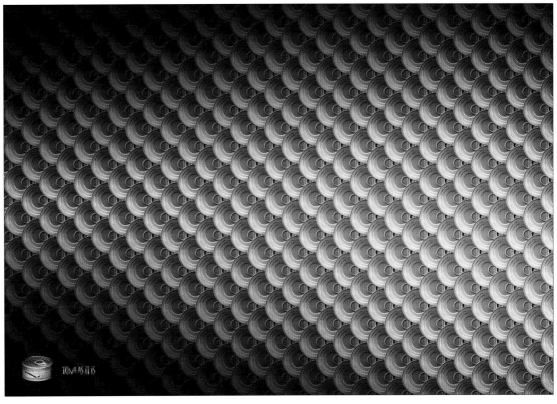

Agency	Markom Leo Burnett, Istanbul	Agency	Publicis MARC, Sofia
Creative Director	Yasar Akbas	Creative Director	Vladilen Achev
Copywriter	Erdinc Mutlu	Illustrator	Givko Popov
Art Director	Erkan Kaya	Client	Ocean Tuna
Photographer	Ilkay Muratoglu		
Client	Trakya Birlik Cooking Oil		

32 **Confectionery & Snacks**

Agency	Fallon London	In extreme close-up, we see the sulky face of a humanoid-looking gorilla. He seems impatient about something. Meanwhile, we hear Phil Collins singing "In the Air Tonight". As the camera pulls slowly back, we see that the gorilla is sitting at a drum kit. Finally, when the pop song's famous drum section begins, the gorilla gets to joyously play along. It's like he's been waiting for this moment all his life. Cadbury's Dairy Milk: a glass and a half full of joy.
Creative Director	Juan Cabral	
Copywriter	Juan Cabral	
Art Director	Juan Cabral	
Production	Blink Productions	
Director	Juan Cabral	
Producers	Matthew Fone	
	Nicky Barnes	
Client	Cadbury's Dairy Milk, "Gorilla"	

Agency	Duval Guillaume Brussels
Creative Directors	Katrien Bottez
	Peter Ampe
Copywriter	Raoul Maris
Art Director	Christian Loos
Photographer	Marcel Veelo
Client	Bazooka Bubblegum

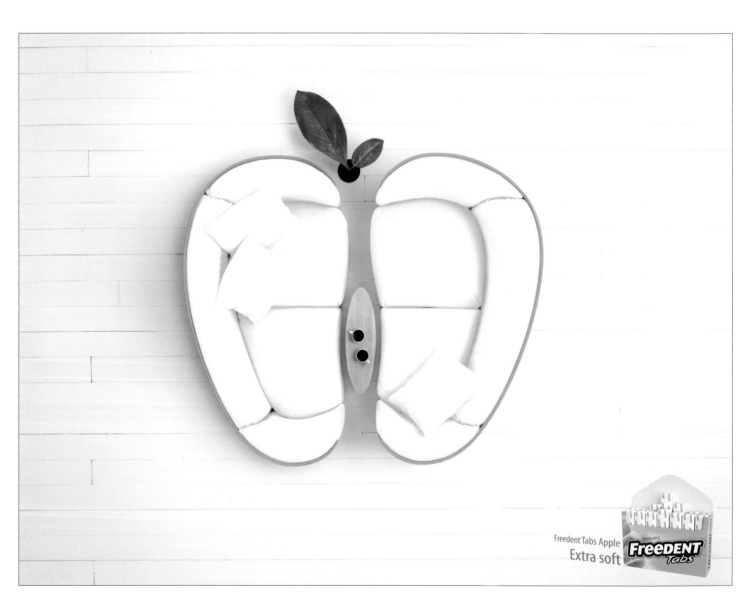

Freedent Tabs Apple
Extra soft

Agency	Impact BBDO, Dubai	The glowing red character on a pedestrian
Creative Director	Jennie Morris	crossing descends from his perch and
Copywriter	Jennie Morris	starts picking a fight with his green rival
Art Director	Sian Binder	below. They fall to the street. Suddenly, all
Production	X-Ray Film,	over town, tiny red and green men leave
	Amsterdam	their places on traffic lights and take part in
Director	Joeri Holsheimer	a gang war. Finally, after a lengthy combat,
Producers	Soeren Schmidt	the green figures defeat the red. From now
	Azza Aboul Magd	on, there will be no waiting at kerbs for
Client	Snickers,	energetic joggers. Snickers: don't stop.
	"Don't Stop"	

Agency	CLM BBDO, Paris
Creative Directors	Jean-Francois Sacco
	Gilles Fichteberg
Copywriter	Paul Kreitmann
Art Director	Paul Kreitmann
Photographer	Gregoire Alexandre
Client	Freedent Tabs Chewing Gum

The healthy fast food.

The healthy fast food.

The healthy fast food.

Agency	Jung von Matt, Zurich
Creative Director	Michael Rottmann
Copywriter	Alexander Holtz
Art Director	David Hanselmann
Photographers	Staudinger + Franke
Client	Dar-Vida

ABOUT THE FIBER TYPE, INTERPLAY AND MOTOR UNITS OF MUSCLE CELLS.

Each muscle contains a large number of muscle bundles. These muscle bundles are surrounded by a layer of connective tissue (muscle fascia). Its purpose is to facilitate gliding against other muscles and give shape to the muscle. Each muscle bundle contains a certain number of muscle cells (myons). These muscle cells are also called muscle fibers. A muscle cell consists of smaller components: myofibrils. Myofibrils lie parallel to each other and are striated under normal light microscopy. This is because the myofibrils are composed of smaller components, myofilaments, which in turn are of two types: actin and myosin. Maybe we should pull up the boat in September this year. The ice came so early last year. And what should we have for dinner tonight? Maybe sausage. But wait, that's what we ate yesterday. We'll have to settle for macaroni and cheese. Have to buy milk, butter, bread, eggs. Maybe we could make an omelette? A German one, the eggs are in the fridge.

 When muscles contract (shorten), the actin is drawn in between the myosin. As a consequence the myofibrils also shorten and thicken, which in turn causes the elastic fibers that surround the muscle cell and the connective tissue (surrounding the muscle and extending out into the muscle tendon) to provide a force that affects the muscle's attachment and origin, so that skeletal movement occurs. MOTOR UNIT. In order for the muscle to contract, a signal is sent from the brain through the spinal cord neurons and down to a nerve which in turn branches and reaches all the way to the muscle cells. This functional unit is called a motor unit and consists of a neuron and all the muscle cells that it innervates. If the motor units contain relatively few cells the muscle is associated with fine motor function and with gross motor function when there are many units. When a motor unit is put to work, all cells in that unit contract with maximum force. The same muscles are always at work when light loads are involved and the same units are always recruited as the load increases. The muscle is protected by two types of neurons: muscle spindles and tendon spindles (Golgi tendon organ). These are hooked up in parallel between muscle cells and passively follow the movement of adjacent muscle cells. When muscle cells are stretched, the muscle spindles are also stretched. If the muscle is stretched too much and there is risk that it will rupture, the muscle spindle sends a contractile signal to the central nervous system, which in turn sends a signal back that stimulates contraction of the muscle, thereby preventing injury. This protective mechanism is called the stretch reflex. The tendon spindles are located in the transition between muscle cells and tendons. In contrast to the muscle spindles, these send a signal that causes the muscle to stop contracting in order to avoid tendon injury. Oh, no! My sister's kids are coming to visit this weekend too. What a pain! Have to clean up and play the good uncle for forty-eight hours. I sure hope they don't have colds. Have to call Dad, too. It's been a while. Good lord! It's probably been three months since the last time we talked. Wonder if they finished replacing the roof yet. Hope I don't have to help with that project. But I suppose I'll have to. Just where do you buy roof tiles anyway?

 FIBER TYPES. We know today that there are two types of fibers: slow fibers (type 1) and fast fibers (type 2). The designation 'slow' does not imply that the muscle is stopped from performing a rapid movement in sports. In these contexts, for example, a smash return in tennis is very slow. Slow fibers receive their energy supply from the blood. Fast fibers are mainly supplied by energy stored in the muscle. Type 2 fibers are then divided into three subcategories: type 2a, type 2b and type 2c. Type 2a: These have the best characteristics of both of the other types; in other words: high strength and good endurance. Type 2b: These are the most explosive, with poor endurance. Type 2c: In recent years researchers have tried to describe how different muscle cells change in response to various training methods. We know that type 1 fibers are controlled by a certain type of neuron (small) and type 2 fibers by a different neuron (big), and neurons do not change. Meanwhile, researchers believe that after lengthy periods of endurance training type 2 muscle fibers learn to use oxygen as an energy source, and are then referred to as type 2c. Boy am I tired. Maybe I'm coming down with the flu or something. That's all I need. Better get to the drugstore right away. Buy tissues. And nose spray. And some of that nasal oil, to keep my nose from getting too dry. I hate pharmacies. Wonder if they get sick often, I mean the pharmacists? Maybe we should rent a movie tonight. Maybe that new one. The one that everyone is talking about. What was it called? The Searchers? No. That's an older film. Hmm.

 TYPE 1 FIBER TRAINING. During relatively low intensity and long-term work, researchers have ascertained that type 1 fibers react with the following changes: the capillary network in the muscle and its ability to provide oxygen to the muscle increases, mainly around type 1 fibers. The mitochondria inside the muscle cell increase and their job is to produce energy. The number of repetitions at submaximal level increases. TYPE 2 FIBER TRAINING. High load training mainly affects type 2 fibers. Principle changes include: the cross-sectional area of the cells increases, as does their ability to develop more power. The cell's capacity to work without oxygen (anaerobic) increases. Nerve and muscle coordination improves. More motor units are recruited (technique). When the muscle changes the joint angle, it is engaged in dynamic work. When it actually contracts it is called concentric contraction. When the muscle tries to contract but is stretched out because external resistance is greater, it is known as eccentric (braking) action. This is when the muscle develops the greatest power. When internal muscle power is equal to external resistance, no movement occurs. This is called isometric contraction or static work. MUSCLE FORCE AND STRENGTH. In order to measure a muscle's strength, we need to know its origin and attachment site, as well as how it passes by the joint; in other words, the perpendicular distance from the line of action of the muscle's force vector to the joint's rotational axis. We need the following data: Moment arm length (l) Weight of equipment (F) Distance between joint axis and the attachment. A muscle can develop a maximum force of about 50N of muscle cross-sectional area. Cross-sectional area refers to the number of myofibrils contained by the muscle. In other words, the muscle's ability to lift a heavy object depends on two conditions: the physiological cross-sectional area and how it passes by the joint. Muscle power can be affected by means of strength training, but the individual is born with the muscle attachment. In other words, certain individuals are better adapted to certain activities. Laundry tonight. What a drag. Hope that grumpy old man from apartment 6 doesn't come and whine that I didn't clean the dryer filter again. Man, you'd think he has better things to do! Maybe everyone gets like that when they get old. Maybe it's unavoidable. Wonder if that shirt my old lady gave me for Christmas needs to be done with the cold wash cycle? Hope it doesn't need dry cleaning. Dry cleaning? How do they do that anyway? How can you wash something without water, weird? I have to buy new jeans one of these days too. Black or blue, that's the question. Black ones would probably be cool. But I suppose I'll get blue ones anyway.

Agency	TBWA\Chiat\Day, New York
Executive CD	Gerry Graf
Creative Directors	Ian Reichenthal
	Scott Vitrone
Copywriter	Eric Kallman
Art Director	Craig Allen
Production	Smith & Sons Films, London
Director	Ulf Johansson
Producers	Philippa Smith
	Lora Schulson
Client	Snickers, "Mechanics"

Two mechanics are bending over the engine of a car, their heads close together. One of them gets out a Snickers chocolate bar and starts to eat it. The other man, unable to resist, starts munching the other end. Inevitably, their lips meet. They jump away from one another as if electrocuted. "Quick – do something manly!" commands one of them. They both grab a handful of their own chest hair and rip it out, roaring cathartically. Snickers: most satisfying.

Agency	Saatchi & Saatchi, Stockholm
Creative Directors	Adam Kerj
	Fredrik Preisler
Copywriter	Magnus Jakobsson
Art Director	Gustav Egerstedt
Photographer	Hans Malm
Client	Gainomax Energy Bar

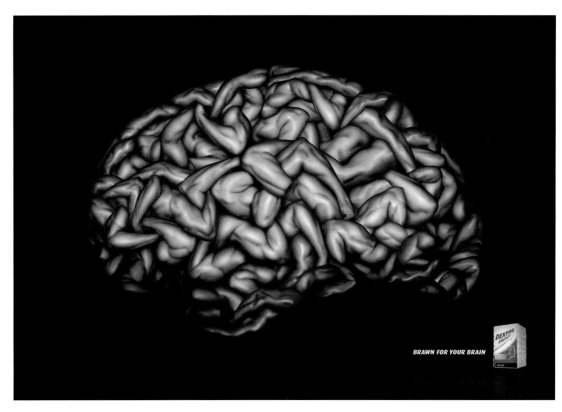

Agency	Markom Leo Burnett, Istanbul		**Agency**	Kempertrautmann, Hamburg
Creative Directors	Yasar Akbas		**Creative Directors**	Jens Theil
	Idil Akoglu Ergulen			Gerrit Zinke
Copywriter	Erdinc Mutlu		**Copywriter**	Michael Götz
Art Directors	Erkan Kaya		**Client**	Dextro Energy
	Haluk Karslioglu			
Photographer	Ilkay Muratoglu			
Client	Crazy Balloon			

38 **Dairy Products**

Agency	Publicis, Zurich
Creative Director	Markus Gut
Copywriter	Roy Spring
Art Director	Viviana Chiosi
Client	Emmentaler

Milk keeps you in shape.

Milk keeps you in shape.

Agency	Ruf Lanz, Zurich		**Agency**	Grey, Oslo
Creative Directors	Danielle Lanz		**Client**	The Blind Cow
	Markus Ruf			Gourmet Cheese
Copywriters	Thomas Schöb			
	Markus Ruf			
Art Director	Lorenz Clormann			
Client	SMP, Swiss Milk Producers			

40   **Dairy Products**

Agency	McCann Erickson, Athens	Agency	KNSK Werbeagentur, Hamburg
Creative Director	Anna Stilianaki	Art Director	Nick Jungclaus
Copywriter	Eleftheria Petropoulou	Illustrator	Nick Jungclaus
Art Director	Yannis Lapatas	Client	Campina Optiwell
Client	Vlachas Evaporated Milk		

Dairy Products   **41**

Agency	Lowe Brindfors, Stockholm
Creative Director	Tove Langseth
Art Director	Rickard Villard
Illustrator	Lotta Külhorn
Client	Yoggi Fruit Yoghurt

42   **Alcoholic Drinks**

Agency	Abbott Mead Vickers BBDO, London	In a dusty Latin American down, a man tips a domino. As the domino effect is unleashed, a line of falling tiles ripples around the room and out of the window. Then we see that the enterprising villagers have taken the game to another level. The falling dominos are replaced by everyday objects: matchboxes, crates, old refrigerators, burning bales of hay, wardrobes, mattresses, oil drums and even cars topple one after the other. Finally, the domino effect turns a giant cylindrical pile of books into a sculpture resembling a pint of Guinness. Good things come to those who wait.
Creative Director	Paul Brazier	
Copywriters	Angus McAdam	
	Paul Jordan	
Art Directors	Angus McAdam	
	Paul Jordan	
Production	MJZ, London	
Director	Nicolai Fugslig	
Producers	Suza Horvat	
	Carol Powell	
Client	Guinness, "Tipping Point"	

Nobody can resist.

Nobody can resist.

Nobody can resist.

 Alcoholic Drinks 43

Agency	DDB&Co, Istanbul
Creative Director	Karpat Polat
Copywriter	Karpat Polat
Art Directors	Ali Bati
	Burak Kunduracioglu
Photographer	Gokce Erenmemisoglu
Client	Villa Doluca Wines

A DAY IS A STEP
A YEAR IS A TANGO

GLENFIDDICH
EVERY YEAR COUNTS

SKILFULLY CRAFTED. ENJOY RESPONSIBLY.

44 **Alcoholic Drinks**

Agency	180 Amsterdam
Creative Directors	Andy Fackrell
	Richard Bullock
Copywriter	Niklas Lilja
Art Director	Antero Jokinen
Production	Trigger Happy Productions, Berlin
Director	Ralf Schmerberg
Producers	Stephan Vens
	Claire Finn
Client	Glenfiddich, "Every Year Counts"

"A day is a step," says the narrator, over an image of dancing shoes. "A year is a tango." Next we see a bustling Indian street. "A day is a tourist. A year is a traveller." A romantic couple: "A day is a chance encounter. A year says love." A man ineffectually blowing a trumpet: "A day is frustration. A year is a melody." And so on, as we grasp the idea that a day is a mere trifle while a year leads to something profound. Years of experience go into a glass of Glenfiddich whisky. And every year counts.

Agency	180 Amsterdam
Creative Directors	Andy Fackrell
	Richard Bullock
Copywriter	Niklas Lilja
Art Director	Antero Jokinen
Photographer	Stephen Shore
Client	Glenfiddich

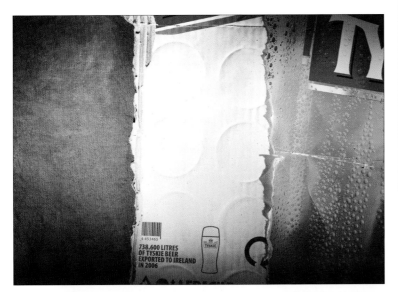

Alcoholic Drinks   **45**

Agency	DDB Warsaw
Creative Directors	Marcin Mroszczak
	Jakub Korolczuk
	Ryszard Sroka
Copywriter	Natalia Dudek
Art Director	Marcin Zaborski
Photographer	Igor Omulecki
Client	Tyskie Beer

Agency	H&C Leo Burnett, Beirut
Creative Director	Bechara Mouzannar
Copywriter	Joyce Zavzavadjian
Art Directors	Celine Khoury
	Roula Ghalayini
Client	Johnnie Walker
	Black Label

With this massive wall poster in central Beirut, Johnnie Walker encouraged the Lebanese to move forward into 2007 with optimism and to put the sad events of 2006 behind them.

Agency	Caldas Naya, Barcelona
Creative Director	Gustavo Caldas
Copywriter	Gustavo Caldas
Art Director	Juanjo Casañas
Photographers	Mike Diver
	Pedro Aguilar
Client	A.K.Damm Beer

BREWED THE SAME WAY SINCE 1870
UNTIL LAST YEAR WHEN
WE COMPLETELY CHANGED IT

WWW.AMSTEL.COM

TASTE LIFE PURE FILTERED

**YOU KNOW THOSE MICROSCOPIC PARTICLES
IN YOUR BEER YOU NEVER KNEW ABOUT?**
THEY'RE GONE NOW

WWW.AMSTEL.COM

TASTE LIFE PURE FILTERED

Alcoholic Drinks **47**

Agency	180 Amsterdam	**Agency**	Irish International BBDO, Dublin
Creative Director	Adam Chasnow	**Creative Director**	Mal Stevenson
Copywriter	Adam Chasnow	**Copywriter**	Mark Nutley
Art Director	Antero Jokinen	**Art Director**	Pat Hamill
Client	Amstel Beer	**Photographer**	Kevin Griffin
		Client	Guinness

Agency	Irish International BBDO, Dublin
Creative Director	Mal Stevenson
Copywriter	Mark Nutley
Art Director	Pat Hamill
Production	Red Bee Media, London
Director	Steve Cope
Producer	Edel Ericson
Client	Guinness, "Music Machine"

Men in sleek white spacesuits are fired from giant trumpets to slam into black drums, where they burst into bubbles. Their co-workers slide down black cables or rocket into an inky sky to clash against a layer of golden symbols. As the camera pulls back and out, we learn that this musical science fiction world is a metaphor for the flavour and goodness that's bubbling away inside a pint of Guinness just after it's been poured. Guinness: it's alive inside.

 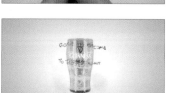

48   Alcoholic Drinks

Agency	Abbott Mead Vickers BBDO, London
Creative Director	Paul Brazier
Copywriter	Tony Strong
Art Director	Michael Durban
Production	Uli Meyer Animation
Director	Michael Schlingmann
Producers	Matt Saxton Carol Powell
Client	Guinness, "Hands"

In this little masterpiece of stop motion animation, we see fingers being drummed against a pale background. As jaunty folk music kicks in, the hands dance and prance in more sophisticated ways, moving to the tune as their owner struggles to keep himself occupied. At the end of the spot, the fingers are flexed and words are typed: "Good things come to those who wait." It's Guinness, of course.

Agency	JWT, London
Executive CD	Nick Bell
Creative Directors	Anita Davis Jonathan Budds
Copywriter	Adam Griffin
Art Director	Rob Spicer
Production	Rattling Stick
Director	Daniel Kleinman
Producers	Johnnie Frankel Sarah Patterson
Client	Smirnoff Vodka, "Sea"

On a fishing boat at sea, a man drains his can of beer, crushes it and chucks it over the side. He's surprised when it's flung back at him. Suddenly, the sea begins throwing back everything that has been dumped into it over the years: tin cans, coins, washing machines, shipwrecks, rusted anchors, ancient statuary, downed fighter planes...they're all coughed up onto land until the sea is totally pure. All that remains is a bottle of Smirnoff Vodka: the ultimate in purity.

WELCOME TO 1366

STELLAARTOIS.COM

Agencies	Lowe Brindfors, Stockholm	Agency	Noble Graphics Creative Studio,
	Lowe Worldwide		Sofia
Creative Director	Matthew Bull	Creative Director	Chavdar Kenarov
Copywriters	Håkan Engler	Copywriter	Ida Daniel
	Johan Holmström	Art Director	George Kasabov
	Mats Brun	Photographer	Bliss
Art Directors	Rickard Villard	Client	Tuborg
	Tim Scheibel		
	Johan Tesch		
	Kalle dos Santos		
Photographer	Jean-Marie Vives		
Client	Stella Artois		

Follow the rabbit and you will find happiness

It was not this rabbit you should have followed

And now you must apologize to the rabbit

Do you think this is black?

100% black

50   **Non-Alcoholic Drinks**

Agency	& Co., Copenhagen
Creative Director	Robert Cerkez
Copywriter	Peter Hansen
Art Director	Robert Cerkez
Production	Bacon, Copenhagen
Director	Martin Werner
Producers	Charlie Gaugler
	Mie Schaffalitzky
Client	Café Noir, "Rabbit"

In Danish, the word "black" denotes something strange or bizarre. That's what our hero discovers when he encounters a black-cloaked figure by the roadside. "Follow the rabbit," says this apparition (in French, naturally), "and you will find happiness." After a brief pursuit, the man in black reappears. He tells our hero that he has chased the wrong rabbit. "Now you'll have to apologise." The baffled hero does so, only to be informed that the rabbit is displeased. We can only guess what happens next. But if you thought that was black, you should try Café Noir.

dare for more

dare for more

 Non-Alcoholic Drinks **51**

Agency	BBDO, Düsseldorf
Creative Directors	Veikko Hille
	Sebastian Hardieck
	Toygar Bazarkaya
Copywriter	Christopher Neumann
Art Director	Michael Plueckhahn
Imaging	Stefan Kranefeld
Client	Pepsi

Agency	Wieden+Kennedy, Amsterdam
Creative Directors	Al Moseley
	John Norman
Copywriters	Al Moseley
	Rick Condos
Art Directors	John Norman
	Hunter Hindman
Production Directors	Psyop, New York
	Todd Mueller
	Kylie Matulick
Producers	Mariya Shikher
	Sandy Reay
Client	Coca-Cola, "Happiness Factory - The Movie"

In this sequel to last year's hit "Happiness Factory" spot, we see what happens when the factory runs out of juice. A brave worker is dispatched to the faraway source of Coca-Cola to investigate the problem and start the factory working again. He experiences all sorts of challenges and adventures on his way, turning this spot into a three-minute epic. At the end, though, he reawakens the source, the Coca-Cola begins to flow and the factory is happier than ever.

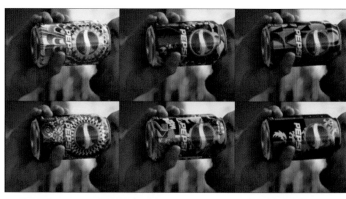

52 **Non-Alcoholic Drinks**

Agency	Shalmor Avnon Amichay/Y&R, Tel Aviv
Creative Directors	Gideon Amichay
	Yoram Levi
Production	POV
Director	Shahar Segal
Producer	Shira Robas
Client	Elite Coffee, "Shanghai"

An airline pilot is staying at a hotel in Shanghai. When reception calls to wake him up, he asks for some hot water. Two porters appear with a tin bath. "No, small glass," he explains. After scouring the city, the porters reappear with small glasses – as in spectacles. Patiently, the pilot explains: "No, hot water in a small glass, for wake-up." Finally, the porters arrive at his door with a small glass of water. They promptly fling it in his face, "for wake up". In fact, all he wanted was some hot water for his Elite Turkish instant coffee.

Agency	CLM BBDO, Paris
Creative Director	Anne de Maupeou
Copywriters	David Bertram
	Leo Berne
Art Directors	Leo Berne
	David Bertram
Production	Irene, Paris
Director	Frédéric Planchon
Producers	Guillaume de Bary
	France Monnet
Client	Pepsi, "Destinies"

The screen is split into six images. Each is a short film featuring the parallel lives of the same young man. By watching them carefully, we can see what happens to him depending on the decisions he makes during the day. He either: gets involved in a football match; joins a rock band; meets the love of his life; foils a robbery and ends up with the spoils; gets a free ride in a limo – or simply trips and spills his drink. Life offers endless possibilities, but at least some things remain reliable, like Pepsi.

Agency	Team Y&R, Dubai
Creative Directors	Shahir Ahmed
	Komal Bedi
Copywriter	Amit Kapoor
Art Director	Rupert Allcock
Client	Rhino Energy Drink

Non-Alcoholic Drinks

Agency	Demner, Merlicek & Bergmann, Vienna		Agency	Marcel, Paris
			Creative Directors	Frédéric Témin
Creative Director	Francesco Bestagno			Anne de Maupeou
Copywriter	Claus Gigler		Copywriter	Nicolas Chauvin
Art Director	Francesco Bestagno		Art Director	Nicolas Chauvin
Illustrator	Daniela Schabernak		Photographer	Peter Lipman
Client	Meinl Coffee		Client	Minute Maid

Agency	Storåkers McCann, Stockholm	This poster is transformed during the night when its back-lighting reveals the silhuettes of various couples behind the Mer bottle.
Copywriter	Mia Cederberg	
Art Director	Mitte Blomqvist	
Photographer	Ragnhild Fors	
Client	Mer	

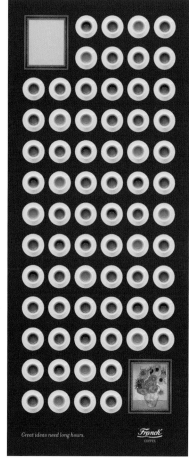

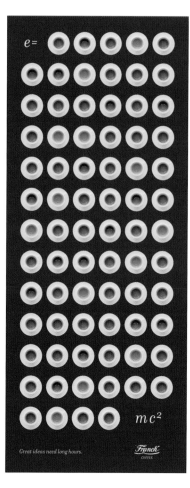

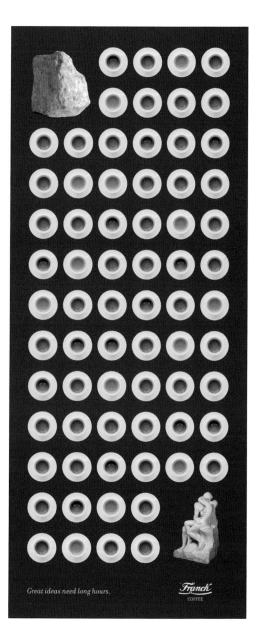

Agency	CLM BBDO, Paris
Creative Directors	Gilles Fichteberg
	Jean-Francois Sacco
Copywriter	Fabien Moreira
Art Director	Paola Nauges
Photographer	Jean-Noel Leblanc-Bontemps
Client	Pepsi Light

Agency	Grey Worldwide, Zagreb
Creative Director	Mirka Modrinić
Copywriter	Mirka Modrinić
Art Director	Joško Jureškin
Photographer	Boris Poljičanin
Client	Franck Coffee

Agency	Armando Testa, Turin	Agency	Graffiti BBDO,
Creative Directors	German Silva		Bucharest
	Ekhi Mendibil	Creative Director	Ema Prisca
	Haitz Mendibil	Copywriter	Dan Stanescu
Copywriters	German Silva	Art Director	Cosmin Simionescu
	Ekhi Mendibil	Illustrator	Cosmin Simionescu
	Haitz Mendibil	Client	Mountain Dew
Art Directors	Haitz Mendibil		
	Andrea Lantelme		
Photographer	Eugenio Recuenco		
Client	Lavazza Coffee		

Agency	DDB Oslo	In a long-ago classroom, a little girl is reading
Copywriter	Eirik Hovland	out her essay about "the future". "In the
Art Director	Morten Varhaug	future, a telephone will be so small that we
Production	Komet Film	can put it in our pocket and take it with us
Director	Jens Lien	everywhere." Her classmates laugh at her.
Producer	Jørgen Mjelva	"You can watch TV shows and the news on
Producer	Cyril Boije	the phone." Now she's dragged up before
Client	Telenor, "The Essay"	the headmaster, doctors and a shrink, who

all think she's crazy. But she insists: "You
can see live football...and make movies." It's
all too much for her mother, who bursts into
tears. But Telenor 3G phones actually can do
all those things...right now.

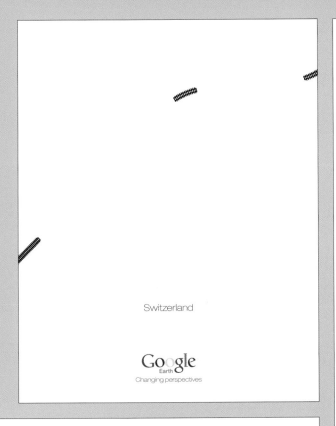

Switzerland

Google
Earth

Changing perspectives

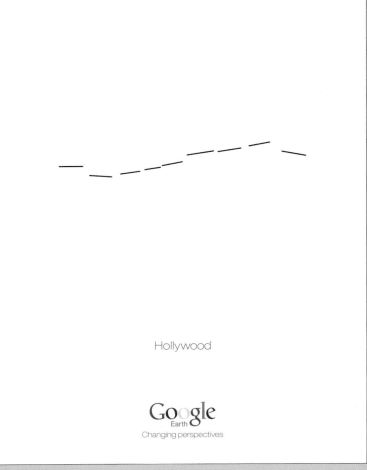

Hollywood

Google
Earth

Changing perspectives

Moscow

Google
Earth

Changing perspectives

Communication Services **59**

Agency	Kolle Rebbe, Hamburg
Creative Directors	Lorenz Ritter
	Sven Klohk
Copywriter	Constantin Sossidi
Art Director	Kay-Owe Tiedemann
Illustrator	Kay-Owe Tiedemann
Client	Google Earth

Agency	Storåkers McCann, Stockholm
Copywriters	Martin Marklund
	Petrus Kukulski
Production	Esteban, Stockholm
Directors	Alexander Brügge
	Markus Erneroth
Producers	Olof Barr
	Maria Widemar
Client	TeliaSonera, "Satellite Dish"

On a balcony, a man is removing his satellite dish. "We'll get a little sun on the balcony," he says. His son offers to help him, but he refuses. Suddenly, the dish slips out of his fingers and drops two floors, crashing onto the roof of a car below. A passing neighbour is furious: "It almost fell on my head!" With his father cringing out of sight below the balcony, the son is forced to take the blame. At least with Telia, they can now watch TV via broadband.

60   **Communication Services**

Agency	Marcel, Paris
Creative Directors	Fred Raillard
	Farid Mockart
Copywriter	Michael Zonnenberg
Art Director	Joseph Dubruque
Production	The Gang Films, Saint-Cloud
Director	Rob Sanders
Producers	Frédéric Mialaud
	Jacques Fouche
Client	Orange, "Flowers"

In this poetic spot, we see expanses of water entirely covered by gorgeous flowers. Young boys, elderly men, a young woman and a little girl: they all swim exuberantly through this exotic floral waterscape. Of course, if we had high definition TV, we'd appreciate the beauty of the scenes even more. HD by Orange: feel the beauty.

Agency	Publicis Conseil, Paris
Creative Director	Olivier Altmann
Copywriter	Olivier Dermaux
Art Director	Mathieu Vinciguerra
Production	Irène
Director	Frédéric Planchon
Producers	Guillaume de Bary
	Pierre Marcus
Client	Orange, "Planet"

All around the world, people are painting panels of wood and other flat surfaces dark blue. Then we see them walking, riding or sailing into position, in what is clearly an epic depiction of teamwork. Finally, on a signal, they hoist the blue panels above their heads. Up in a space ship, astronauts suddenly see planet earth turn dark, as if it's vanished. Down below, everybody laughs, pleased with the cosmic prank. It's a giant equivalent of a "flash mob". The internet from Orange: more fun together.

Agency	Forsman & Bodenfors, Gothenburg
Production	Hungry Man
Director	Scott Vincent
Producer	Martin Box
Client	Tele2, "Answer"

A father is teaching his daughter to ride a bike – but when his mobile phone rings, he abandons her to answer it. In a supermarket, a kid drops an armful of groceries so he doesn't have to miss a call, bottles smashing to the ground. Another man drops a new flat-screen TV that he's installing with his wife just to answer the phone. And a dog-walker lets go of his ravenous charges in order to pick up a call. Phone calls are so cheap with Tele2 that people feel compelled to answer their phones in the most inadvisable situations.

Agency	Duval Guillaume Brussels
Creative Directors	Katrien Bottez
	Peter Ampe
Copywriter	Benoît Menetret
Art Director	Jean-Marc Wachsmann
Production	Caviar Brussels
Director	Bram Van Riet
Producers	Eva Custers
	Lies Muys
	Dieter Lebbe
Client	Belgacom, "Swimming Pool"

A man inflates a cheap plastic bathing pool in the back garden for his kids. But he only has to tap the pump lightly with his foot and the shapeless piece of plastic unfurls into a huge aquatic play-land, complete with turrets, water slide and fountains in the shape of dolphins. Belgacom also gives its customers more than they expect.

Agency	Duval Guillaume Brussels
Creative Directors	Katrien Bottez
	Peter Ampe
Copywriter	Benoît Menetret
Art Director	Jean-Marc Wachsmann
Production	Latcho Drom Brussels
Director	Manu Coeman
Producers	Yves Legrève
	Bruno Dejonghe
	Dieter Lebbe
Client	Belgacom, "Lotto"

A man is watching the TV lottery when he realises that he's about to score the jackpot. Suspecting that the final number will also match his ticket, he uses the remote to pause the TV show. Then he opens his front door, cries "Help!" to alert the neighbours, and arranges cushions on the floor. He starts the show again. Sure enough, the last number matches his. He falls into a faint, with no danger of injury. Pause live TV, with Belgacom.

Agency   Publicis Conseil, Paris
Creative Director Olivier Altmann
Copywriters   Laurent Dravet
                  Axel Orliac
Production   Irène, Paris
Director   Matthijs Van Heiningen
Producers   Pierre Marcus
                  Hélène Daubert
Client   Orange,
                  "Rugby World Cup
                  Zidane"

During the Rugby World Cup, the French team has an unexpected new recruit: the soccer star Zinedine Zidane. We see that while Zidane may be a football genius, his slender physique is somewhat out of place on the rugby field. After some rough tackles, he uses his soccer skills to his advantage, weaving around the other players and finally achieving a great header. Unfortunately, he forgets that the ball is supposed to go over the bar. Everyone can experience the Rugby World Cup, with Orange internet.

62   Communication Services

Agency   Garbergs Reklambyrå,
              Stockholm
Copywriters   Stefan Pagréus
              Henning Wijkmark
Art Directors Malin von Werder
              Sebastian Smedberg
Production   Flodellfilm Stockholm
Director   Tomas Jonsgården
Producers   Magnus Åkerstedt
              Anna Adamson
Client   Telenor,
              "Telenor Mobile TV"

Over several decades, starting in 1957, we see rock'n'roll stars following the tradition of chucking televisions out of hotel windows. No matter what the era, the fans clustered outside the hotels scream their approval of this act of rebellion and destruction. And of course, a big TV set makes a very satisfying scrunch when it hits the ground. That's until 2007, when a rocker throws his mobile phone out of the window. His fans simply look bemused. TV on your mobile, from Telenor.

Agency   Garbergs Reklambyrå,
              Stockholm
Copywriter   Stefan Pagréus
Art Directors Sebastian Smedberg
              Mattias Dahlqvist
Production   Stylewar
Directors   Martin Sjöström
              Jacob Dahlström
Producers   Christer Kildén
              Anna Adamson
Client   Telenor, "Come Together"

Ring tones, dial tones, slamming laptop lids and various household objects are cleverly used as instruments by a family performing a familiar tune: "Come Together" by the Rolling Stones. With Telenor, mobile, broadband and fixed all come together in the perfect communications package.

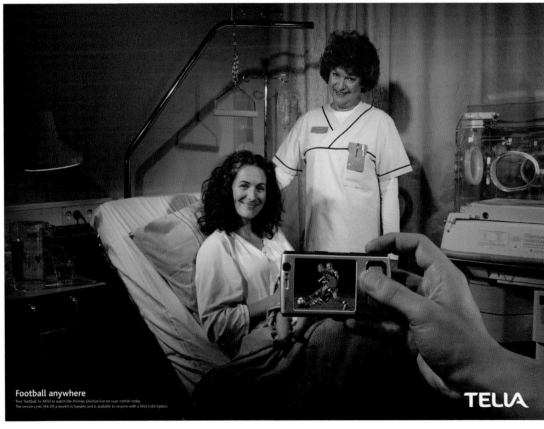

Football anywhere
Text 'Football' to 4450 to watch the Premier Division live on your mobile today.
The service costs SEK 69 a month in Sweden and is available to anyone with a Telia subscription.

Agency	Storåkers McCann, Stockholm	The magazine centre-fold brought the two faces in this double page press ad even closer together.	**Agency**	Storåkers McCann, Stockholm
Copywriter	Hanna Belander		**Copywriter**	Christian Sundgren
Art Director	Jonas Frank		**Art Director**	Jonas Frank
Photographers	Andreas Ackerup, Adamsky		**Photographers**	Bisse / Adamsky
Client	TeliaSonera		**Client**	TeliaSonera

64   **Communication Services**

Agency	Grabarz & Partner, Hamburg	Agency	Publicis, Stockholm
Executive CD	Ralf Heuel	Copywriter	Malin Åkersten Triumf
Creative Directors	Martin Grass	Art Director	Yasin Lekorchi
	Djik Ouchiian	Photographer	Niklas Ahlm
Copywriter	Martin Grass	Client	Neonode N2
Art Director	Djik Ouchiian		
Photographer	Djik Ouchiian		
Illustrators	Maren Wiegmann		
	Lena Ritthaler		
Client	Arcor Spam Blocker		

Agency	Fallon London	Agency	Jung von Matt, Berlin
Executive CD	Richard Flintham	Creative Directors	Mathias Stiller
Creative Director	Micah Walker		Wolfgang Schneider
Copywriters	Sam Akesson		David Mously
	Tomas Mankovsky		Jan Harbeck
Art Directors	Sam Akesson	Copywriter	Jan Harbeck
	Tomas Mankovsky	Art Director	David Mously
Photographers	Stijn & Marie	Client	DHL
Client	Orange		

Agency	Metropolitan Republic/
	Jupiter Drawing Room,
	Johannesburg
Creative Directors	Paul Warner
	Peter Khoury
	George Low
Copywriters	Konstant van Huyssteen
	Cara Messias
	James Cloete
Art Directors	Shane Forbes
	Wesley Phelan
Production	Velocity Films,
	Johannesburg
Director	Greg Gray
Producers	Helena Woodfine
	Noeleen Burley
Client	MTN, "Clap"

Mobile communications can link a community. As a metaphor for this, the agency takes its cameras to the Hillbrow district of Johannesburg, where a dance school from Soweto performs a brilliantly choreographed routine to "The Clapping Song" by Shirley Ellis. Before long, it seems that almost every local resident is in on the act, clapping and dancing in time to the music. The result is joyous and uplifting. MTN: go start something.

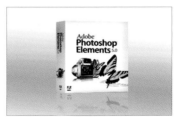

Agency	Metropolitan Republic/
	JDR, Johannesburg
Creative Directors	Paul Warner
	Peter Khoury
	George Low
Copywriters	Konstant van Huyssteen
	Cara Messias
Art Directors	Shane Forbes
	Wesley Phelan
Production	Wicked Pixels
Producers	Dennis Dyas
	Noeleen Burley
Client	MTN, "Stickies"

A cool urban art collective decorates the side of a skyscraper with thousands of sticky Post-It notes, creating a giant piece of graffiti. Not content with one example, they create sticky figures all around the city – and thanks to stunning animation, these shapes actually move. Meanwhile, people are excitedly telephoning the local radio station, eager to share what they've seen. Others take photos with their phones. MTN: go make magic.

Agency	Jung von Matt, Hamburg
CDs	Arno Lindemann
	Bernhard Lukas
Copywriter	Caroline Ellert
Art Director	Joanna Swistowski
Production	Erste Liebe Filmproduktion,
	Hamburg
Director	Sven Bollinger
Producers	Torben Ferkau
	Sybille Krafft
	Marie Wagner
Client	Adobe Systems,
	"Sauna"

At a dinner with friends, a man is passing around photos from his recent trip to Finland. They make polite comments about his snaps, until he hands his best friend's wife a photo of himself "at the sauna". Her jaw drops and her eyes pop. She wordlessly passes the photo to her husband, whose expression is a mixture of shock and admiration. Finally he asks "John, have you really got such a big...? You could jack your car up with that!" The man looks smug. But the pack shot reveals that he has been using Adobe Photoshop.

Agency	TBWA\PHS, Helsinki		**Agency**	Forsman & Bodenfors, Gothenburg
Copywriter	Erkko Mannila		**Photographer**	Mattias Edwall
Art Directors	Pia Pitkanen		**Client**	Tele2
	Jukka Rosti			
Illustrator	Pia Pitkanen			
Client	Finnish Post Office			

Agency	DDB Amsterdam	The flip-flapping departures board of a railway station is the inspiration behind this effects-driven fantasy. The timetable of Dutch railways is changing, so commuters must change their morning routine. To illustrate what might happen if they don't, we see people disappearing and magically reappearing at earlier or later points in their schedule. For instance, a man is transported rather too early from his bathroom to the office, while a woman reappears back in bed. The effects mimic the "flip-card" display system used by departures boards.
Creative Directors	Sanne Braam	
	Sikko Gerkema	
Copywriter	Daniël Snelders	
Art Directors	Niels de Wit	
	Robert van der Lans	
Production	Bäst	
Director	Daan Hocks	
Producers	Menno Koop	
	Marco van Prooijen	
Client	Nederlandse Spoorwegen/ Dutch Railways, "New Timetable"	

Minimal environmental impact

SJ
National Rail
Read more about our environmental work at www.sj.com

Agency	King, Stockholm
Creative Director	Frank Hollingworth
Copywriters	Niclas Carlsson
	Christian Karlsson
Art Directors	Josephine Wallin
	Tommy Carlsson
Client	SJ, Swedish Railways

At first glance, the railway track is hidden in the magazine's centre-fold and only becomes apparent when the pages are spread apart.

Agency	Publicis QMP, Dublin
Creative Director	Anton McClelland
Copywriter	Eugene Ruane
Art Director	Anton McClelland
Production	Red Rage Films, Dublin
Director	Brian Durnin
Producers	Gary Moore
	Niamh Skelly
	Jessica Wright
Client	Failte Ireland, "Chicken"

In a posh restaurant, a woman asks the trainee waiter: "How's the chicken prepared?" Conscious that the headwaiter beside him is watching his every move, the young man hesitates. Then he replies: "I think they just tell them, 'You're going to die'." The headwaiter smiles ingratiatingly at the diners and explains: "He's being trained." Careers in tourism, sponsored by Failte Ireland, the Irish Tourist Board.

Agency	McCann Erickson, Madrid
Creative Director	Monica Moro
Copywriter	Isabel Lopez
Art Directors	Ricardo Rovira
	Raquel Martínez
Production	Lee Films Madrid
Director	Sega
Producers	Iván Fernandéz
	Diego Mañas
Client	Madrid Metro, "A Short Story"

When a man discovers that his girlfriend is cheating on him, he feels so small that he literally shrinks. The tiny disconsolate figure shambles onto the metro. On a train, however, he meets an attractive woman who's also shrunk. Drawn together, they begin to enjoy their diminutive stature. In fact, they have a romantic day out on the metro. When they surface, they're back to normal size. Madrid Metro: "It's not the new trains; it's not the new stations – it's how it makes you feel."

Agency	DDB Amsterdam
Creative Directors	Sanne Braam
	Sikko Gerkema
Copywriter	Sikko Gerkema
Art Director	Sanne Braam
Production	25 FPS, Amsterdam
Director	Maarten Treurniet
Producers	Bas Pinkse
	Wikke van der Burg
	Marloes van den Berg
Client	Nederlandse Spoor-wegen/Dutch Railways, "Business Man"

A businessman arrives in a Dutch city to do an important deal with a Japanese company. In the boardroom, he compliments his opposite number's elegant silk suit. Far from being shocked, the Japanese man asks if he'd like to try it on. They jovially swap suits. This bonding experience instantly turns them into best friends. We see them sharing childhood memories, larking about with the photocopier and casually finalising the deal while using the urinals. When you travel relaxed, you do business relaxed.

Agency	Publicis Helsinki
Creative Director	Anthony Wolch
Copywriter	Timo Heikkilä
Art Director	Pekka Rouhiainen
Production	Otto Tuotanto, Helsinki
Director	Jappe Päivinen
Producer	Katariina Lehtonen
Client	Sun Tours, "Young Sir"

A little boy is on vacation with his parents in an exotic country. At night they go to a restaurant, where the boy is treated with courtesy and respect – just like a grown-up! The waiter gives him a menu, but he knows exactly what he wants: a giant lobster like the one being eaten at a neighbouring table. The plate duly arrives when "thud!" the boy is back at the school canteen, facing a plate of stodgy battered fish and mashed potato. He's been daydreaming. Thinking of a holiday? Sun Tours.

Agency	Kitchen Leo Burnett, Oslo
Copywriter	Kristoffer Carlin
Art Director	Martin Thorsen
Production	Paradox Produksjon, Oslo
Director	Andreas J. Riiser
Producer	Gry Sætre
Client	Oslo Sporveier, "Big Bus"

This grittily-directed spot begins with a huge traffic jam. Apparently frustrated, one of the drivers pulls out of line and accelerates. Improbably, the other cars follow him. Now we see they're whizzing around an airport runway. It's all very impressive – but there's method in their madness. Sure enough, the cars get into formation. As the camera pulls back, we see that the parked cars have formed the outline of a giant bus. Slowly, it starts to trundle forwards. A single bus can eliminate a one kilometre traffic jam.

Agency	King, Stockholm
Creative Director	Frank Hollingworth
Copywriter	Niclas Carlsson
Art Director	Josephine Wallin
Production	Social Club, Stockholm
Director	Jesper Ericstam
Producers	Richard Edholm
	Lena Ivarsson
Client	SJ Swedish Railways, "Heroes"

The David Bowie song "Heroes" plays over shots of some very ordinary people on a train. Awkward teenagers, passengers with their feet on the seats, noisy kids, a man eating smelly fast food, grumpy older people and self-absorbed younger ones...what could possibly be heroic about this lot? The endline reveals it all: "Thank you for choosing the greenest way to travel." Taking the train helps the fight against climate change.

Agency	Ruf Lanz, Zurich
Creative Directors	Danielle Lanz
	Markus Ruf
Copywriter	Markus Ruf
Art Director	Danielle Lanz
Production	Rosas'n'co Films
Director	Benjamin Kempf
Producer	Nadia Rosasco
Client	VBZ Zurich
	Public Transport,
	"La Cucaracha"

A Mexican song-and-dance trio, complete with sombreros, boards a tram in Zurich. Then they begin performing the familiar song La Cucaracha at mind-boggling speed. What's all the rush? In Zurich, there's a tram stop every 300 metres. Apologies to all musicians.

72   Transport & Tourism

Agency	King James,
	Cape Town
Creative Director	Alistair King
Copywriter	Paige Nick
Art Director	Christan Boshoff
Illustrator	Lev Yilmaz
Director	Lev Yilmaz
Producer	Caz Friedman
Client	Kulula.com Airline,
	"Flying With Kids" &
	"Tourists"

In this animated campaign, users of the South African airline recall funny incidents from their flights. Here, a man explains how, on one flight, a kid in the next row stuck his tongue out at him. The man pulled a funny face. The kid pulled an even funnier, scarier one. The pair continued to grimace one another until the man made the most "awful, scary face I knew how to do". The kid burst into tears. Then his mother turned around, furious. Kulula.com: come fun with us.

In the second spot, a woman remembers sitting on a flight next to two tourists identifiable by their sunburns and giant wooden giraffe. When the man asked her what Johannesburg was like, she teased him by saying that elephants were the main form of transport, everyone lived in mud huts, men carried spears, women had no tops and there was no electricity. Incredibly, the man believed her. "I think he may have wet himself a little." Flying Kulula is always fun.

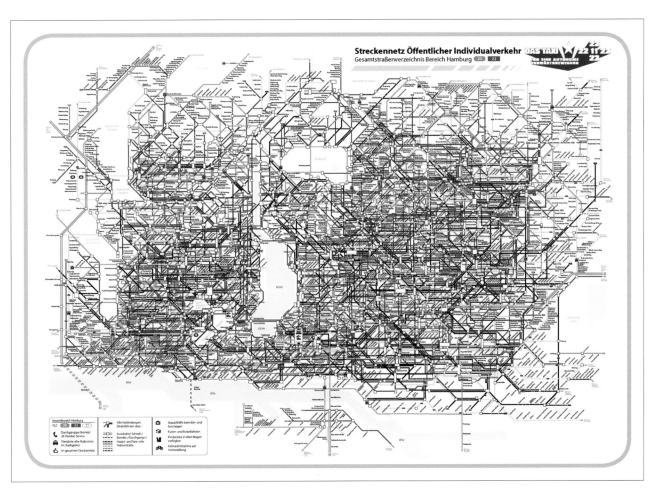

Agency	BDDP & Fils, Paris	Agency	Nordpol+ Hamburg	Public transportation network for
Creative Directors	Manoelle Van Der Vaeren	**Creative Director**	Lars Ruehmann	individual traffic. (To compete with the
	Guillaume Chifflot	**Copywriters**	Sebastian Behrendt	public transport systems, this poster for a
Copywriter	François Faure		Ingmar Bartels	Hamburg taxi service shows every street
Art Director	Antoine Mathon	**Art Directors**	Tim Schierwater	in the city. The posters were removed
Photographer	Cédric Delsaux		Christoph Bielefeldt	from the Hamburg underground when
Client	C'est So Paris,		Stephanie Schneider	passengers leaned dangerously close to
	Tourism Website		Bertrand Kirschenhofer	the tracks in order to read them.)
		Client	Das Taxi	

74   Transport & Tourism

Agency	DDB Paris
Creative Directors	Alexandre Hervé
	Sylvain Thirache
Copywriter	Jérôme Langlade
Art Director	Sébastien Pierre
Photographer	Olivier Amsellem
Client	Voyages-sncf.com

Agency	Leo Burnett, Paris	Agency	King, Helsinki
Creative Director	Stephan Ferens	**Creative Director**	Jouko Laune
Copywriters	Edward Capelle	**Copywriter**	Timo Koskinen
	Stéphane Santana	**Art Director**	Jouko Laune
Art Directors	Edward Capelle	**Photographer**	Kari Ylitalo
	Stéphane Santana	**Client**	Carpark
Photographer	Locomotiv		
Client	Motocab		

Because they deserve a break.

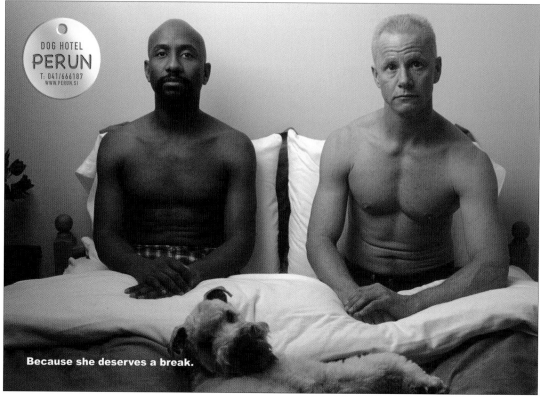

Because she deserves a break.

Agency	DDB Oslo	Agency	Mayer McCann,
Copywriter	Camilla Bjørnhaug		Ljubljana
Art Directors	Preben Moan	Creative Director	Vojka Zgavec
	Joachim Bjørndahl	Copywriter	Barbara Brodnik
Photographer	Billy Bonkers	Art Director	Tina Brezovnik
Client	Flytoget	Client	Perun Dog Hotel

Agency   TBWA\Paris
Creative Director   Erik Vervroegen
Copywriter   Ghislaine de Germon
Art Director   Marianne Fonferrier
Photographer   David Harriman
Client   SNCF, French Railways
                Téoz Trains

The power of flowers.

Agency	Walker, Zurich	An elderly woman visits the grave of her late husband on their wedding anniversary. Unexpectedly, a delivery man appears with a bouquet of flowers and a letter. We hear the voice of the husband as the woman reads: "My darling – I knew I'd find you here, today of all days, our special anniversary. Thank you for thinking of me. These flowers are to let you know I'm thinking of you. As I always do. As I always will." Interflora – the power of flowers.
Creative Director	Pius Walker	
Copywriter	Pius Walker	
Production	Paul Weiland Film, London	
Director	Anthony Minghella	
Producer	Mary Francis	
Client	Fleurop Interflora, "Anniversary"	

THE
HARVEY NICHOLS
SALE

THE
HARVEY NICHOLS
SALE

THE
HARVEY NICHOLS
SALE

 Retail Services **79**

Agency	DDB London
Creative Directors	Adam Tucker
	Justin Tindall
Copywriter	Jonathan John
Art Director	David Mackersey
Photographer	Tim Flach
Client	Harvey Nichols

Agency	King, Helsinki
Copywriter	Timo Koskinen
Art Director	Kimmo Korhonen
Production	Also Starring
Director	Vellu Valla
Producer	Johannes Lassila
Client	Itakeskus, "The Period of Darkness"

Finns have to suffer a two month period when the sun barely rises. Here we see a Finnish family loafing morosely around their gloomy, under-lit home. Suddenly, fingers of sunshine peep through the curtains and the family becomes hysterically happy as golden light pours into the apartment. Then, just as abruptly, it vanishes and they are plunged back into gloom. Get a life: buy a lamp.

Agency	SMFB, Oslo
Copywriters	Stig Bjølbakk
	Hans Martin Rønneseth
Art Directors	Stig Bjølbakk
	Hans Martin Rønneseth
Production	Moland Film
Directors	Johan Skog
	Niklas Froberg
Producer	Mone Mikkelsen
Client	Kiwi Grocery Stores, "Camping"

On a campsite, a woman leaves her family's modest caravan to do some shopping at the local Kiwi supermarket. But with each purchase she makes, their camping conditions grow more comfortable: the chairs become more luxurious, a white picket fence appears, the paddling pool expands inside. By the time the woman has finished shopping, even the caravan itself has doubled in size. With the money you save shopping at Kiwi, you can afford a few luxuries.

Agency	Walker, Zurich
Creative Director	Pius Walker
Copywriter	Pius Walker
Art Director	Mr. G
Production	Cobblestone Hamburg
	Socialclub, Stockholm
Director	Axel Laubscher
Producers	Pieter Lony
	Markus Ahlm
Client	Fleurop Interflora, "Tent"

On a lengthy camping expedition, a group of men are writing to their loved ones. One of them reads out his missive: "Dear Catherine, your hair is blonde and nice, like the beer in my hand." Don't look for words – say it with flowers. Interflora.

Agency	GMP Advertising, Bucharest	We see a large apartment building at night. A few lights are on – but one light keeps going on and off very rapidly. On the screen, the explanation appears: phosphorescent condoms. Available at the Erotica online sex shop.
Creative Director	Oliver Kapusta	
Copywriter	Cosmin Ezaru	
Art Director	Cosmin Ezaru	
Production	Multimedia Est, Bucharest	
Client	Erotica.ro, "The Light"	

Retail Services 81

Agency	DDB Oslo	At the office canteen, three women are fretting about their diets. One admits she skipped breakfast. Another wants to know the "glycemic index" of an asparagus. "I haven't eaten anything I like since June 2002," admits a third. But at the dinner table, they are joined by a svelte colleague who intends to eat a big lunch. When they ask if she's on a secret diet, she replies "No, I just started walking to work." Sometimes simple is better – like Rema 1000 grocery store.
Copywriters	Kenneth Lamond Johansen Jørgen Gjærum	
Art Directors	Tone Garmann Pål Jespersen	
Production	Monster Commercials	
Director	Peter Næss	
Producers	Helene Hovda Lunde Jessica Paine	
Client	Rema 1000, "Walking"	

Agency	Young & Rubicam, Paris	We're at an archaeological dig in Egypt. An Indiana Jones type unearths a valuable artefact, wraps it in cloth and cycles off with it at full speed. He effortlessly negotiates rugged terrain, narrow alleys, potholes and seething traffic in order to make it to the Cairo museum of antiquities. Proudly, he places the ancient Egyptian statue on a trolley. But as it is wheeled away, the trolley wheel hits a pebble – and the artefact disintegrates. Not every vehicle has the suspension of B-Twin bikes, available at Décathlon.
Creative Directors	The Six	
Copywriter	Jean-François Bouchet	
Art Directors	Jessica Gérard-Huet	
Production	La Pac, Paris	
Director	Matthias Schut	
Producer	Valérie Montiel	
Client	Décathlon, "Egypt"	

– Bought something nice?
– Yes, sausages for my grandchildren.

You're putting napkins on the dinner table?

fakta
It only takes 5 minutes

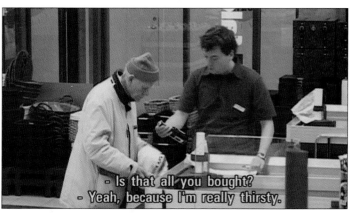

– Is that all you bought?
– Yeah, because I'm really thirsty.

– What now?
– I just want to check it ...

fakta
It only takes 5 minutes

so, you wanna go home for pizza and a fuck?

Louis Nielsen
THE DISCOUNT OPTICIAN

Louis Nielsen
THE DISCOUNT OPTICIAN

82   Retail Services

Agency	Uncle Grey, Aarhus	
Creative Director	Per Pedersen	
Copywriters	Michael Paterson	
	Thomas Falkenberg	
Art Director	Jesper Hansen	
Production	Lassie Film,	
	Copenhagen	
Director	Jan Gleie	
Producers	Stig Weiss	
	Jan Pedersen	
Client	Fakta Supermarkets,	
	"Small Talk" &	
	"Quality Control"	

Fakta employees try various ploys to get customers to stay longer. In the first film, a cashier engages a customer in a long conversation about her lunch plans, which involve having sausages with her grandkids, as the next customer in line fumes impatiently. "Is that all you bought?" asks a cashier in the second spot, when a man pays for a single beer. He is astonished when the cashier opens the beer and has a sip to "test" it. Shopping at Fakta only takes five minutes – but they wish you'd stay longer.

Agency	Uncle Grey, Aarhus	
Creative Director	Per Pedersen	
Copywriter	Ulrik Feldskov Juul	
Art Director	Rasmus Dunvad	
Production	Moland Film,	
	Copenhagen	
Director	Peter Harton	
Producers	Sandra Heavy	
	Jan Pedersen	
Client	Louis Nielsen	
	Opticians, "Twins" &	
	"Husband and Dog"	

Identical twins test designer glasses vs cheaper ones from Louis Nielsen. The men approach twin women. In unison they ask: "So, you wanna go home for a pizza and a fuck?" They are both slapped in the face. "Ahh," they say, "you don't like pizza?" Another slap. In the second spot a woman watches her husband play with their dog, first with cheap glasses and then an expensive pair. His oafish behaviour only goes from bad to worse. Conclusion: expensive glasses do not make you more attractive, nor do they make life prettier.

Make sure you have a room to send them to.

Kids room for only €499

top ▦ interior

www.hornbach.com

You helped rebuild Germany after the war.
So don't let anyone tell you
how to renovate.

HORNBACH ⧄
Home Improvement Superstores

Retail Services 83

Agency	Duval Guillaume Brussels	Agency	Heimat, Berlin
Creative Directors	Katrien Bottez	**Creative Directors**	Guido Heffels
	Peter Ampe		Juergen Vossen
Copywriters	Raoul Maris	**Copywriters**	Sebastian Kainz
	Hans Kerkhoff		Guido Heffels
Art Directors	Raoul Maris		Till Eckel
	Hans Kerkhoff	**Art Directors**	Tim Schneider
Client	Top Interior		Marc Wientzek
		Photographer	Wolfgang Stahr
		Illustrator	Michael Mackens
		Client	Hornbach

Agency	Ruf Lanz, Zurich	Agency	Selmore, Amsterdam
Creative Directors	Markus Ruf	Creative Directors	Bas Korsten
	Danielle Lanz		Michael Jansen
Copywriters	George W. Bush	Copywriter	Bas Korsten
	Markus Ruf	Art Director	Michael Jansen
Art Director	Grit Wolany	Photographer	Arthur Mebius
Client	Sport Factory Outlet	Client	Bijenkorf

Agency	King, Stockholm
Creative Director	Frank Hollingworth
Copywriters	Hedvig Hagwall Bruckner
	Pontus Ekström
Art Directors	Helena Redman
	Alexander Elers
	Daniel Söderstedt
Photographer	Peter Gehrke
Client	Åhléns Department Stores

Each of these press executions used three consecutive pages; the single page "teaser" ads being followed by "revelations" on the next two pages.

Everything is more beautiful with flowers.

Agency	McCann Erickson, Geneva	Agency	Zapping/M&C Saatchi, Madrid
Creative Director	Timo Kirez	Creative Directors	Uschi Henkes
Copywriter	David von Ritter		Manolo Moreno
Art Director	Olivier Renaud		Urs Frick
Photographer	Marie Deillon	Copywriter	Carlos García Janini
Client	Fantasia Flowers	Art Director	Carlos Alvarez
		Photographer	Miguel Toledano
		Client	Anemone Flower Shop

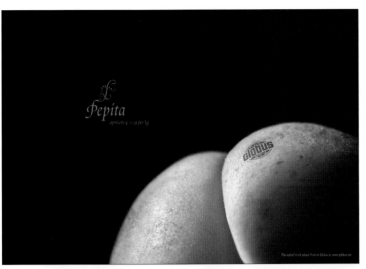

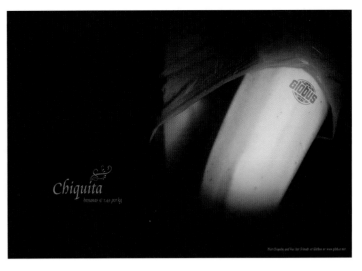

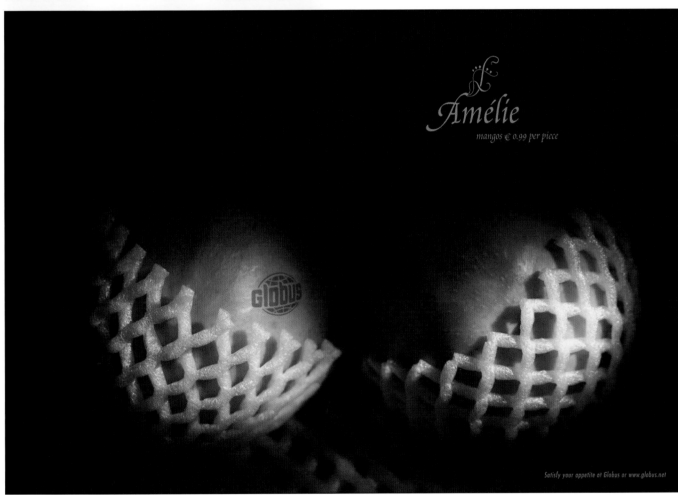

Agency	Ogilvy, Frankfurt
Creative Directors	Gregor Seitz
	Wolfgang Zimmerer
Copywriter	Marc Oehlcke
Art Director	Daniel Schweinzer
Photographer	Jo Bacherl
Client	Globus Supermarket

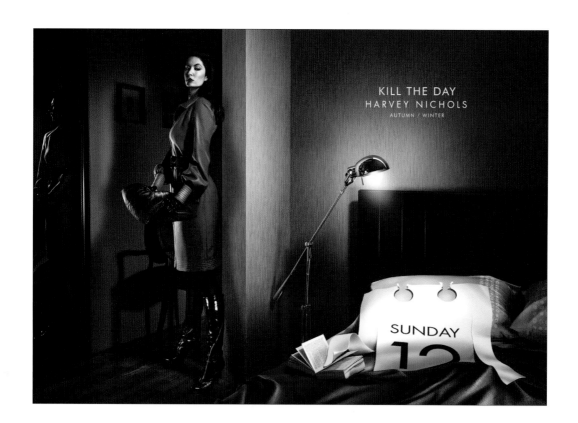

88 **Retail Services**

Agency	Team Y&R, Dubai	Agency	DDB London
Creative Directors	Shahir Ahmed	Creative Director	Adam Tucker
	Komal Bedi	Copywriter	Matt Lee
Copywriters	Shahir Ahmed	Art Director	Peter Heyes
	Amit Kapoor	Photographer	Robert Wyatt
Art Directors	Mohanad Shuraideh	Client	Harvey Nichols
	Komal Bedi		
Illustrators	Gitten Tom		
	Abhijeet Vartak		
Photographer	Tejal Patni		
Client	Harvey Nichols		

HARVEY NICHOLS
WOMENSWEAR

HARVEY NICHOLS
MENSWEAR

HARVEY NICHOLS
BEAUTY

Agency	DDB London
Creative Directors	Adam Tucker
	Justin Tindall
Copywriters	Emer Stamp
	Ben Tollett
Art Directors	Emer Stamp
	Ben Tollett
Photographer	Dimitri Daniloff
Client	Harvey Nichols

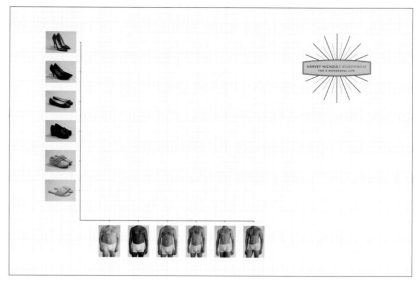

Agency	Ruf Lanz, Zurich
Creative Directors	Markus Ruf
	Danielle Lanz
Copywriter	Nicole Glaus
Art Director	Lorenz Clormann
Photographers	Stefan Minder
	Felix Schregenberger
Client	Hiltl Vegetarian Restaurant

Agency	DDB London
Creative Director	Adam Tucker
Copywriters	Joanna Wenley
	Grant Parker
Art Directors	Grant Parker
	Joanna Wenley
Photographers	Beate Sonnenberg
	Wayne Parker
Client	Harvey Nichols

NOW EVEN UNGENEROUS PEOPLE CAN AFFORD A NEW SKI SUIT.

Agencies	Publicis, Amsterdam	Our free interior architect refines	**Agency**	Ruf Lanz, Zurich

Agencies   Publicis, Amsterdam
            Publicis Dialog, Amsterdam
Creative Directors   Bram Holzapfel
            Annemiek Klijn
Copywriter   Arnout Robbe
Art Director   Paul Wagemaker
Photographer   Eddo Hartmann
Client   Villa Arena

Our free interior architect refines
your home, not your habits.

Agency   Ruf Lanz, Zurich
Creative Directors   Markus Ruf
            Danielle Lanz
Copywriter   Markus Ruf
Art Director   Marcel Schläfle
Client   Sport Factory Outlet

Just call us.

Centraal Beheer

The insurance company
in Apeldoorn. (055) 579 8000

Agency	DDB Amsterdam	We're introduced to a bumbling ambulance
Creative Director	Martin Cornelissen	crew. One of them is so busy doing the
Copywriter	Daniël Snelders	crossword that he almost loses an old guy
Art Director	Niels de Wit	– only to be alerted by the rapid bleeping of
Production	Stink, London	the life support machine. He electrocutes the
Director	Ivan Zacharias	codger back to life. The arrival of a brand
Producers	Nick Landon	new ambulance makes the pair's day. But the
	Vanessa Janssen	technology confuses them. At one point, the
Client	Centraal Beheer Insurance,	emergency operative in the back confuses
	"Ambulance"	the reversing signal with the life support
		machine, and electrocutes a perfectly healthy
		patient. It's always best to have insurance.

Should you name her Anna, Vera or Nicole? We suggest David.

Many doors have opened to women in today's business world. But the doors of many of the major board rooms remain closed. Of the 271 companies listed on the Swedish stock exchange, only 5 have a woman CEO. And 22 of these companies don't have a single woman in top management at all.

But who cares?

You should, since it's your money. One day, most of us will be collecting a retirement pension that is generated at least in part by investments in Swedish corporations. It's in our mutual interest that these companies have done everything in their power to maximize financial growth. And we don't believe this is done with only men in charge. And we are not alone. Countless financial reports show that businesses with more women in top management are more profitable.

When you become a Folksam client, we can influence more companies to offer the same opportunities to our daughters as to our sons. We might not be able to change everything. But over time, we will make a difference – particularly when it comes to mutual fund growth. So if you think this makes good sense, invest your retirement pension savings with us. Remember, you still have the chance to change the future. Particularly your daughter's.

Folksam®
Ethical Investments

Harvard or Cambridge? Start by calling her Michael.

The first step toward a succesful corporate career is to be born a man. Simply because men are the ones in charge. Among the 271 companies listed on the Swedish stock exchange, only 5 have a woman CEO. And 22 of these companies don't have a single woman in top management at all.

So who cares?

You should, since it's your money. One day, most of us will be collecting a retirement pension that is generated at least in part by investments in Swedish corporations. It's in our mutual interest that these companies have done everything in their power to maximize financial growth. And we don't believe this is done with only men in charge. And we are not alone. Countless financial reports show that businesses with more women in top management are more profitable.

When you become a Folksam client, we can influence more companies to offer the same opportunities to our daughters as to our sons. We might not be able to change everything. But over time, we will make a difference – particularly when it comes to mutual fund growth. So if you think this makes good sense, invest your retirement pension savings with us. A good question to ask yourself could be that if you have a chance to help modernize the gender structure of the corporate world, shouldn't you take it? One day your daughter might ask you that very same question.

Folksam®
Ethical Investments

Give your daughter the right career opportunities: name her William.

Today, you can find more Williams than female CEOs in companies traded on the Swedish stock exchange. It sounds like a bad joke, but it's actually nothing to laugh about. Because even if all these Williams probably are doing a good job, there's got to be something wrong when only 5 out of 271 publicly traded companies have women in the top management slot.

So who cares?

You should, since it's your money. One day, most of us will be collecting a retirement pension that is generated at least in part by investments in Swedish corporations. It's in our mutual interest that these companies have done everything in their power to maximize financial growth. And we don't believe this is done with only men in charge. And we are not alone. Countless financial reports show that businesses with more women in top management are more profitable.

When you become a Folksam client, we can influence more companies to offer the same opportunities to our daughters as to our sons. We might not be able to change everything. But over time, we will make a difference – particularly when it comes to mutual fund growth. So if you think this makes good sense, invest your retirement pension savings with us. High returns and low fees are something you can count on. A clean conscience comes as a bonus.

Folksam®
Ethical Investments

 Financial Services   **93**

Agency	ANR.BBDO Sweden, Gothenburg & Stockholm
Copywriter	Olle Nordell
Art Directors	Andreas Lönn
	Marcus Göransson
Photographer	Alexander Crispin
Illustrators	Marie Wanberg
	Jeanett Aschman
Client	Folksam

Agency	MUW Saatchi & Saatchi, Bratislava	
Creative Director	Rasto Ulicny	
Copywriter	Matus Svirloch	
Art Director	Rasto Ulicny	
Production	Hitchhiker Films	
Director	Roman Valent	
Client	Kooperativa Insurance, "Ketchup"	

In his parked car, a man is about to tuck into a tasty hotdog slathered with ketchup. A pretty blonde woman gets into her car behind him – and promptly rear-ends him. Splat! In the impact, he gets ketchup all over his face. But when the woman comes to apologise, she thinks he's covered in blood. She screams. And the man screams too. After all, this could mean a bigger insurance payout!

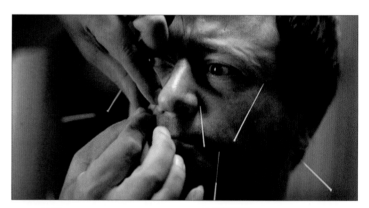

Agency	DDB Amsterdam
Creative Director	Marin Cornelissen
Copywriter	Niels Westra
Art Director	Jakko Achterberg
Production	Bike Films, Amsterdam
Director	Frank Devos
Producers	Monique van Beckhoven Yuka Kambayashi
Client	Centraal Beheer Insurance, "Prison Guard"

In another hilarious spot from Dutch insurer Centraal Beheer, a young man is being trained as a prison guard. A veteran colleague shows him the ropes – which consist of taunting the powerless prisoners. Then the rookie is given the job of delivering a love letter to a prisoner in a barred cell. Warming to his task, the novice guard threatens to set fire to the letter. But when it really does catch alight, the smoke alarms go off and all the cell doors automatically open. Let's hope he's insured.

Agency	DDB Amsterdam
Creative Director	Martin Cornelissen
Copywriters	Dylan de Backer André Dammers
Art Directors	André Dammers Joris Kuijpers
Production	Czar.nl, Amsterdam
Director	Bart Timmer
Producers	Sybrig Stork Vanessa Janssen
Client	Centraal Beheer Insurance, "Acupuncture"

A man turns up at a seedy Asian acupuncture clinic and soon finds himself stripped down to his underpants and stuck full of pins. The "therapist" works happily away, humming along to the radio, until he sniffs smoke. Opening a door, he sees a fire raging outside. He bolts for it. His prickly patient hobbles onto the balcony, where far below the fire brigade urge him to jump onto their spread canvas. Understandably, he's not keen. At times like this, it's best to be insured with Centraal Beheer.

This is not a hammer.

This is a common finger squasher. Hopefully Allianz Insurance.

Allianz (Ⅲ)

This is not a roof tile.

This is a painful bump provocateur. Hopefully Allianz Insurance.

Allianz (Ⅲ)

This is not a banana peel.

This is a malicious back bruiser. Hopefully Allianz Insurance.

Allianz (Ⅲ)

Agencies	Atletico Germany, Düsseldorf
	Atletico International, Barcelona
Creative Directors	Roland Vanoni
	Arndt Dallmann
Copywriter	Anne Katrin Trybek
Art Director	Lars Hodeige
Illustrator	Aleix Pons
Client	Allianz Insurance

Agency	DDB Stockholm
Creative Director	Johan Holmström
Copywriter	Mattias Manitski
Art Directors	Ted Mellström
	Simon Higby
Production	Sonny London
	FLX Stockholm
Directors	Fredrik Bond
	Emil Möller
Producers	Helen Kenny
	Emil Möller
	Fabian Mannheimer
Client	EnterCard, "Impulses"

As they sit together on a bridge, a girl gets a sudden impulse to give her boyfriend a shove, just to see what happens. We all have bizarre and dramatic impulses, explains the narrator, over scenes of a man jumping from a building, a half-naked woman driving a bus, a car rampaging through a field of crops...and so on. But self-control prevents us from doing such insane, dangerous things. So why are we so afraid of losing control of our credit cards? Remember – with EnterCard, you're in control.

96   **Financial Services**

Agency	Abby Norm, Stockholm
Copywriter	Håkan Nyberg
Art Director	Emil Frid
Production	Social Club, Stockholm
Director	Jesper Ohlsson
Producers	Rickard Edholm
	Sarah Grey
	Copeland
Client	KPA Pension, "Anti Personnel Mines"

In the troubled Middle East, we see a kid leaving his home and larking about in the streets with his friend, like any normal youngster. This is inter-cut with images of a mysterious cargo being delivered. As the kid decides to walk home across country, we see a group of soldiers pulling up in a jeep not far away. They are planting anti-personnel mines on the route the kid is about to take. Do you know how your pension fund is being invested? Invest ethically, with KPA.

Agency	Papaya Advertising, Bucharest
Creative Director	Robert Tiderle
Copywriter	Robert Tiderle
Art Director	Dan Samoila
Production	Smart Film, Bucharest
Director	Razvan Marculescu
Producers	Stefan Angheluta
	Vlad Caprarescu
Client	BCR Property Insurance, "Petrol - The Giant"

As his kid enjoys a birthday party indoors, a man is digging in the back garden so he can plant a sapling. His wife emerges: "Not on your son's birthday!" The man waves her away. At the next stroke, his pickaxe hits a seam of oil. The huge gusher soaks the man. He rushes into the house to tell everyone, but they are all terrified of the blackened apparition. His wife drops the birthday cake, whose candles set the petrol ablaze. Maybe the man isn't so lucky after all. Let's hope he's got property insurance!

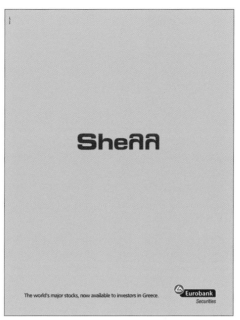

ΣONY

The world's major stocks, now available to investors in Greece.

Eurobank
Securities

SheΛΛ

The world's major stocks, now available to investors in Greece.

Eurobank
Securities

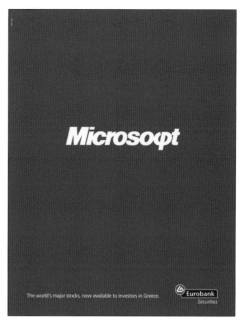

Microsoφt

The world's major stocks, now available to investors in Greece.

Eurobank
Securities

CA Crédito Agrícola
HOME LOANS

SOMETIMES YOU JUST NEED
A BIGGER PLACE.

Agency	Spot JWT, Athens	Agency	Leo Burnett, Lisbon
Executive CD	Takis Liarmakopoulos	Creative Director	Fernando Bellotti
Creative Director	Alexandros Tsoutis	Copywriter	Chacho Puebla
Copywriter	Maria Tzanidou	Art Director	Bruno Ribeiro
Art Director	Alexandros Tsoutis	Photographer	Omar Hamdan
Client	Eurobank	Client	Crédito Agricola

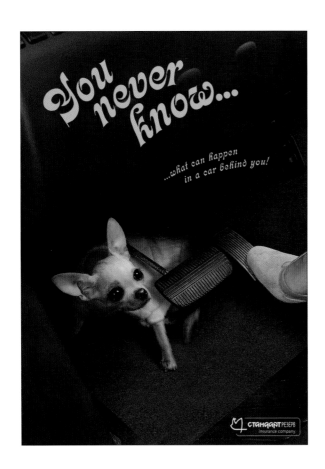

98   Financial Services

Agency	Creative Agency Avrora, Moscow	Agency	Ogilvy, Frankfurt
Creative Director	Pawel Khijnakov	**Creative Directors**	Simon Oppmann
			Peter Roemmelt
Copywriter	Anna Pershina	**Copywriter**	Joerg Schrod
Art Director	Andrey Sitalov	**Art Director**	Jens Frank
Client	Standard Reserve Insurance	**Client**	Dresdner Kleinwort

Agency	Selmore, Amsterdam
Creative Directors	Poppe van Pelt
	Diederick Hillenius
Copywriter	Poppe van Pelt
Art Director	Diederick Hillenius
Client	Fortis ASR Insurance

Agency	Garbergs Reklambyrå, Stockholm
Copywriter	Johan van der Schoot
Art Director	Lotta Mårlind
Production	Spader Knekt
Director	Patrik Bergh
Producers	Mattias Bengtsson
	Fredrik Heinig
	Camilla Geijer
Client	Skandia, "Pool" & "Coaster"

Exuberant young people strip to their underwear, charge across the grounds of a hotel and leap into the swimming pool. All except one, moderately older man, who descends gingerly via the ladder and embarks on a careful breast stroke. Time to think about pensions?

A bunch of young guys are sitting on a sofa watching the match. One comes in from the kitchen with beers – and coasters, to protect the nice coffee table from rings. His friends look at him askance. Time to think about pensions? Time to visit the Skandia website.

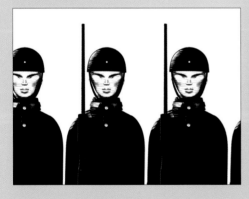

Your signature
is more powerful than you think.

Agency	TBWA\Paris
Creative Director	Erik Vervroegen
Copywriters	Stéphane Gaubert
	Stéphanie Thomasson
Art Directors	Stéphane Gaubert
	Stéphanie Thomasson
Production	Mr Hyde
Director	Philippe Grammaticopoulos
Client	Amnesty International, "Signatures"

This dark animated film demonstrates how signing an Amnesty petition brings hope. The spot begins with a signature that unravels to become a door, allowing a prisoner to escape. In the next scene, a woman fends off lascivious prison guards with a signature that unfurls into a whip. Signatures allow one man to escape his torturers, and another to deflect firing squad bullets. Finally, a signature is transformed into a balloon that lifts a child soldier out of a war zone. Your signature is more powerful than you think.

Agency   Kolle Rebbe, Hamburg
Creative Directors Sven Klohk
                  Lorenz Ritter
Copywriter   Elena Bartrina y Manns
Art Directors   Maik Beimdieck
                  Jens Lausenmeyer
Illustrator   Eva Salzmann
Client   Misereor Charity

IT'S NOT HAPPENING HERE
BUT IT IS HAPPENING NOW

amnesty international

Agency	Walker, Zurich
Creative Director	Pius Walker
Production	Gorgeous Enterprises, London
Director	Chris Palmer
Producer	Rupert Smithe
Client	Amnesty International, "Channel Hop"

As we hop from channel to channel, familiar TV presenters tell us appalling facts: "There are 27 million people enslaved worldwide," says a chirpy blonde. On a kids' quiz show, we're told that Colombia has the highest number of child soldiers. A TV chef informs us that people in China are tortured by having bamboo shoots forced under their fingernails. And a TV exercise queen points out that half a million girls are abducted into sexual slavery every year. None of this stuff is happening near you – but it is happening now. Show your concern by joining Amnesty.

How much to pay for apple?

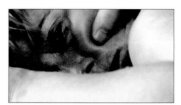

Women enslaved by sex trafficking lose more than just their names

Trafficking is Torture.

Trafficking is Torture.

102   Public Interest

Agency	Quiet Storm, London
Copywriter	Neal Colyer
Art Director	Neal Colyer
Production	Quiet Storm Films, London
Directors	Kevin Chicken
	Steven Sander
Producer	Kate Pirouet
Client	Helen Bamber Foundation, "Trafficking is Torture " Campaign

A young woman is struggling with the English language. When trying to ask for fruit, she says: "How much to pay for cock suck?" (while what she really means is subtitled on the screen). Later on, instead of asking for directions, she asks: "You fuck me good, yes?" She messes up a job interview the same way. Everyone is confused and embarrassed by her language, but it's clear that she has no idea what she's saying. In fact, these "useful" phrases have been taught to her by the human traffickers who sold her into prostitution.

Addressing the camera, an actress (Emma Thompson, a Trustee of the Helen Bamber Foundation) tells the story of two apparently unrelated women called Elena and Maria. Elena worked in the market and wanted to move to England. Maria is now forced to work as a prostitute and is "beaten if she says no". Inter-cut images suggest that the actress is being beaten and raped. "Elena's family thinks she's dead," says the actress. In fact, Elena has simply changed her name to Maria. She fell into the hands of human traffickers. Trafficking is torture.

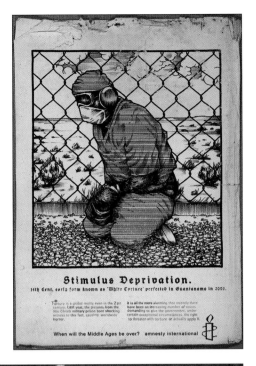

Stimulus Deprivation.
14th Cent, early form known as 'White Torture' perfected in Guantanamo in 2005.

Torture is a global reality even in the 21st century. Last year, the pictures from the Abu Ghraib military prison bore shocking witness to this fact, causing worldwide horror.

It is all the more alarming that recently there have been an increasing number of voices demanding to give the government, under certain exceptional circumstances, the right to threaten with torture or actually apply it.

When will the Middle Ages be over? amnesty international

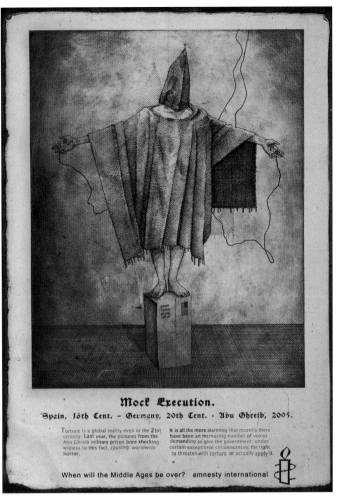

Mock Execution.
Spain, 16th Cent. – Germany, 20th Cent. – Abu Ghreib, 2005.

Torture is a global reality even in the 21st century. Last year, the pictures from the Abu Ghraib military prison bore shocking witness to this fact, causing worldwide horror.

It is all the more alarming that recently there have been an increasing number of voices demanding no give the government, under certain exceptional circumstances, the right to threaten with torture or actually apply it.

When will the Middle Ages be over? amnesty international

Humiliation.
Medieval method of torture, from about 1250 to 2006

Torture is a global reality even in the 21st century. Last year, the pictures from the Abu Ghraib military prison bore shocking witness to this fact, causing worldwide horror.

It is all the more alarming that recently there have been an increasing number of voices demanding to give the government, under certain-exceptional circumstances, the right to threaten with torture or actually apply it.

When will the Middle Ages be over? amnesty international

Torturesome Interrogation.
Also known as 'torture' or 'ordeal', 1350-2006.

Torture is a global reality even in the 21st century. Last year, the pictures from the Abu Ghraib military prison bore shocking witness to this fact, causing worldwide horror.

It is all the more alarming that recently there have been an increasing number of voices demanding to give the government, under certain exceptional circumstances, the right to threaten with torture or actually apply it.

When will the Middle Ages be over? amnesty international

Agency	Ogilvy, Frankfurt
Creative Directors	Simon Oppmann
	Peter Roemmelt
Copywriters	Peter Roemmelt
	Daniel Cojocaru
Art Directors	Simon Oppmann
	Daniel Cojocaru
Illustrator	Daniel Cojocaru
Client	Amnesty International

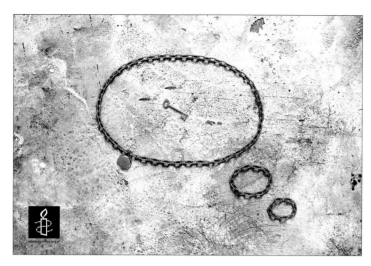 

Agency	DDB&Co, Istanbul	**Agency**	Contrapunto, Madrid
Creative Director	Karpat Polat	**Creative Directors**	Antonio Montero
Client	Amnesty International		Félix del Valle
			Carlos Jorge
		Copywriters	Eduardo Vea Keating
			David Cervera
		Art Director	Alvaro Guzmán
		Photographer	Cristina López
		Client	Amnesty International

Agency	Y&R/Team Advertising, Bucharest	Agency	Philipp und Keuntje, Hamburg
Creative Directors	Anca Puiu	Creative Director	Holger Lindhardt
	Dragos Popescu	Copywriter	Heiko Notter
Copywriter	Dragos Popescu	Art Director	Oliver Brkitsch
Art Director	Dan Serbanescu	Client	Amnesty International
Photographer	Carioca		
Client	Christmas Trees Festival		

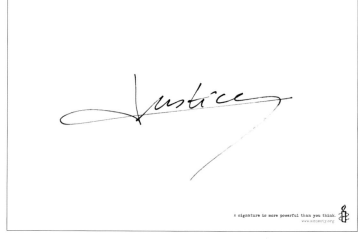

A signature is more powerful than you think.
www.amnesty.org

A signature is more powerful than you think.
www.amnesty.org

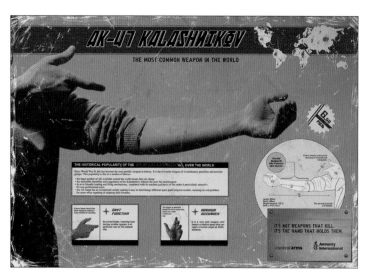

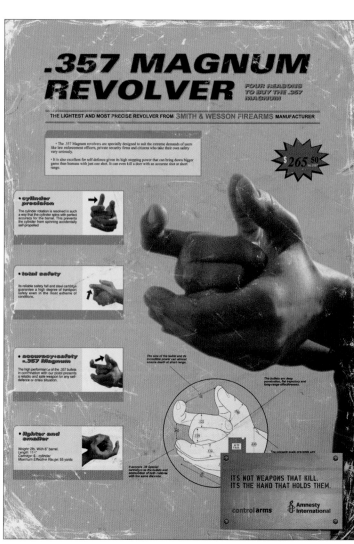

Public Interest

Agency	TBWA\Paris	**Agency**	Contrapunto, Madrid
Creative Director	Erik Vervroegen	**Creative Directors**	Antonio Montero
Copywriter	Thierry Buriez		Félix del Valle
Art Directors	Thierry Buriez		Carlos Jorge
	Alexandre Henry	**Copywriter**	Guillermo Santa Isabel
Client	Amnesty International	**Art Director**	Clara Hernández
		Illustrator	Clara Hernández
		Client	Amnesty International

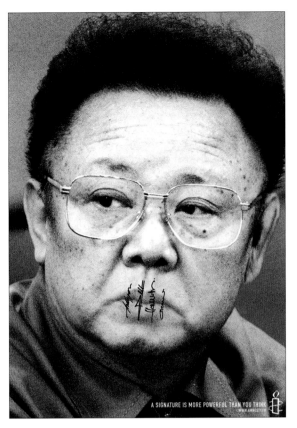

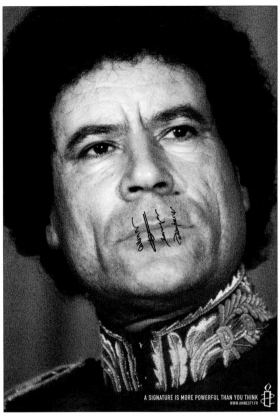

Agency	TBWA\Paris	Agency	TBWA\Paris
Creative Director	Erik Vervroegen	Creative Director	Erik Vervroegen
Copywriters	Ghislaine de Germon	Copywriters	Veronique Sels
	Jean-François Bouchet		Daniel Perez
Art Directors	Marianne Fonferrier	Art Directors	Ingrid Varetz
	Jessica Gerard-Huet		Javier Rodriguez
Client	Amnesty International	Photographer	Michael Lewis
		Client	Amnesty International

Agency	McCann Erickson, Warsaw	
Copywriters	Robert Olszewski	
	Magda Komorek	
Art Director	Blanka Lipinska	
Director	Frank Vroegop	
Producers	Mira Klajnberg	
	Pawel Mrowka	
Client	Child in the Net	
	"Execution"	

In a brutal scene, soldiers drag a man from his home – having shoved a black hood over his head – and prepare to shoot him. He's down on his knees, pleading for his life beside a grave that's already been dug. Suddenly, the camera pans over to a young kid in a baseball cap, who's looking on from a safe distance. He's calmly eating crisps. "What are you doing here, kiddo?" asks the cameraman. "I'm surfing the net," replies the boy. We must protect children from unsuitable material on the web.

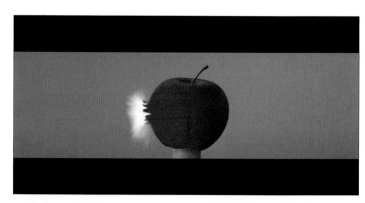

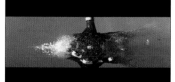

Agency	TBWA\Paris	
Creative Director	Erik Vervroegen	
Copywriter	Nicolas Moreau	
Art Director	Nicolas Moreau	
Director	Les Blin	
Producer	Festen Films	
Client	Amnesty International,	
	"Bullet"	

A prisoner is about to be executed. But as the bullet is fired, thousands of pieces of paper drift down like snowflakes. Each one is filled with signatures. The sheets of paper line up, forming a thick barrier in front of the condemned man. The bullet begins to lose speed as it is forced to punch through each piece of paper. Finally, its velocity exhausted, it drops uselessly to the floor. Join Amnesty: your petition is more powerful than you think.

Agency	Abbott Mead Vickers	
	BBDO, London	
Creative Director	Paul Brazier	
Copywriter	Gary Walker	
Art Director	Huw Williams	
Production	Therapy Films	
Directors	Malcolm Venville	
	Sean de Sparengo	
Producers	Nicola Sims	
	Yvonne Chalkley	
Client	Choice FM,	
	"Gun Crime"	

We see the explosive power of a bullet as it hits an egg, a glass of milk, an apple, a bottle of ketchup, a keg of water and a melon, all in slow-motion. To our horror, we then see a young boy's face. But instead of a bullet, the words "Stop the bullets, kill the gun" speed towards his head. Inner city radio station Choice FM is campaigning for peace on the streets.

Agency	Saatchi & Saatchi, Amsterdam
Creative Director	Magnus Olsson
Copywriter	Rick Coolegem
Art Directors	Alexandre Lagoet
	Tim Bishop
Photographer	Damien Grenon
Client	Stichting LaLuz

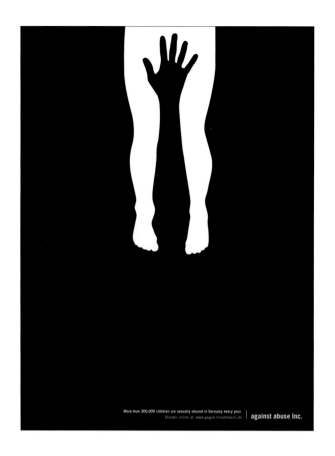

Agency	Grabarz & Partner, Hamburg	Agency	Saatchi & Saatchi, Amsterdam
Creative Directors	Ralf Heuel Patricia Pätzold Ralf Nolting	Creative Director	Magnus Olsson
		Copywriter	Magnus Olsson
		Art Director	Magnus Olsson
Copywriter	Laura Müller-Rossbach	Photographer	Chris Beeldschoon
Art Director	Julia Elles	Illustrator	Simon Spilsbury
Illustrator	Julia Elles	Client	Hidden Violence
Client	Against Abuse Inc.		

Agency	Chemistry, Dublin	**Agency**	Y&R/Team Advertising, Bucharest
Creative Director	Mike Garner	**Creative Directors**	Anca Puiu
Copywriter	Ann Fleming		Dragos Popescu
Art Director	Nicole Sykes	**Copywriters**	Dragos Popescu
Client	Focus Ireland		Antonio Marzavan
		Art Director	Dan Serbanescu
		Photographer	Carioca
		Client	Save the Children

Agency	Forsman & Bodenfors, Gothenburg	**Agency**	Abbott Mead Vickers BBDO, London

Agency Forsman & Bodenfors, Gothenburg
Photographer Marcus Ohlsson
Client BRIS

Agency Abbott Mead Vickers BBDO, London
Creative Director Paul Brazier
Copywriter Mike Sutherland
Art Director Antony Nelson
Client The Samaritans

These poster were actually knitted and then pulled apart to reveal the text and the Samaritans helpline.

Malaria multiplies deaths from drought

Red Cross

Malaria multiplies deaths from war

Red Cross

BAD WATER KILLS MORE CHILDREN THAN WAR.
SUPPORT THE "ONE DROP OF WATER" PROJECT. SMS "DROP" TO 72 900 TO DONATE 50 SEK. WWW.UNICEF.SE

unicef

Agency	Grey España, Madrid	**Agency**	Jung von Matt, Stockholm
Creative Director	Marcos García	**Copywriters**	Magnus Andersson
Copywriter	Teresa Galante		Fredric Thunholm
Art Director	Alvaro Sanchez Carvajales	**Art Directors**	Johan Jäger
Client	Red Cross		Max Larsson von Reybekiel
		Photographers	Henrik Halvarsson
			Marina Kereklidou
		Client	Unicef

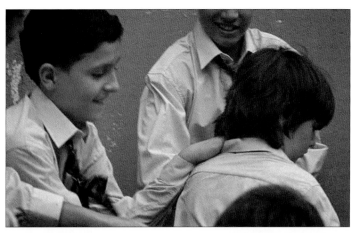

Agency	Markom Leo Burnett, Istanbul
Creative Directors	Yasar Akbas
	Idil Akoglu Ergulen
Copywriter	Selva Bayyurt
Art Director	Atilla Karabay
Production	Kala Film
Director	Fatih Kizilgok
Client	BGD Stray Animals Foundation, "Dog"

A little boy is living on the street. Other kids throw stones at him. He risks his life crossing busy roads. He is forced to wash using public drinking fountains. Pedestrians avoid him; parents drag their kids away from him. He is pursued and beaten by a band of young men. Exhausted, he crawls into his home: a cardboard box. Before our eyes, the street child transforms into a stray dog. Do you still find his plight outrageous? The Stray Animals Foundation believes animals should be treated like humans.

114   **Public Interest**

Agency	Mortierbrigade, Brussels
Creative Director	Philippe De Ceuster
Copywriter	Antoine Wellens
Art Director	Mehdi Dewalle
Production	Czar.be, Brussels
Director	Fien Troch
Producers	Arnaud Uyttenhove
	Veerle De Vos
Client	Zijkant Equal Payday, "Executive Cow"

As a woman executive enters an office, she is greeted with a cheery "Hey, bitch!" by one of her male colleagues. In fact, everywhere she goes, her male co-workers insult her. "How was your weekend?" she asks one of them, in the elevator. He replies: "None of your business, you stupid fuck." Surprisingly, the woman remains perfectly calm. Finally arriving at her office, she shuts the door behind her. A sign on it reads: "Executive cow." The real insult is that women are paid 24% less than men.

Agency	BBDO Portugal, Lisbon
Creative Director	Nuno Cardoso
Copywriter	Nuno Cardoso
Art Director	André Moreira
Production	Krypton
Director	Rui Brito
Producer	Carlos Jorge Antunes
Client	Acção Animal, "Bullfights"

A young woman is tied to a post in a city square. A deranged crowd hurls rocks and stones at her. Their faces are contorted as they shout and jeer. Finally the woman slumps to the ground, half-conscious and bleeding. This is a metaphor for the bloody ritual of the bullfight. "Suffering can't form part of our tradition," states the Portuguese charity Acção Animal – against cruelty to animals.

PINT OF BEER € 4.50
50 liters of fresh water € 1.50

Text 'aid' to 2255 and donate € 1.50   People in Need
Cordaid

AFTERSHAVE € 35.-
basics for a new home € 6.50

Text 'aid' to 2255 and donate € 1.50   People in Need
Cordaid

HANDBAG € 32.-
Food for a week € 4.-

Text 'aid' to 2255 and donate € 1.50   People in Need
Cordaid

Agency	Saatchi & Saatchi, Amsterdam
Creative Director	Magnus Olsson
Art Director	Tim Bishop
Photographer	Carl Stolze
Client	Cordaid/People in Need

5.4 million die of smoking related causes every year.
That's 2000 times a 9/11.

Issued in public interest by **Khaleej Times**

THERE'S NO SUCH THING AS AN OLD JUNKIE
TAKE BACK YOUR FUTURE. CALL 01284 701 702

FOCUS 12
Rehab Centre

THERE'S NO SUCH THING AS AN OLD JUNKIE
TAKE BACK YOUR FUTURE. CALL 01284 701 702

FOCUS 12
Rehab Centre

116   Public Interest

Agency	Percept Gulf, Dubai	**Agency**	Abbott Mead Vickers BBDO, London
Creative Director	Prashant Sankhe		
Copywriter	Sudeep Koshy	**Creative Director**	Paul Brazier
Art Director	Prashant Yeware	**Copywriter**	Bern Hunter
Client	Khaleej Times	**Art Director**	Mike Bond
		Photographer	Spike Watson
		Client	Focus 12

Agency	DraftFCB, Paris	We see a woman on a sofa in a 1970s
Creative Director	Thomas Stern	home. Addressing the camera, she says:
Copywriter	Dominique Marchand	"When I smoke next to my baby, the
Art Director	Jean Michel Alirol	chances of him dying of Sudden Infant
Production	Mr Hyde, Paris	Death Syndrome are increased by 50%."
Director	Keith Bearden	She adds: "But I don't know this yet." In
Producer	Anne Boucher	a series of 1970s scenes, smokers admit
Client	INPES, "Années 70"	that their habit affects those around them

that their habit affects those around them
– but protest that they are not yet aware of
the dangers of passive smoking. Finally, we
see a 1970s mother and father smoking in
a car, their children practically suffocating.
They have the excuse of ignorance – but
you don't.

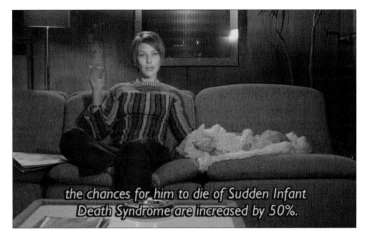

Agency	Abbott Mead Vickers BBDO, London	At first it looks as though we are in a normal
Creative Director	Paul Brazier	old peoples' home – but then things take
Copywriter	Bern Hunter	a sinister turn. One elderly woman begins
Art Director	Mike Bond	snorting coke, another injects heroin. Other
Production	12 Foot 6	residents are chasing the dragon or smoking
Director	Arran Bowyn	crack. Why does all this look so improbable?
Producers	Helen Hadfield	Because there's no such thing as an old
	Larry Holland	junkie. Focus 12 is a rehab clinic.
	Francine Linsey	
	Nicci Clark	
Client	Focus 12, "No Such Thing"	

Agency	McCann-Erickson Belgium, Hoeilaart	As our hero demonstrates, life is hard
Creative Director	Jean-Luc Walraff	when you're one-handed. You play the
Copywriter	Gregory Defay	guitar tunelessly. Pushing a wheelbarrow
Art Director	Salvatore Carlino	is almost impossible. When you row a
Directors	Olivier Tollet	boat, you go around in circles. And you
	Julien Collette	can't walk your dog and hold an umbrella
Client	Bordet Tobacco & Detoxification Centre, "The Hand"	at the same time. But when we see the

at the same time. But when we see the
man playing pinball – with great difficulty
– we learn that he hasn't lost a hand after
all. In fact, he's holding a cigarette in it.
Smoking is a handicap. It's time to quit.

118   **Public Interest**

Agency	TBWA\Athens	**Agency**	ATTP, Athens	Therapeutic programme for substance abusers and their families.
Creative Director	Vangelis Vrouvas	**Creative Director**	Vassilis Panagiotopoulos	
Copywriters	George Loukoumis	**Copywriter**	Antonis Roussos	
	Vassilis Kleisouras	**Art Directors**	Manos Leontis	
Art Director	Christos Kliafas		Mary Valonasi	
Client	World No Tobacco Day	**Client**	Kethea,	
			Nostos Drug	
			Rehab Programme	

Tolerance helps us all.

The world is too small for religious conflict. Too small for warfare. Too small for the narrow-minded. The Interreligious Fellowship Council of Switzerland (IRAS COTIS) fosters dialogue with other cultures to make everyone in this world feel at home. With confidence-building. With you: www.iras-cotis.ch **IRAS COTIS**

Scarf

Headscarf

The difference is in your head

MINORITY FORUM

Agency	Euro RSCG Group Switzerland, Zurich	**Agency**	Duval Guillaume Brussels
Executive CD	Frank Bodin	**Creative Directors**	Katrien Bottez
Creative Director	Dominik Oberwiler		Peter Ampe
Photographer	Andrea Vedovo	**Art Directors**	Vanessa Hendrickx
Client	Interreligious Council of Switzerland		Alexander Cha'ban
		Photographer	Gregor Collienne
		Client	Minority Forum

Agency	Duval Guillaume Brussels
Creative Directors	Katrien Bottez Peter Ampe
Copywriters	Benoît Menetret Peter Ampe
Art Directors	Jean-Marc Wachsmann Katrien Bottez
Production	Latcho Drom, Brussels
Director	Manu Coeman
Producers	Yves Legrève Dieter Lebbe Bruno Dejonghe Emily Rammant
Client	Brailleliga, "A Blind Call"

A stocky young man is trimming his garden hedge when he gets a phone call. Spotting the name on the screen, he says, "Hi Dad!" The voice says: "Listen, son, I'm not your real dad. Your real dad is Robert, an estate agent..." Cut to the man's dad, who is watching a soap opera – the real source of the heartbreaking confession. Next time you call by mistake, make sure it does some good. Put the number of the Braille League charity for the blind at the top of your speed dial list, and it gets a donation each time you dial it by mistake.

120   Public Interest

Agency	Grey, Stockholm
Copywriter	Martin Stadhammar
Art Director	Oskar Bård
Production	Hobby Film, Stockholm
Director	Oskar Bård
Client	Anorexi Bulimi Kontakt, "The Mirror"

Reflected in a mirror, we see a slightly plump but my no means unattractive teenage girl. She studies herself critically. As she pinches a roll of flesh at her waist, her eyes fill with tears. Perfectly normal though her body may be, she clearly hates her looks. When the camera pulls back, we are horrified to see the real girl in front of the mirror, who has the wasted, skeletal figure of an anorexic. Anorexia is a serious psychological illness.

Agency	BBDO Portugal, Lisbon
Creative Director	Nuno Cardoso
Copywriter	Nuno Cardoso
Art Director	Fabiano Bonfim
Production	Ministério dos Filmes
Director	José Pedro Sousa
Producers	Alberto Rodrigues, Maria João Monteiro
Client	Portuguese Federation of Sports for the Disabled, "Thanks - Beijing 2008"

A disabled man in a wheelchair finds his way blocked by a parked car. But using his ingenuity and a bit of muscle, he manages to get over the obstacle and continue on his way. Thanks to supporters of the Portuguese Federation of Sports for the Disabled, sportsmen and women with disabilities have overcome all the obstacles and are ready to participate in the Beijing Olympic Games. This ad is a way of saying "thank you".

Stop the oppression of women in
the Islamic world: www.ishr.org

Every month a child dies through not wearing a seatbelt in the back

Agency	Grabarz & Partner, Hamburg		**Agency**	Ogilvy, Amsterdam
Creative Directors	Ralf Heuel		**Copywriter**	Edsard Schutte
	Dirk Siebenhaar		**Art Director**	Jan-Willem Smits
Copywriter	Bent Hartmann		**Photographer**	Arno Bosma
Art Director	Julia Elbers		**Client**	Dutch Association of
Photographer	Veronika Faustmann			Traffic Victims
Client	ISHR, International Society			
	for Human Rights			

Agency	Lyle Bailie International, Belfast
Creative Directors	David Lyle
	Julie Anne Bailie
Copywriters	David Lyle
	Julie Anne Bailie
Art Directors	David Lyle
	Julie Anne Bailie
Production	Russell Curran Productions, Dublin
Director	Syd Macartney
Producers	Carrie Hart
	Russ Russell
	Anne Marie Curran
	Sonia Laughlin
Client	N. Ireland Road Safety Authority, "Mess"

A couple embrace beside a roadside wall in an idyllic country scene. At that moment a horrific three-car car crash ends their romance forever. The young man is killed and pinned against the girl by a car that slams into him. Everyone else dies – apart from the driver who caused the accident. At the inquest, we see that the girl is crippled. The surviving driver recalls that he lost control of his speeding car when he swerved to avoid a dog. The faster the speed, the bigger the mess.

Turn off the music.

Turn on to the road.

EDINBURGH BICYCLE COOPERATIVE

Agency	Far From Hollywood, Copenhagen
Creative Directors	Charlie Fisher
	Morten Hoffmann Larsen
Copywriters	Charlie Fisher
	Morten Hoffmann Larsen
Production	Far From Hollywood
Director	Kim Jacobsen
Producer	Morten Hoffmann Larsen
Client	Danish Road Safety Council, "2-Wheel Driving"

Stunt driver Tristan Jönsson is about to break the world record for driving on two wheels. After 126 kilometres, his fans greet him rapturously at the finish line. With a flourish, he stops coolly at a red traffic light and allows a man to cross. Finally settling his car onto all four wheels, he prepares to take a lap of honour. But a van hurtles into his car at an intersection, killing him outright. We realise he wasn't wearing a safety belt. Just because you're a great driver, it doesn't mean everyone else is. Buckle up.

Agency	Family Advertising, Edinburgh
Creative Directors	Kevin Bird
	David Isaac
Copywriter	David Isaac
Art Director	Kevin Bird
Photographer	Mark Seager
Client	Edinburgh Bicycle Cooperative

Agency	Ogilvy, Frankfurt
Creative Directors	Christian Mommertz
	Dr. Stephan Vogel
Copywriter	Dr. Stephan Vogel
Art Director	Christian Mommertz
Photographer	Jo Bacherl
Client	Malteser
	Ambulance Service

Agency	Leo Burnett, Paris
Creative Director	Stephan Ferens
Copywriters	Edward Capelle
	Stéphane Santana
Art Directors	Stéphane Santana
	Edward Capelle
Production	Marcassin, Paris
Director	Dimitri Daniloff
Producers	Jérémie Morichon
	Gabriel Duforesto
	Bertrand Ayache Anguenot
Client	Sidaction, "The Hourglass"

Sensuously filmed, this writhing mass of naked bodies looks more like a beautifully choreographed dance than an orgy. Then one of the bodies falls away as if tumbling into an abyss. When the camera pulls back, we see that the coupling bodies are contained in the top half of an hour glass. But each moment, another body drops lifelessly into the bottom half – onto a pile of corpses. Every ten seconds, someone in the world dies of AIDS.

Agency	Ogilvy Portugal, Lisbon
Creative Directors	Edson Athayde
	Paul Smith
Copywriters	Edson Athayde
	Sergio Costa
Production	Stink
Director	Neil Harris
Producers	Jess aan de Wiel
	Russell Benson
	Sally Miller
Client	MTV AIDS Awareness, "Shot"

We see couples making love in a variety of circumstances: in a car, in a hotel bedroom, or at home. But on each occasion, after they've finished, the man produces a gun. Although we don't see the men murdering their lovers, we hear the shots. The fastest growing group of people affected by AIDS and HIV is heterosexual women under 30. Insist that your lover wears a condom. Otherwise, he might as well be carrying a loaded gun.

Agency	Shalmor Avnon Amichay/Y&R, Tel Aviv
Creative Directors	Gideon Amichay
	Tzur Golan
Copywriter	Yaneev Avital
Art Director	Galit Attia
Production	Shosi & Udi
Director	Oded Ben-Nun
Producer	Sigal Nugasy
Client	Israel Aids Task Force, "Oh My God"

After a seductive candlelit dinner at home, a young man and his girlfriend are getting down to business. "Oh God," says the woman, as she approaches orgasm, "Oh my God!" But if he's not wearing a condom, praying to God won't help. That's the message from the Israel Aids Task Force.

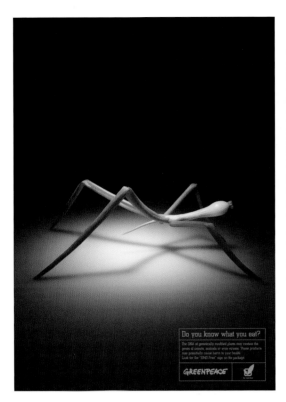

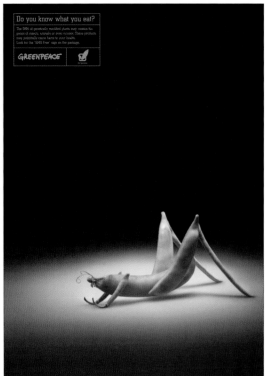

Be careful.
Demand that your
partner wears
a condom.

Agency	BBDO, Moscow	Agency	Ogilvy Portugal, Lisbon
Creative Director	Andrey Iliassov		
Copywriters	Tanya Moseeva	Creative Director	Edson Athayde
	Ilya Petrov	Copywriter	Edson Athayde
Art Director	Giorgi Popiashvili	Art Director	Maria Amorim
Photographer	Goran Tacevski	Client	MTV AIDS Awareness
Client	GreenPeace		

Agency	Forsman & Bodenfors, Gothenburg
Production	RAF
Director	Johan Renck
Producer	Sarah Grey
Client	SOS Live Earth, "Cow"

This unlikely film shows a row of cows' arses in close-up. It gets even worse when all the cows start shitting. But there's a message behind the madness: the titles explain that cows produce more greenhouse gases than cars and trucks combined. So we should help reduce the need for beef by eating vegetarian at least once a week. That way we'd help the environment, and probably be healthier too, according to SOS Live Earth.

Agency	Ogilvy Portugal, Lisbon
Creative Directors	Edson Athayde
	Paul Smith
Copywriters	Rui Silva
	João Guimarães
	André Pereira
Art Director	André Pereira
Production	Krypton, Lisbon
Director	Joana Areal
Producers	Gabriela Nogueira
	Paulo Carrapito
Client	MTV Global Warming, "Mute"

On a beach, various individuals use sign language to recount terrifying facts about climate change. "The earth is warming faster than at any time during the past 10,000 years," signs one. "The 1990s was the warmest decade on global record," explains another. "40% of arctic ice has gone since the 1970s" and yet "25,000 people died in a heat wave". The last person to appear, a young boy, sums up the message: "The time for talking is over. It's time to use your hands." Stop global warming.

Agency	TBWA\Paris
Creative Director	Erik Vervroegen
Copywriter	Veronique Sels
Art Director	Eve Roussou
Director	Wilfrid Brimo
Producer	Wanda
Client	AIDES,
	AIDS Awareness,
	"Love Story"

In this animated tale, a sexually active young man enjoys a variety of different liaisons: with his first girlfriend, with a waitress, with a sexy farmhand and with a dominatrix. He visits an upmarket brothel and even spends a vacation at "Orgy Land". But no matter what he gets up to, he never forgets to wear a condom. That way, he can enjoy a sex life that's long as well as action-packed.

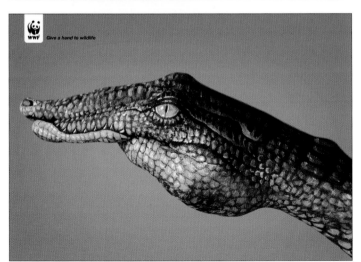

Agency	Ogilvy & Mather, Bucharest	Agency	Saatchi & Saatchi Simko, Geneva
Creative Directors	Albert Nica	Creative Director	Olivier Girard
	Dani Macarie	Copywriter	Jean-Michel larsen
Copywriter	Corina Bompa	Art Director	Nicolas Poulain
Art Director	Catalin Popescu	Illustrator	Guido Daniele
Client	WWF	Client	WWF

128 **Public Interest**

Agency	Ogilvy, Frankfurt	Agency	Contrapunto, Madrid
Creative Directors	Simon Oppmann	**Creative Directors**	Antonio Montero
	Peter Roemmelt		Jaime Chavarri
Copywriter	Olga Potempa		Ivan de Dios
Art Director	Daniela Friedel	**Copywriter**	Jaime Chavarri
Photographer	Jo Bacherl	**Art Director**	Ivan de Dios
Client	OroVerde	**Client**	WWF
	Rainforest Foundation		

JUST ONE PIECE OF GARBAGE IS NOT GARBAGE.
That is what you and the other 7 720 000 Bulgarians think.

Agency	DDB&Co, Istanbul	Agency	Ogilvy & Mather, Sofia
Creative Director	Karpat Polat	**Creative Director**	Maria Todorova
Copywriter	Karpat Polat	**Copywriter**	Milena Krumova
Art Director	Ali Bati	**Art Director**	Veneta Nikolova
Photographer	Ilkay Muratoglu	**Client**	WWF
Client	Turmepa		

130   **Public Interest**

Agency	Young & Rubicam, Paris
Creative Directors	The Six
Copywriter	Pierre Philippe Sardon
Art Director	Guillaume Auboyneau
Photographer	Régis Fialaire
Client	Surfrider Foundation

Agency	Young & Rubicam, Paris
Creative Directors	The Six
Copywriter	Rémy Hadjadj
Art Director	Akim Zérouali
Illustrator	Bernard Mallangier
Client	Surfrider Foundation

Agency	Young & Rubicam, Paris
Creative Directors	The Six
Copywriter	Louis Carpentier
Art Director	Louis Carpentier
Client	Surfrider Foundation

Stop second hand smoking

Agency	Gulf Promoaction DDB, Dubai	Agency	Drive Communication, Jeddah
Creative Director	Rishad Lawyer	Creative Directors	Ramzi Barakat
Copywriter	Rishad Lawyer		Serge Zahar
Art Director	Laith Hafez	Copywriter	Chahid El-Khouri
Client	Anti-Second-Hand Smoking Campaign	Art Director	Hadi Syriani
		Client	Anti-Smoking Creative Competition

Agency Ogilvy, Frankfurt
Creative Directors Simon Oppmann
Peter Roemmelt
Copywriter Olga Potempa
Art Director Daniela Friedel
Client German Foundation for
the Preservation of
Historic Monuments

Complete series now available.

MUSICA
LISTEN WITH YOUR SOUL

Agency	The Jupiter Drawing Room, Cape Town	Over a warning triangle, a censor warns viewers that the DVD of provocative comedy
Executive CD	Ross Chowles	series "Little Britain" may contain scenes
Creative Director	Darren McKay	of "sex, nudity, violence, strong language,
Copywriter	Dave Topham	profanity, blasphemy, obscenity, racism,
Art Director	Gareth McPherson	ageism, chauvinism, anti-Semitism, anti-
Production	Wicked Pixels	Arabism, hetero-sexism, homo-sexism,
Director	Andrew Shaw	mono-sexism, sexism, misogyny, misandry,
Producers	Kamila Pisula	heterophobia, homophobia, toilet humour and
	Leila Isaacs	an adult breast feeding scene which we're
Client	Musica DVDs,	just not certain which category it fits into".
	"Little Britain"	A caption reads: "You have been warned."

Digicams with super zoom. **NiEDERMEYER**
DIE BESTSELLERZONE

 Audiovisual Equipment & Accessories **135**

Agency	TBWA\Vienna
Creative Directors	Robert Wohlgemuth
	Gerd Turetschek
	Elli Hummer
Copywriter	Karin Schalko
Art Director	Jeff Stenzenberger
Photographer	Arnd Ötting
Illustrator	Christian Pfeifer
Client	Niedermeyer

Agency	McCann Erickson, Bucharest
Creative Directors	Adrian Botan
	Alexandru Dumitrescu
Copywriter	Adela Dan
Art Directors	Adriana Pascanu
	Catalin Paduretu
Client	Foton Batteries, "Sleeping"

Whether they're eating breakfast, playing or even on the toilet, this bunch of toddlers can't seem to stop nodding off. What's causing their exhaustion? You can put the blame on Foton Master Batteries, which keep toys working day and night – meaning kids don't get to sleep.

136   Audiovisual Equipment & Accessories

Agency	TBWA\España, Madrid
Creative Directors	Guillermo Gines
	Angel Iglesias
Copywriter	Vicente Rodriguez
Art Director	Ely Sanchez
Production	RCR, Madrid
Director	Dani Benmayor
Producers	Daniel Monedero
	Enrique Domenech
Client	PlayStation, "Shadows"

We see a man's shadow flickering over rooftops. Strangely, it has no owner. Jumping to the ground, the shadow lands in the middle of a street football game and steals the ball. One of the teenage players gives chase, but the shadow outruns him. Then it accidentally jostles a rich woman – although it doesn't steal her handbag. Even a small dog is unable to catch up with it. Finally, the errant silhouette arrives at the feet of its owner – racing driver Fernando Alonso - engrossed in his PlayStation Formula 1 game.

Agency	TBWA\London
Executive CD	Steve Henry
Creative Directors	Danny Brooke Taylor
	Tony McTear
Art Director	Richard Beesening
Production	MJZ, London
Director	Dante Ariola
Producers	Debbie Turner
	Natalie Hill
	Tracie Stokes
Client	PlayStation, "Grenade"

A campaign for PS3 features a spooky hotel and its eccentric residents. In this episode, a macho Italian crook and his long-suffering girlfriend arrive with a suitcase full of cash. Meanwhile, a gay resident's pet poodle has found a grenade belonging to another guest – a deranged Vietnam veteran. When the poodle's flamboyant owner snatches the grenade and throws it away, it lands beside the suitcase and explodes. Thousands of banknotes are scattered to the four winds. "This is living!" exclaims the hotel's concierge.

Agency	Leo Burnett, Milan	The legendary characters of classic
Creative Directors	Sergio Rodriguez	videogames were re-created with Post-its
	Enrico Dorizza	on the streets of Milan. On the back of
Copywriter	Davide Rossi	each Post-it a message invited readers
Art Director	Francesco Epifani	to bring these vintage games back to life
Photographer	Francesco Epifani	with a Nintendo Wii virtual console.
Client	Nintendo Wii	

138   **Audiovisual Equipment & Accessories**

Agency	TBWA\España, Madrid		Agency	TBWA\España, Madrid
Creative Directors	Juan Sanchez		Creative Directors	Juan Sánchez
	Guillermo Gines			Guillermo Ginés
	Cesar Olivas			Bernardo Hernández
	Montse Pastor			Montse Pastor
	Cristina Davila		Copywriters	Vicente Rodríguez
Copywriter	Pablo Farres		Art Directors	Ely Sánchez
Art Director	Gonzalo Vergara		Photographer	Gonzalo Puertas
Photographers	Diego Dominguez		Client	PlayStation
	Inaki Domingo			
Client	PlayStation			

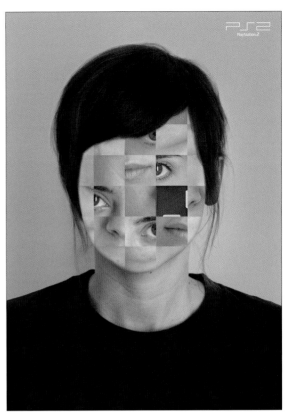

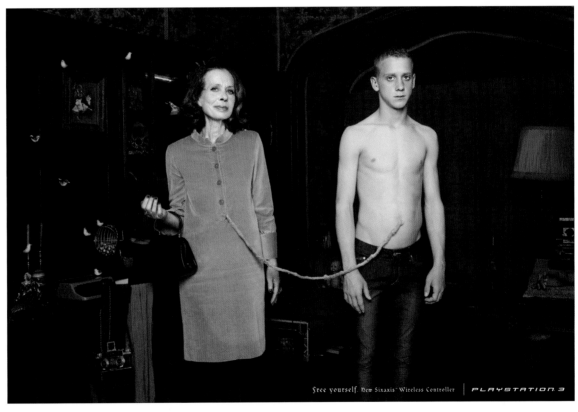

Free yourself. New Sixaxis™ Wireless Controller | *PLAYSTATION 3*

Agency	TBWA\España, Madrid	Agency	TBWA\España, Madrid
Creative Directors	Juan Sanchez	Creative Directors	Guillermo Gines
	Guillermo Gines		Juan Sanchez
	Montse Pastor		Bernardo Hernandez
	Cesar Olivas	Copywriter	Vicente Rodríguez
	Cristina Davila	Art Director	Ely Sanchez
Copywriter	Cesar Olivas	Photographer	Sara Zorraquino
Art Director	Cristina Davila	Client	PlayStation
Photographer	Cristina Davila		
Client	PlayStation		

Agency	Young & Rubicam, Singapore	We're in Cairo, looking at the pyramids. From the top of one of the pyramids, reels of coloured cotton begin to fall. The cotton reels bounce and tumble over the rough stones, leaving their vivid threads behind them. Finally, Cairo residents are astonished to see that one of the pyramids is covered with all the colours of the rainbow. The Sony Bravia TV offers "live colour creation" like no other.
Executive CD	Rowan Chanen	
Copywriters	Edward Ong	
	Rowan Chanen	
Art Directors	Kirsten Ackland	
	Scott McClelland	
Production	Velocity Films, Cape Town	
Director	Keith Rose	
Producers	Karen Kloppers	
	Kim Lim	
Client	Sony Bravia, "Threads"	

Agency	Fallon London
Creative Director	Juan Cabral
Copywriters	Chris Bovill
	John Allison
Art Directors	Chris Bovill
	John Allison
Photographer	Tim Gutt
Client	Sony Cybershot

Agency	TBWA\Paris		**Agency**	TBWA\Paris
Creative Director	Erik Vervroegen		**Creative Director**	Erik Vervroegen
Copywriter	Benoit Leroux		**Copywriter**	Veronique Sels
Art Director	Philippe Taroux		**Art Directors**	Eve Roussou
Client	PlayStation			Veronique Sels
				Viken Guzel
			Photographer	Matthieu Deluc
			Client	PlayStation

FIGHT AGING

2007   2017

Canon photo paper gives you durability that will last for generations

Photo Paper Pro, PR-101
The ultimate printer paper for glossy photos. For pictures with
the look and feel of traditional photographs. The unique glossy
treatment protects the paper from aging for a long time.

you can
Canon

Extremly high resolution TVs

NiEDERMEYER
BESTSELLERZONE

Extremly high resolution TVs

NiEDERMEYER
BESTSELLERZONE

142   Audiovisual Equipment & Accessories

Agency	802 Kommunikation, Stockholm	**Agency**	DraftFCB Kobza, Vienna
Creative Directors	Max Hansson	**Creative Director**	Joachim Glawion
	Par Axelson	**Copywriter**	Rita-Maria Spielvogel
Copywriter	Par Axelson	**Art Director**	Edith Büyükdoganay
Art Director	Max Hansson	**Client**	Niedermayer
Client	Canon Photo Paper		

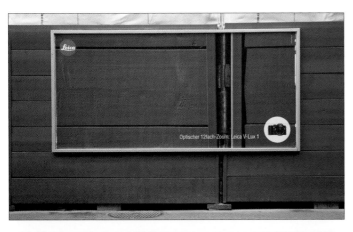

Agency	Advico Young & Rubicam, Zurich
Creative Directors	Urs Schrepfer
	Christian Bobst
Copywriter	Johannes Raggio
Art Directors	Christian Bobst
	Isabelle Hauser
Photographer	Christian Bobst
Client	Leica

Let's put his energy to good use.

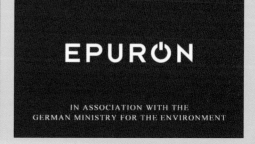

EPURON

IN ASSOCIATION WITH THE
GERMAN MINISTRY FOR THE ENVIRONMENT

Agency	Nordpol+ Hamburg	A strange black-clad character with a jutting
Creative Director	Lars Ruehmann	jaw and a bowler hat perched on his massive
Copywriter	Matthew Branning	head is telling his life story. "I was always
Art Directors	Bjoern Ruehmann	misunderstood," he says, as we see a
	Joakim Reveman	flashback of him lifting a woman's skirt on the
Production	Paranoid Projects, Paris	street. Then he throws sand in a little girl's face
Directors	The Vikings	at a playground. "People didn't like me – I got
Producers	Melanie Robert-Kaminka,	on their nerves," he continues, as we see more
	Virginie Dinh	anti-social behaviour. Lately, though, he has
Client	Epuron, "Power of Wind"	been accepted by society. He turns to spin
		the model wind turbine behind him. The man
		personifies the wind, a source of clean energy.

ALVINE BUKETT bed linen
100% cotton.
150x200/50x60 cm
98,-

SNACK box
renewable material (wood)
W56xD39, H30 cm
129,-

STATIV clothing rack
225,-

ALVINE BLOM bed linen
100% cotton.
150x200/50x60 cm
98,-

BUMERANG clothes hanger
Solid wood
35,-/8 pack

STOLMEN combination
Renewable wood.
110-35 cm
1.005,-

ALVINE FRÖ pillow case
100% cotton. 65x65 cm
79,-

TRAKTOR stool
with castors. W63xD63 cm.
198,-

▲ **Homes, Furnishings & Appliances**   **145**

Agency	DDB Oslo
Copywriter	Espen Dysvik Hagen
Art Director	Morten Foss
Photographer	Massimo Leardini
Client	Ikea

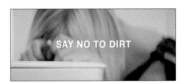

Agency	Jung von Matt, Hamburg
Creative Directors	Willy Kaussen
	Hans Weishaeupl
Copywriter	André Hennen
Art Director	Kim Ney
Production	FilmDeluxe, Berlin
Director	Owen Harris
Producers	Juergen Kraus
	Stefan Pauli
	Ana Lopez
Client	CWS, "Say No to Dirt"

At a nightclub, a fashionable beauty enters the washroom and locks herself in a stall. Removing a fold of paper from her purse, she sprinkles a small mound of coke onto the spotless toilet seat and prepares to snort it. Unfortunately, the self-cleaning CWS loo has detected the intrusion and begins automatically wiping the toilet seat. Before the pretty coke-head can react, her drug of choice has been cleaned away. She screams in frustration. Seconds later, she hears a similar scream from a neighbouring stall. CWS toilets "say no to dirt".

Agency	Just/Kidde, Copenhagen
Creative Director	Carsten Kidde
Copywriter	Rasmus Springborg
Art Director	Bengt Persson
Production	Just/Kidde
Director	Øystein Borge
Producers	Martin Bardrum
	Uffe Just
Client	Miele Dishwashers, "Carwash"

Parents arrive home just in time to see their young son lifting a tricycle out of the dishwasher. They look on, bemused, as he hands the trike over to another little kid who's waiting at the kitchen door. The kid pays him. Now a second customer arrives with another 3-wheeler, which our little entrepreneur once again loads into the dishwasher. In fact, children with trikes are queuing around the block to take advantage of the "car wash". Miele Dishwashers are very spacious.

Agency	La Chose, Paris
Creative Director	Pascal Grégoire
Copywriters	Benjamin Parent
	Guillaume Rebbot
Art Directors	Benjamin Parent
	Guillaume Rebbot
Production	Les Telecreateurs, Paris
Director	David Horowitz
Producers	Arno Moria
	David Batusanski
Client	Ikea

On a rainy day, a man is sitting on the sofa reading the newspaper. When his dog arrives clutching its leash in its jaws, the man shakes his head: there'll be no walk this afternoon. In protest, the dog leaves a muddy paw-print on the cream sofa. The man ignores it. Now the dog puts both paws on the sofa and leaves a lot more prints. So the man picks up his coffee cup and deliberately spills its contents over the sofa. Ikea sofas have washable covers. Realising it can't win, the dog slopes off.

Made of Genuine Leather.

NATUZZI
FURNITURE BOUTIQUE

Agency	Realpro, Novokuznetsk	**Agency**	Leo Burnett, Budapest
Creative Director	Igor Yarigin	**Creative Director**	Peter Tordai,
Copywriter	Vladimir Cherepanov	**Copywriters**	Anikó Hohol
Art Director	Vladimir Cherepanov		Vilmos Farkas
Photographers	Stas Zhuravlev	**Art Directors**	Renata Nemeth
	Oleg Beloborodov		Robert Rosenberg
Client	Natuzzi Leather Furniture	**Client**	Samsung Vacuums

Extremely sharp knives: the WMF knife collection Yamato.

For those who value precision: WMF Grand Gourmet blades. Unsurpassably sharp and manufactured from unique special blade steel. You can find more information on WMF Grand Gourmet blades on the Internet at www.wmf.de or of course at our WMF branches.

148 **Homes, Furnishings & Appliances**

Agency	KNSK Werbeagentur, Hamburg	Agency	KNSK Werbeagentur, Hamburg
Creative Directors	Anke Winschewski Vappu Singer	Creative Directors	Tim Krink Niels Holle Ulrike Wegert
Copywriters	Anke WInschewski Birgit Bauer	Copywriter	Steffen Steffens
Client	WMF knives	Art Director	Thomas Thiele
		Client	WMF Knives

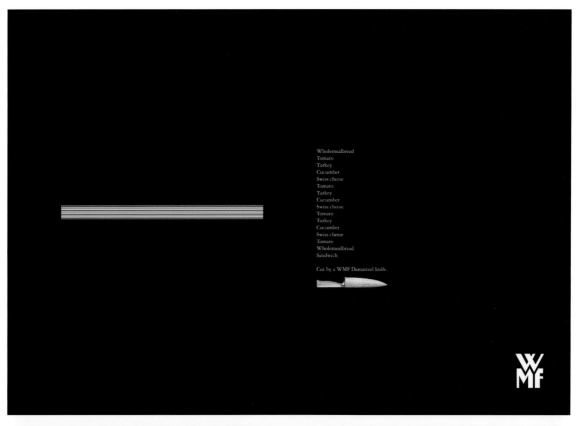

Wholemealbread
Tomato
Turkey
Cucumber
Swiss cheese
Tomato
Turkey
Cucumber
Swiss cheese
Tomato
Turkey
Cucumber
Swiss cheese
Tomato
Wholemealbread
Sandwich

Cut by a WMF Damasteel knife.

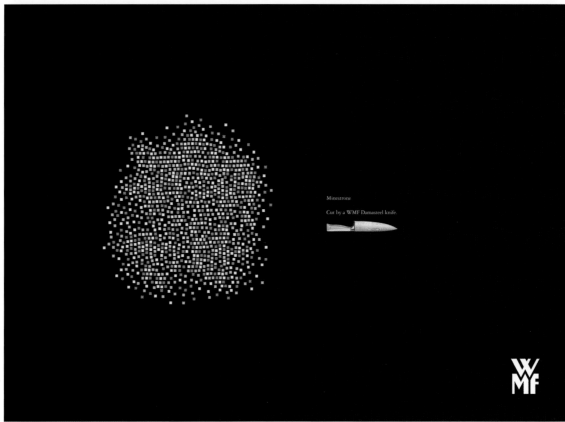

Minestrone

Cut by a WMF Damasteel knife.

Agency	KNSK Werbeagentur, Hamburg
Creative Directors	Tim Krink
	Niels Holle
Copywriter	Berend Brüdgam
Art Director	Tim Krink
Client	WMF Knives

Homes, Furnishings & Appliances

Agency	Saatchi & Saatchi Poland, Warsaw	Agency	Publicis Conseil, Paris
Creative Director	Max Olech	Creative Directors	Olivier Altmann
Copywriter	Piotr Skarbek		Hervé Plumet
Art Director	Aneta Szeweluk	Copywriter	Olivier Dermaux
Photographers	Mejor Samrai	Art Director	Mathieu Vinciguerra
Client	Keso Door Locks	Photographer	Jean-Yves Lemoigne
		Client	Stihl

Agency	Memac Ogilvy, Tunis	Agency	Zelig, Stockholm
Creative Director	Nicolas Courant	Creative Directors	Peo Olsson
Art Directors	Michaël Zampol		Fredrik Lewander
	Wilfrid Guérin	Copywriter	Peo Olsson
Client	Eclipstore Shutters	Art Directors	Fredrik Lewander
			Anders Lindgren
		Photographer	Pål Allan
		Client	Mora Armatur Taps

152 **Homes, Furnishings & Appliances**

Agency	Starlink Creative Services, Bucharest		Agency	Scholz & Friends, Berlin
Creative Director	Stefan Voloaca		Creative Directors	Jan Leube
Copywriter	Andrei Gurau			Matthias Spaetgens
Art Director	Catalin Burcea		Copywriter	Michael Haeussler
Photographer	Catalin Burcea		Art Directors	Tim Stockmar
Client	Altipo Windows			Kay Luebke
			Photographer	Ralph Baiker
			Client	Weru Windows

Cushions
€10

Cooler bag
€12

Chair
€39

Oil lamp
€35

ÅHLÉNS
DEPARTMENT STORES
ENDLESS POSSIBILITIES

Brandt

DON'T LET SMELLS MIX
BIOLYSE SYSTEM REFRIGERATOR

Brandt

DON'T LET SMELLS MIX
BIOLYSE SYSTEM REFRIGERATOR

Homes, Furnishings & Appliances **153**

Agency	King, Stockholm		**Agency**	DDB Paris
Creative Director	Frank Hollingworth		**Creative Directors**	Alexandre Hervé
Copywriters	Hedvig Hagwall Bruckner			Sylvain Thirache
	Pontus Ekström		**Copywriter**	Edouard Pérarnaud
Art Directors	Helena Redman		**Art Director**	Martin Darfeuille
	Alexander Elers		**Photographer**	Jenny van Sommers
	Daniel Söderstedt		**Client**	Brandt
Photographer	Petrus Olsson			
Client	Åhléns Department Stores			

154 **Household Maintenace**

Agency	Heimat, Berlin	Before leaving home, a man takes a disheartened
Creative Directors	Guido Heffels	glance at his faded and leaking bathroom. As he
	Juergen Vossen	walks to work, we see that the entire bathroom
Copywriters	Alexander Ardelean	has uprooted and followed him, as if to taunt him
	Till Eckel	about his neglect. Even on the tram, the bathroom
	Sebastian Kainz	is in pursuit. When he turns a corner, it is lying in
Art Directors	Mike Brand	ambush. Finally, he ends up fighting it. Cut to a
	Tim Schneider	scene of the man installing a shower head in his
	Marc Wientzek	gleaming new bathroom. Finish the decorating –
Production	Markenfilm, Berlin	before it finishes you.
Director	Carl Erik Rinsch	
Producers	Lutz Mueller, Kerstin Breuer	
Client	Hornbach, "Haunted"	

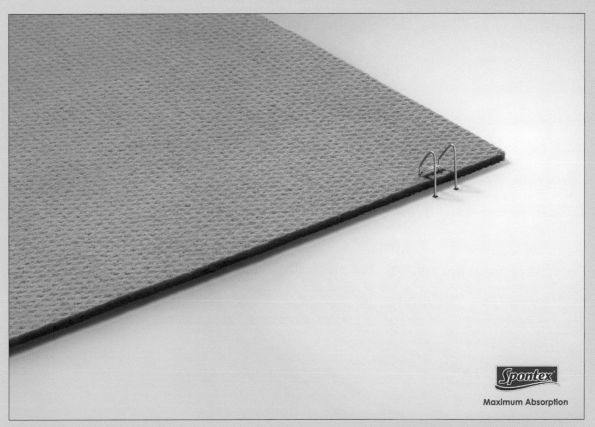

Maximum Absorption

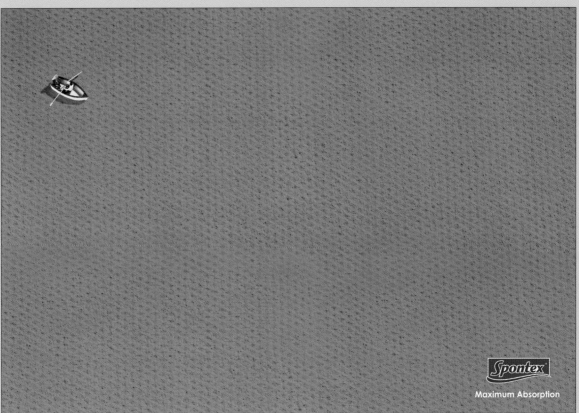

Maximum Absorption

 Household Maintenace **155**

Agency	TBWA\España, Barcelona
Creative Director	Ramón Sala
Copywriters	Carlos Riau
	Javi Gimeno
Art Directors	Vicky Desvalls
	Enio Sarrias
Photographer	Miguel Fernández
Client	Spontex

Agency	BBDO, Düsseldorf
Creative Directors	Stefan Vonderstein
	Ralf Zilligen
	David Carter
	David Lubars
Copywriters	Hans-Holger Pollack
	Fiona Grace
	Julian Witzel
Art Directors	Sharon Jessen
	Concetta Milione
	Michael Plueckhahn
Photographer	Andrew Zuckerman
Client	Braun Multiquick

156   **Household Maintenace**

Agency	Heimat, Berlin
Creative Directors	Bastian Kuhn
	Alexander Weber-Gruen
Art Director	Bastian Kuhn
Production	Markenfilm Wedel
Director	Bastian Kuhn
Producer	Acki Heldens
Client	Wallpaper Association

In a fast-moving series of still photographs, we see a young man ageing in front of his constantly changing wallpaper. Just as his hairstyles, clothes and physical appearance alter, so does his wallpaper – with the major difference that it always appears fresh and exciting, even long after he has disappeared. The Wallpaper Association offers endless opportunities.

Agency	Leo Burnett, Moscow
Creative Director	Mikhail Kudashkin
Copywriter	Viktor Lander
Art Director	Alexandra Scherbovich
Production	Postpro 18 Moscow
Producers	Olga Anosova
	Philipp Yakovlev
Client	Tide, "White Screen"

This cinema ad was designed to be shown just before the main feature. A woman emerges from her house and begins to hang a sheet on the clothesline. Thanks to Tide detergent, the sheet is so blinding white that you could easily project a film on it. And indeed, after the Tide logo and the words "Enjoy the movie" have appeared, that's exactly what happens. Tide is all about whiteness.

Agency	JWT, Paris	Agency	TBWA\Vienna
Creative Directors	Andrea Stillacci	Creative Directors	Robert Wohlgemuth
	Pascal Manry		Gerd Turetschek
Copywriter	Yann-Gaël Cobigo		Elli Hummer
Art Director	Xavier Beauregard	Copywriter	Niki Link
Photographer	Vincnet Dixon	Art Director	Jan Christ
Client	O'Cedar	Photographer	Markus Rössle
		Client	Bic Permanent Markers

158   **Household Maintenace**

Agency	BBDO Athens		**Agency**	Memac Ogilvy, Tunis
Creative Director	Theodosis Papanikolaou		**Creative Director**	Nicolas Courant
Copywriter	Daphne Patrikiou		**Copywriter**	Thomas Thelliez
Art Director	David Kaneen		**Art Director**	Wilfrid Guérin
Illustrator	David Kaneen		**Photographer**	Kamel Agrebi
Client	Post-it Notes		**Client**	Bufalo Leather Polish

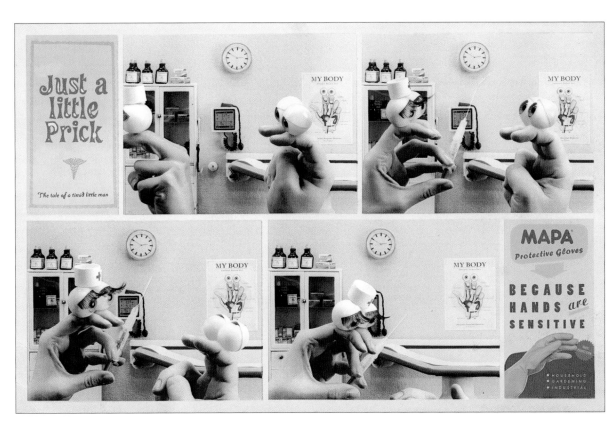

Agency	TBWA\Paris		Agency	TBWA\Paris
Creative Director	Erik Vervroegen		**Creative Director**	Erik Vervroegen
Copywriter	Thierry Buriez		**Copywriter**	Xander Smith
Art Directors	Thierry Buriez		**Art Directors**	Jonathan Santana
	Alexandre Henry			Bjoern Ruehmann
				Joakim Reveman
Photographer	Vincent Dixon		**Photographer**	Sven Glage
Client	Spontex Classic Sponges		**Client**	Mapa Protective Gloves

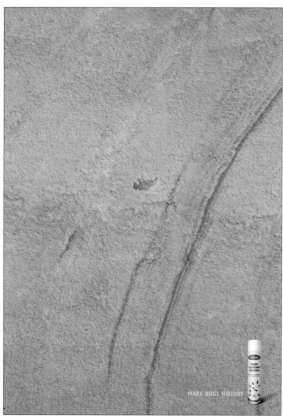

160 **Household Maintenace**

Agency	New Moment New Ideas Company, Belgrade	Agency	Ogilvy, Amsterdam
Creative Director	Dragan Sakan	Creative Director	Carl Le Blond
Copywriter	Slavisa Savic	Copywriter	Edsard Schutte
Art Director	Slavisa Savic	Art Director	Jan-Willem Smits
Client	Loctite Superbond	Photographer	Pieter van der Meer
		Client	Aeroxon

Agency	DDB Madrid	Send your mistakes where nobody can see
Creative Director	Mario Gascon	them. (The abandoned letter in each visual
Copywriter	Guille Ramirez	is the spelling mistake in the text that has
Art Director	Lisi Lluch	been corrected with Pritt).
Client	Pritt	

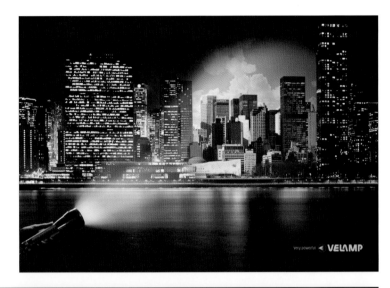

162   Household Maintenace

Agency	10 Advertising, Antwerp	Agency	1861 United (Red Cell), Milan
Creative Director	Marc Leyssens	Creative Directors	Pino Rozzi
Copywriter	Robin Dhondt		Roberto Battaglia
Art Director	Steven de Vreese	Copywriter	Luca Beato
Photographer	Raf Coolen	Art Director	Micol Talso
Client	Ecover	Photographer	Pierpaolo Ferrari
		Client	Velamp

Agency	Saatchi & Saatchi Poland, Warsaw
Creative Director	Max Olech
Copywriter	Daniel Piecka
Art Director	Bartek Grala
Photographer	Tomek Albin
Client	Ariel Color

FÜR VOLUMEN,
DAS LANGE HÄLT.

HAARSPRAY EXTRA STARK

Agency	Young & Rubicam, Frankfurt	For volume that lasts longer.
Creative Director	Uwe Marquardt	
Copywriter	Kai-Oliver Sass	
Art Director	Harald Schumacher	
Graphic	Julia Sturm	
Client	Gard Hair Spray	

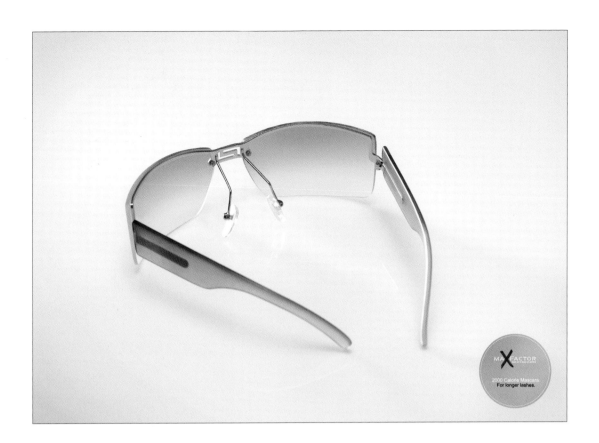

Agency	Markom Leo Burnett, Istanbul	Agency	Lowe MENA, Dubai
Creative Directors	Yasar Akbas	Creative Directors	Dominic Stallard
	Idil Akoglu Ergulen		Clinton Manson
Copywriter	Selva Bayyurt	Copywriter	Clinton Manson
Art Director	Yucel Bilgin	Art Director	Dominic Stallard
Photographer	Ilkay Muratoglu	Photographer	Clive Stewart
Client	Max Factor Mascara	Client	Axe Shower Gel

Agency	Grey Worldwide, Dubai	Agency	Lowe MENA, Dubai
Creative Director	Alisdair Miller	Creative Directors	Dominic Stallard
			Clinton Manson
Copywriter	Vidya Manmohan	Copywriter	Clinton Manson
Art Director	Prasad Pradhan	Art Director	Dominic Stallard
Photographer	Suresh Subramaniam	Photographer	Clive Stewart
Client	Juice Hair Salon	Client	Axe Shower Gel

ENJOY THE SUN.

PIZ BUIN self tan

For all skin types.

Agency	Grey, Stockholm	**Agency**	Lowe Brindfors, Stockholm
Creative Director	Martin Stadhammar	**Creative Director**	Tove Langseth
Copywriter	Marcus Nyström	**Copywriter**	Olle Langseth
Art Director	Daniel Backman	**Art Director**	Tove Langseth
Graphic	Sara Bellafesta	**Photographer**	Markus Ohlsson
Client	Hawaiian Tropic	**Client**	Piz Buin

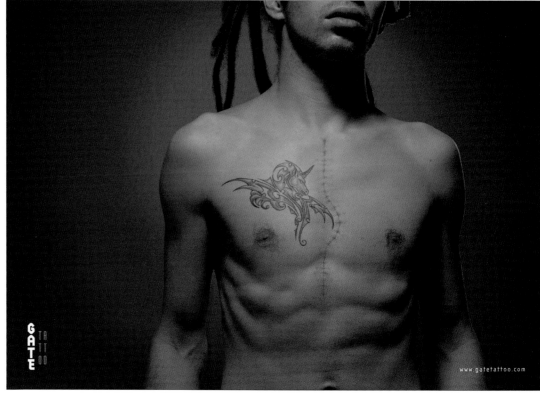

168 Beauty Products & Services

Agency	Mark BBDO, Prague	Agency	Alice BBDO,
Creative Directors	Leon Sverdlin		Istanbul
	Martin Charvat	Creative Director	Ozan Varışlı
Copywriters	Viktor Spala	Copywriter	Ali Göral
	Leon Sverdlin	Art Director	Kutlay Sındırgı
Art Director	Michal Nemecek	Photographer	Erbil Balta
Photographer	Goran Tacevski	Illustrator	Hüseyin Yıldız
Client	Zen Asian Wellness Spas	Client	Gate Tattoos

Agency	McCann Erickson, Bucharest	Agency	TBWA\Istanbul
Creative Directors	Adrian Botan	Creative Directors	Pemra Atac
	Alexandru Dumitrescu		Ilkay Gurpinar
Copywriter	Craita Coman	Copywriter	Ilkay Gurpinar
Art Director	Raluca Negoita	Art Director	Pemra Atac
Photographer	Cosmin Bumbut	Photographer	Emre Dogru
Client	Geta Voinea Hair Salons	Illustrator	Diagonal
		Client	YKM Fragrances

170   **Toiletries & Health Care**

Agency	JWT, Paris
Creative Directors	Xavier Beauregard
	Vincent Pedrocchi
Copywriter	Vincent Pedrocchi
Art Director	Xavier Beauregard
Production	Wanda, Paris
Director	Claude Fayolle
Producers	Claude Fayolle
	Elisabeth Boitte
Client	Wilkinson Quattro Titanium, "Fight for Kisses"

In the opening scene, we see an animated baby using a bra as a skipping rope. The narrator explains: "There was a time when babies had a great life." In flashback, we see the baby being embraced by his mother. "The softness of their skin got them all their mom's attention." But things change when the father discovers the Wilkinson Quattro razor. This makes his skin so soft that his wife wants to kiss him again. Mad with jealousy, the baby realises that he is going to have to "fight for kisses". So he gets into training, martial arts style.

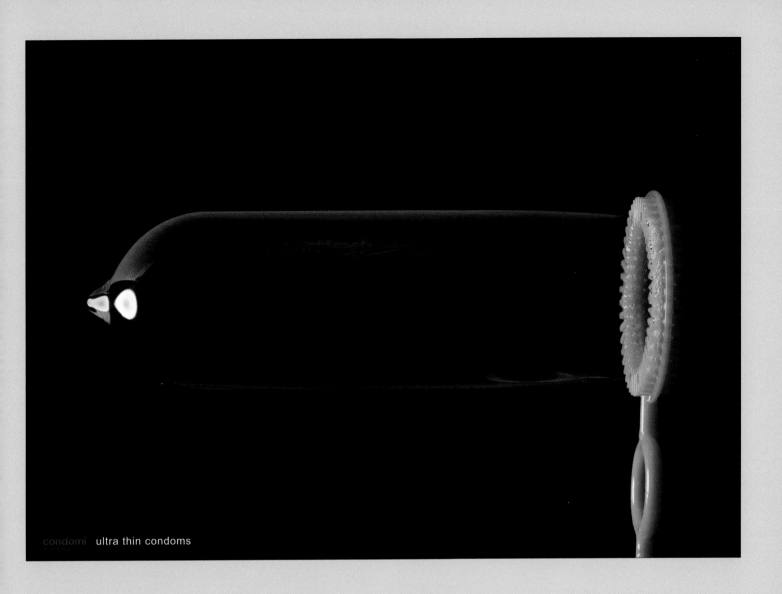

condomi   ultra thin condoms

 Toiletries & Health Care   **171**

Agency	DraftFCB Kobza, Vienna
Creative Director	Patrik Partl
Copywriters	Eva Sommeregger
	Florian Schwab
Art Directors	Andreas Gesierich
	Daniel Senitschnig
Client	Condomi

Agency	Forsman & Bodenfors, Gothenburg
Production	Anders Skog Films
Director	Anders Skog
Producer	Sonia Maggioni
Client	Libero Diapers, "Yoga"

We see a yoga class. The men and women attending the class contort themselves into ever more extreme positions. After a moment the camera swivels around to show us a diaper-clad baby. It takes us a moment to realise that he is actually leading the class. When he sits down, they sit down. And when he sucks his own foot, his "pupils" are obliged follow suit! The baby claps his hands, delighted by all this. Libero has just made its most stretchy diaper ever.

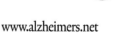

172   **Toiletries & Health Care**

Agency	Try Advertising Agency, Oslo
Creative Director	Kjetil Try
Copywriter	Øystein Halvorsen
Art Director	Karin Lund
Production	Monster, Oslo Moonlighting, Bucharest
Director	Mathis Fürst
Producers	Trond Sandø Gro Marwold Helene Hovda Lunde
Client	Solidox, "Symphony"

An orchestra takes the stage, with a woman who appears to be a singer. But no: in fact, whenever she smiles, a little sparkling 'ting!' sound accompanies the gesture. As the symphony continues, the conductor grimaces, makes faces and sticks his tongue out at her to ensure that she grins in the right places, guaranteeing that the woman will add that 'ting!' of freshness to the music. Solidox toothpaste provides whiteness like no other.

Agency	TBWA\PHS, Helsinki
Copywriter	Erkko Mannila
Art Director	Mikko Torvinen
Production	Woodpecker Film, Helsinki
Director	Tommi Pietilainen
Producer	Jukka Valtanen
Client	Pfizer Aricept, "Alzheimer's Day"

A doctor addresses the camera. "Today is National Alzheimer's Day", he says. "The disease begins slowly. Everyday matters are forgotten; new and old events are mixed up. You may forget what you have just heard and seen." He explains that it's important to detect the symptoms of the disease quickly, so it can be treated. And sure enough, after a short break, the commercial is repeated exactly as before. A caption reads: "If you are seeing this commercial for the first time, you may be suffering from Alzheimer's Disease."

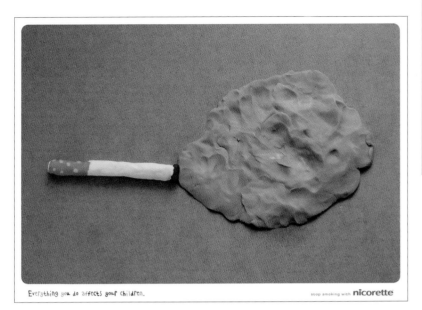

Everything you do affects your children.
stop smoking with **nicorette**

Everything you do affects your children.
stop smoking with **nicorette**

Everything you do affects your children.
stop smoking with **nicorette**

Toiletries & Health Care   **173**

Agency	DraftFCB Kobza, Vienna
Creative Directors	Erich Falkner Patrik Partl
Copywriter	Florian Schwab
Art Directors	Andreas Gesierich Daniel Senitschnig
Client	Nicorette

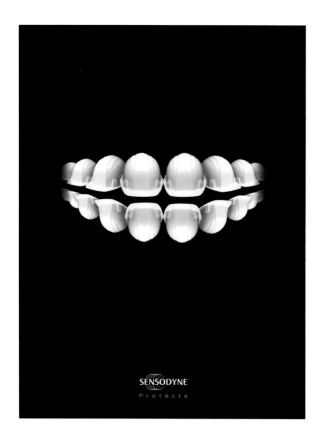

174   **Toiletries & Health Care**

Agency	Callegari Berville Grey, Paris	Agency	Callegari Berville Grey, Paris
Creative Director	Andrea Stillacci	**Creative Director**	Andrea Stillacci
Copywriter	Pascal Poinsot	**Copywriter**	Yannick Savioz
Art Director	Gregory Renault	**Art Director**	Jérôme Gonfond
Photographer	Laurent de Broca	**Photographer**	Ilario Magali
Client	Sensodyne Toothpaste	**Client**	Aquafresh Toothbrushes

Agency	Saatchi & Saatchi Simko, Geneva	Agency	DDB&Co, Istanbul
Creative Directors	Jean-François Fournon	Creative Director	Karpat Polat
	Olivier Girard	Copywriter	Karpat Polat
Copywriter	Jean-François Fournon	Art Director	Ali Bati
Art Director	Isabelle Carvalho	Photographer	Ilkay Muratoglu
Illustrator	Fred Van Deelen	Client	Able Touch Depiliatory Wax
Client	Otrivin		

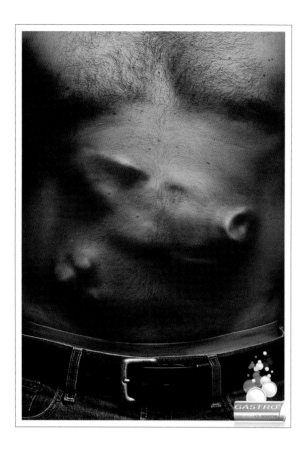

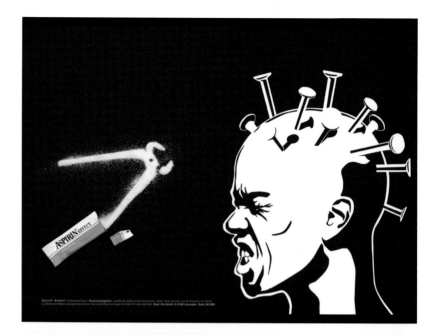

Agency	Callegari Berville Grey, Paris	Agency	BBDO Germany, Düsseldorf
Creative Director	Andrea Stillacci	Creative Directors	Marie-Theres Schwingeler
Copywriter	Luissandro Del Gobbo		Toygar Bazarkaya
Art Director	Giovanni Setteesoldi	Copywriter	Kenny Blumenschein
Photographer	Riccardo Bagnoli	Art Director	Christian Steuler
Illustrator	Claudio Luparelli	Photographer	Michael Dunlap
Client	Gastro Autociel	Illustrator	Christian Steuler
		Client	Aspirin Effect

For stomachs on holiday.

TAMPAX®

Agency	Saatchi & Saatchi, Stockholm	Agency	Leo Burnett & Target, Bucharest
Creative Directors	Adam Kerj	Creative Director	Emilian Arsenoaiei
	Fredrik Preisler	Copywriter	Mihai Botarel
Copywriter	Magnus Jakobsson	Art Director	Ghica Popa
Art Director	Nima Stillerud	Client	Tampax
Client	Bifacid		

durex **play** lubricants at **www.durex.gr**

Agency	McCann Erickson, Athens		**Agency**	DraftFCB Kobza, Vienna
Creative Director	Anna Stilianaki		**Creative Director**	Patrik Partl
Copywriter	Michael Laios		**Copywriter**	Florian Schwab
Art Director	Popi Dimakou		**Art Directors**	Andreas Gesierich
Photographer	Popi Dimakou			Daniel Senitschnig
Client	Durex Lubricants		**Client**	Condomi Lubricants

Agency   McCann Erickson, Madrid
Creative Director Monica Moro
Copywriter   Isabel López
Art Director   Ricardo Rovira
Photographer   Artefacto Visual
Client   Durex Stimulators

Toiletries & Health Care

Agency	The Jupiter Drawing Room, Johannesburg
Creative Directors	Graham Warsop
	Michael Blore
Copywriter	Clint Bechus
Art Directors	Shane Forbes
	Liam Wielopolski
Photographer	Michael Meyersfeld
Client	Durex

Agency	Venividi, Forst an der Weinstrasse
Creative Directors	Benito Babuscio
	Steffen Hofmann
Copywriter	Benito Babuscio
Art Director	Steffen Hofmann
Client	Copamour Condoms

Agency	Leo Burnett, Brussels		Agency	Duval Guillaume, Antwerp
Creative Directors	Jean-Paul Lefebvre		Creative Directors	Geoffrey Hantson
	Michel De Lauw			Dirk Domen
Art Director	Mathieu Dubray		Copywriter	Kristof Snels
Photographer	Thierry Siebrant		Art Director	Sebastien De Valck
Client	Extase Condoms		Photographer	Koen Demuynck
			Client	ReSkin

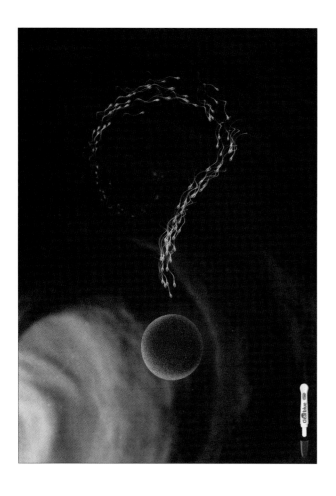

182 Toiletries & Health Care

Agency	Hilanders, Helsingborg
Copywriter	Jessica Cederberg
Art Director	Markus Lindsjö
Illustrator	Tobias Dahlén
Client	Clearblue Digital Pregnancy Test

Agency	DraftFCB Kobza, Vienna
Creative Director	Patrik Partl
Copywriter	Florian Schwab
Art Directors	Andreas Gesierich
	Daniel Senitschnig
Client	Condomi

MORE PRECISION

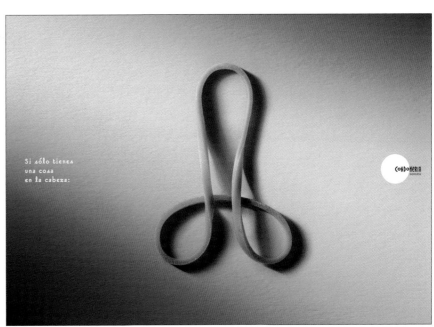

Agency	JWT, Paris	Agency	The Partner, Barcelona	- If you turn everything around.
Creative Director	Pascal Manry	**Creative Director**	Ferran Llopart	
Copywriter	Vincent Pedrocchi	**Copywriter**	Pau Marquès Seguí	- If you know where you want to get to.
Art Director	Xavier Beauregard	**Art Directors**	Diego Otero Rodríguez	
Photographer	Yann Lepape		Ion Fernández Pikazarri	- If you only have one thing on your mind.
Client	Wilkinson	**Photographer**	Raul Ortega	
		Client	La Condonería	

184 **Clothing & Fabrics**

Agency	Nitro, London	A hip-hop princess and a waiflike ballerina
Creative Director	Paul Shearer	dance in a deserted ballroom. At first they
Copywriter	Paul Shearer	seem to provoke one another: the curvy
Art Director	Paul Shearer	yet tomboyish hip-hop fan's moves are fast
Production	Great Guns	and aggressive, while the ballerina dances
Director	Paul Shearer	gracefully, lighter than air. After a few
Producers	Laura Gregory	moments, though, their dance styles start
	Amy Sherwin	to synchronise, until finally they are dancing
Client	Nike Russia, "Ballerina"	as a duo. Nike has sports gear for every
		style and shape. Don't let your body stop
		you – just do it.

Men don't want to look at naked men

 Clothing & Fabrics   **185**

Agency	& Co., Copenhagen
Creative Director	Thomas Hoffmann
Art Directors	Thomas Hoffmann
	Martin Storegaard
Photographers	Rasmus Mogensen
	Morten Laursen
Client	JBS Underwear

Agency   Compagnie 360
                Euro RSCG,
                Suresnes
Creative Director   Jean-François Goize
Copywriter   Antoine Colin
Art Director   Jean-Philippe Magnaval
Production   Marcassin
Director   Gabriel Malaprade
Producers   Jérémie Morichon
                Christophe Demeure
Client   Shock Absorber
                Sports Bra, "Cheeks"

We see a female athlete running in extreme slow motion. With each stride, her cheeks and lips wobble violently. After a few seconds of this, a caption appears: "Imagine her breasts." A voice then informs us that, luckily for her and sportswomen everywhere, a Shock Absorber sports bra can reduce the movements of her chest by 74 per cent.

186   **Clothing & Fabrics**

Agency   Trigger Momentum,
                    Gothenburg
Creative Director   Marios Forslund
Copywriter   Anna Blomdahl
Art Director   Marcus Hessel
Production   Hobby Film
Director   Oskar Bård
Producer   John R Hallström
Client   Intersport,
                    "The Scale" &
                    "The Bus"

A pale, flabby bloke steps gingerly onto his bathroom scales and looks at the result. Hardly believing his eyes, he leaps off like a scalded cat. Gathering his courage, he tries once again. Obviously, his weight has not changed. He jumps off the scales and ponders what to do next. A faint smile appears on his face as he mounts the scales once more – and then steps off them again. He repeats the process, smiling broadly. Our overweight friend has discovered step classes. Intersport: love the challenge.

Leaving his home, a man sees the local bus coming. But he's still several hundred metres from the nearest stop. And so he takes to his heels and runs, careening around baby carriages and taking shortcuts across bridges and down steps – always staying only a few steps ahead of the speeding bus. He arrives at the bus stop in the nick of time, panting with exertion. The driver opens the door for him, but the runner merely grins and waves the bus on. He was only in it for the challenge.

Agency	Friendly Fire, Vienna	Agency	DDB Milan
Creative Directors	Thomas Schmid	Creative Director	Vicky Gitto
	Norbert Horvath	Copywriter	Vicky Gitto
Copywriter	Thomas Schmid	Art Director	Andrea Maggioni
Art Director	Norbert Horvath	Client	Mariella Merendino
Photographer	Clemens Horvath		
Illustrator	Norbert Horvath		
Client	Linda Zlok Fashions		

188 **Clothing & Fabrics**

Agency	Bruketa & Zinic, Zagreb	Small text at the bottom of the poster:	**Agency**	Publicis, Zurich
Creative Director	Moe Minkara	At this moment your bum is completely
Art Directors	Krunoslav Franetic	exposed. If it was in a sexy pair of jeans
	Daniel Vukovic	it would attract attention all the time.
Client	Je*s Jeans	

Agency Bruketa & Zinic, Zagreb
Creative Director Moe Minkara
Art Directors Krunoslav Franetic
Daniel Vukovic
Client Je*s Jeans

Small text at the bottom of the poster:
At this moment your bum is completely
exposed. If it was in a sexy pair of jeans
it would attract attention all the time.

Agency Publicis, Zurich
Copywriter Florian Beck
Art Director Florian Beck
Photographer Giuliano Di Marco
Illustrator Matthias Günter
Client Melvins Fashions

AIGLE OUTDOOR CLOTHES FOR THE REINTRODUCTION OF MAN INTO NATURE

AIGLE OUTDOOR CLOTHES FOR THE REINTRODUCTION OF MAN INTO NATURE

Agency	BETC Euro RSCG, Paris
Creative Director	Rémi Babinet
Copywriter	Valérie Chidlovsky
Art Director	Florence Bellisson
Photographer	Paul Wakefield
Client	Aigle

Wearing stiches is horrifying.

gzl
seamless underwear

ICHI JEANS

ICHI JEANS

Agency	Propaganda Reklam Fikirleri, Istanbul		**Agency**	& Co., Copenhagen
Creative Director	Mahir Uraz		**Creative Director**	Thomas Hoffmann
Copywriter	Mahir Uraz		**Art Directors**	Thomas Hoffmann
Art Director	Engin Oztekin			Martin Storegaard
Illustrator	Bugra Atici		**Photographer**	Casper Sejersen
Client	GZL Underwear		**Client**	Ichi Jeans

Agency	Serviceplan Munich/Hamburg	**Agency**	Saatchi & Saatchi, Stockholm	The pencil 'held' in the gutter of the magazine demonstrates the tight cleavage a Wonderbra offers; this is the Wonderbra pencil test.
Creative Director	Karsten Gessulat	**Creative Directors**	Adam Kerj	
Copywriters	Niels van Hoek		Fredrik Preisler	
	Susanna Schreibauer	**Copywriter**	Hans Malm	
Art Director	Martin Graf	**Art Directors**	Gustav Egerstedt	
Photographer	Denis Pernath		Nima Stillerud	
Client	Speedo Swimwear	**Client**	Wonderbra	

192   **Clothing & Fabrics**

Agency	ANR.BBDO, Gothenburg & Stockholm	Myrorna is a chain that sells second-hand clothes to raise money for the homeless. The campaign recycled real ads from the seventies and eighties to make its point.
Creative Director	Haman Larsson	
Copywriter	Haman Larsson	
Art Director	Marita Kuntonen	
Client	Myrorna	

Agency	& Co., Copenhagen
Creative Director	Thomas Hoffmann
Art Directors	Thomas Hoffmann
	Martin Storegaard
Photographer	Dennis Stenild
Client	JBS Underwear

Agency	Marcel, Paris
Creative Directors	Frédéric Témin
	Anne de Maupeou
Copywriters	Eric Jannon
	Dimitri Guerassimov
Art Directors	Romin Favre
	Nicolas Chauvin
Photographer	Johan Renck
Client	Diesel

194   **Clothing & Fabrics**

Agency	McCann Erickson, Milan	**Agency**	Lorenzo Marini & Associati, Milan
Creative Directors	Federica Ariagno		
	Giorgio Natale	**Copywriter**	Alba Minadeo
Copywriter	Paolo Chiabrando	**Art Director**	Paolo Bianchini
Art Director	Gaetano del Pizzo	**Photographer**	Max Cardelli
Client	Sauber Stockings	**Client**	Caractère Fashions

Basketball hoop
€80

Jeans
€15

ÅHLÉNS
DEPARTMENT STORES
ENDLESS POSSIBILITIES

T-shirt
2 for €10

Motorboat
€140

ÅHLÉNS
DEPARTMENT STORES
ENDLESS POSSIBILITIES

Napkin
€12/metre

Dress
€14

ÅHLÉNS
DEPARTMENT STORES
ENDLESS POSSIBILITIES

While waiting in the living room,
Chloe and Louis made 359 changes to this picture.

Can you spot the differences?

Kidproof clothes

Agency	King, Stockholm	**Agency**	BETC Euro RSCG, Paris
Creative Director	Frank Hollingworth	**Creative Director**	Rémi Babinet
Copywriters	Hedvig Hawall Bruckner	**Copywriter**	Olivier Couradjut
	Pontus Ekström	**Art Director**	Rémy Tricot
Art Directors	Helena Redman	**Photographer**	Stefan Ruiz
	Alexander Elers	**Client**	Petit Bateau Children's Clothing
	Daniel Söderstedt		
Photographer	Petrus Olsson		
Client	Åhléns Department Stores		

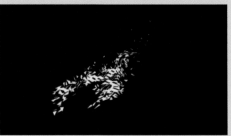
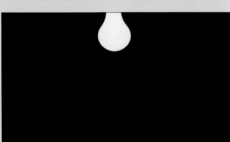

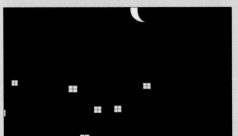
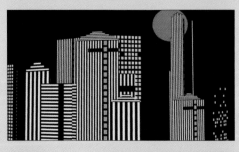

Agency	Grey & Trace, Barcelona	On a black screen, a glowing yellow dot
Creative Directors	Jürgen Krieger	explodes into a kaleidoscope of lights
	Jose Miguel Tortajada	representing the Big Bang. Soon the vortex
Copywriter	Carla Olaortúa	is replaced by flashes of lightning signalling
Art Directors	Dani Páez	the birth of planet earth. Then sparks
	Saül Serradesanferm	from a flint become a blazing fire. In quick
Production	Arena Shots, Barcelona	succession, we see the start of electric light
Director	Joan Gil	and the growth of cities, roads and airport
Producers	Angeles González	runways. A view of the earth from space
	Minerva Liste	transforms into a void lit only by a yellow dot.
Client	Pilot V Liquid Light Marker,	The new Pilot V Liquid Light marker, which
	"History of Light"	provides dramatically bright colours, has just
		treated us to a history of light.

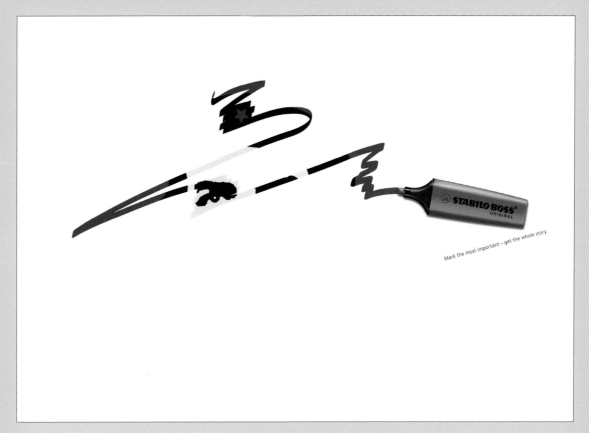

Mark the most important – get the whole story.

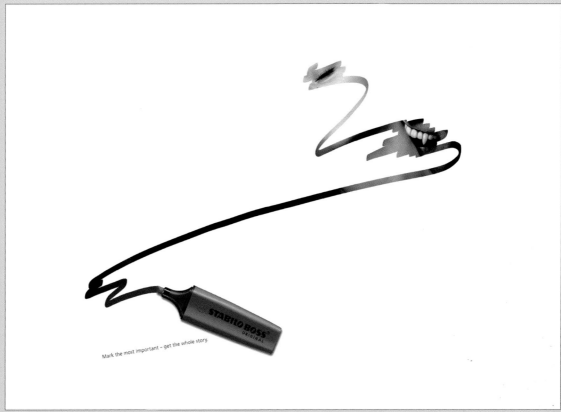

Mark the most important – get the whole story.

Footwear & Personal Accessories 197

Agency	Serviceplan Munich/Hamburg
Creative Directors	Alexander Schill
	Axel Thomsen
Copywriter	Francisca Maass
Art Director	Jonathan Schupp
Client	Stabilo Boss Original

Agency	Coffein, Düsseldorf
Creative Directors	Andreas Beckmann
	Gunnar Eicker
Production	PI_group Production
	International, Hamburg
Director	Harry Patramanis
Producers	Reinhard Gedack
	Sabine Schröder
	Martina Heckner
Client	Rimowa,
	"Troubleshooter"

Scenes of a man fishing from a jetty in the wild are inter-cut with those of a seaplane taking off. Meanwhile, a huge grizzly bear wanders down to the lakeside. It spies the fisherman and ambles on to the jetty. At that moment, the seaplane arrives and drops a metallic Rimowa suitcase. As the ravenous bear rears above the man, the suitcase skips over the lake like a bouncing bomb and clobbers the grizzly. The bear falls into the water, out cold. The indestructible case lands unmarked on the jetty. Rimowa: every case tells a story.

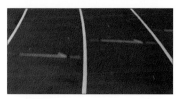

198   Footwear & Personal Accessories

Agency	Wieden+Kennedy,
	Amsterdam
Creative Directors	Alvaro Sotomayor
	Hunter Hindman
	Rick Condos
Art Director	Hunter Hindman
Production	MJZ, London
Director	Dante Ariola
Producers	Natalie Hill
	Elissa Singstock
Client	Nike+, "Addicted"

The narrator – actor Ed Norton – explains his addiction to running. "I've collected footsteps before dawn, seen places I never knew existed, run to the moon and back, been a rabbit for the neighbourhood dogs, obeyed the voice in my head, let music carry me when I couldn't, raced against yesterday, let the world be my witness, measured myself in metres, kilometres and finally character. I've plugged into a higher purpose, left this world and come back changed. I am addicted." Run like you've never run before: Nikeplus.com.

Agency	Wieden+Kennedy,
	Amsterdam
Creative Directors	Alvaro Sotomayor
	Boyd Coyner
Copywriter	Patrick Almaguer
Art Director	Blake Kidder
Production	Between the Eyes,
	London
Director	Eran Creevy
Producers	Ben Pugh
	Orlando Wood
Client	Nike+, "Paula"

Athlete Paula Radcliffe provides the narration, over scenes from her running life: "I am a runner. For as long as I can remember, I have run hundreds, thousands, tens of thousands of miles. I've beaten everyone in the world – even myself. And now, I have to start all over again." Radcliffe's iPod says "Pausing workout" as she stops to check her newborn baby in the pram she is pushing. Nikeplus is a running workout devised by Nike and iPod.

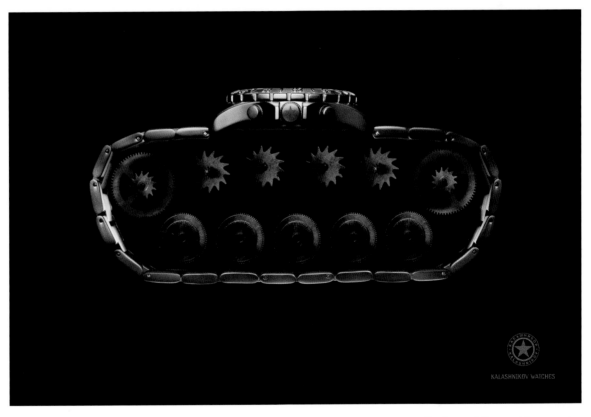

Agency	Impact/BBDO, Jeddah	**Agency**	Grabarz & Partner
Creative Director	Ahmad Beck		Werbeagentur, Hamburg
Copywriter	Ahmad Beck	**Creative Director**	Ralf Heuel
Art Director	Ahmad Beck	**Copywriter**	Holger Paasch
Photographer	Steve Kosman	**Art Directors**	Holger Paasch
Client	Samsonite		Christoph Stricker
		Photographer	Joris van Velzen
		Client	Kalashnikov Watches

Made from fine
Italian canvas

Sometimes, home is just a feeling. Catherine Deneuve. Take three, last day of shooting. Paris.

LOUIS VUITTON

A journey brings us face to face with ourselves. Mikhail Gorbachev. Berlin Wall. Returning from a conference.

LOUIS VUITTON

200 **Footwear & Personal Accessories**

Agency	Grey Copenhagen	**Agency**	Ogilvy & Mather, Paris
Copywriter	Lotte Nyholm	**Creative Director**	Christian Reuilly
Art Directors	Anders Møller	**Copywriter**	Edgard Montjean
	Mikkel Krøijer	**Art Director**	Antoaneta Metchanova
Client	Kappa	**Photographer**	Annie Leibovitz
		Client	Louis Vuitton

THE SWISS SURF AND SNOWBOARD SHOP

Agency	King, Stockholm	Agency	Jung von Matt, Zurich
Creative Director	Frank Hollingworth	Creative Directors	Alexander Jaggy
Copywriter	Patrick Herold		Michael Rottmann
Art Director	Tim Zastera	Art Director	Axel Eckstein
Photographers	Bohman, Sjöstrand	Client	Beach Mountain
Client	Leatherman		

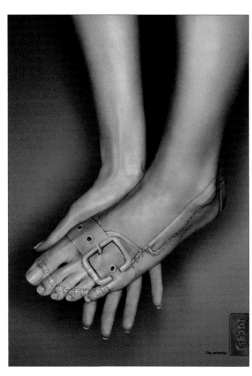

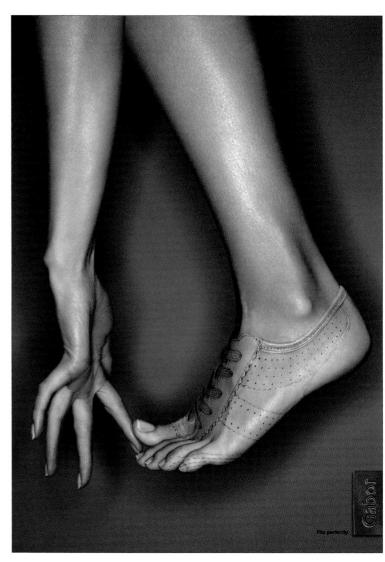

202 **Footwear & Personal Accessories**

Agency	JWT, Warsaw	**Agency**	Serviceplan Munich/Hamburg
Creative Director	Darek Zatorski	**Creative Directors**	Winfried Bergmann
Copywriter	Kamil Nazarewicz		Christoph Everke
Art Director	Katarzyna Macharz	**Copywriter**	Tim Strathus
Photographer	Andrzej Dragan	**Art Director**	Claudia Schmidt-Runge
Client	Converse	**Photographer**	Michael Leis
		Graphic Design	Jasmin Speth
			Monika Steiner
		Client	Gabor Shoes

Sunglasses $159

Footwear & Personal Accessories 203

Agency	King, Stockholm
Creative Director	Frank Hollingworth
Copywriter	Christian Karlsson
Art Director	Tommy Carlsson
Photographer	Calle Stoltz
Client	WeSC Eyewear

204 Automobiles

Agency	Contrapunto, Madrid	A young couple asks a pedestrian the
Creative Directors	Antonio Montero	directions to Oak Street. The pedestrian
	Félix del Valle	points in the direction of a parked Chrysler
	Carlos Jorge	Voyager: "You see that car over there?" he
Copywriter	Félix del Valle	asks. "Yeah," says the woman. The man
Art Director	Carlos Jorge	says smugly: "It's mine." Then, pointing in
Production	Lee Films, Madrid	completely the opposite direction, he says:
Director	Luis Alonso	"It's the second on the right."
Producers	Jacobo Saiz	
	Mamen Puyot	
	Yolanda Galant	
Client	Chrysler Voyager,	
	"It is Mino"	

New Smart ECO. Consuming 3.4 litres every 100 km makes very little difference to the environment. ● smart

New Smart ECO. Consuming 3.4 litres every 100 km makes very little difference to the environment. ● smart

New Smart ECO. Consuming 3.4 litres every 100 km makes very little difference to the environment. ● smart

Automobiles 205

Agency	Contrapunto, Madrid
Creative Directors	Antonio Montero
	Jose Maria Cornejo
	Fernando Galindo
Copywriter	Fernando Galindo
Art Director	José Maria Cornejo
Client	Smart Fortwo

Isn't it beautiful
what hands can do?

The Phaeton.
Handmade Perfection.

Agency	Grabarz & Partner, Hamburg	A "galanty show" is a theatre of shadows. This is a particularly sophisticated version, as many human hands perform an incredible ballet. The payoff comes at the end: "Isn't it beautiful what hands can do?" The Volkswagen Phaeton is "handmade perfection".
Creative Directors	Ralf Heuel	
	Ralf Nolting	
Copywriter	Paul von Mühlendahl	
Art Director	Christoph Stricker	
Production	Deli Pictures	
	Postproduktion	
Director	Michael Reissinger	
Producers	Bianca Mack	
	Anne Hoffmann	
	Patrick Cahill	
Client	Volkswagen Phaeton, "Galanty Show"	

Wonder why you never see
a Volkswagen in horror movies?

Golf
The power of understatement

206 Automobiles

Agency	DDB Germany, Berlin	It's a classic horror movie scenario: while pursued by unspeakable evil, somebody jumps into a car and turns the key in the ignition. With a rasping, grinding noise, the engine fails to start. Meanwhile, the danger edges closer...This ad gathers a selection of scenes suggesting that the horror genre is filled with unreliable vehicles. Then a caption asks: "Wonder why you never see a Volkswagen in horror movies?"
Executive CD	Amir Kassaei	
Creative Directors	Stefan Schulte	
	Bert Peulecke	
Copywriter	Sebastian Kainz	
Art Director	Marc Wientzek	
Producers	Christiane Schwabe	
	Patrick Scharf	
Client	Volkswagen, "Horror Movie"	

Agency	DDB London	Thanks to the soundtrack of this spot, we learn that its protagonist is a "great pretender". In meetings, at the office, or while out shopping, he's a flashy, self-confident type. But his attitude hasn't won him any friends. He spends his nights at the gym or eating alone. When he enters a posh hotel – tossing the keys of his sports car disdainfully to the porter – he's alarmed to see a mirror image of himself. But his double politely thanks the porter for bringing his car around. It's a Golf: cool yet understated.
Creative Director	Jeremy Craigen	
Copywriter	Sam Oliver	
Art Director	Shishir Patel	
Production	Partizan	
Director	Patrik Bergh	
Producers	James Tomkinson	
	Maggie Blundell	
Client	Volkswagen Golf, "Great Pretender"	

You don't need to have children to drive a Touran.

Parking made easy.
The Volkswagen Golf with Park Distance Control.

Agency	DDB Germany, Düsseldorf	Agency	DDB Germany, Berlin
Executive CD	Amir Kassaei	Executive CD	Amir Kassaei
Creative Directors	Heiko Freyland	Creative Directors	Bert Peulecke
	Raphael Milczarek		Stefan Schulte
Copywriters	Felix Lemcke	Copywriters	Jan Hendrik Ott
	Jan Propach		Gen Sadakane
Art Directors	Fabian Kirner	Art Directors	Gen Sadakane
	Michael Kittel		Jan Hendrik Ott
Client	Volkswagen Touran		Tim Stübane
		Photographer	David Cuenca
		Client	Volkswagen Golf

Agency	DDB Amsterdam	
Creative Directors	Joris Kuijpers	
	Dylan de Backer	
Copywriter	Dylan de Backer	
Art Director	Joris Kuijpers	
Production	Czar.nl, Amsterdam	
Director	Bart Timmer	
Producers	Sytske Rijkens	
	Robert Nan	
	Yuka Kambayashi	
Client	Volkswagen Touareg, "Keep it Clean"	

A suspiciously urban-looking VW salesman is out in the countryside, explaining how the Volkswagen Touareg can make quick work of rough terrain. He parks the car beside a ravine, a rocky hillside and then a deep, muddy puddle. "With the Touareg it's vroom! – straight through!" he declares. But each scene is cut before we can witness any off-road action. In fact, despite all the man's macho talk, the car remains suspiciously spotless throughout. "54% buy a Touareg for its looks," explains the caption. "So we'd rather not make it dirty."

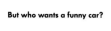

Agency	DDB Germany, Berlin	Art Directors	Christian Jakimowitsch
Executive CD	Amir Kassaei		Marc Isken
Creative Directors	Bert Peulecke	Production	Radicalmedia Berlin
	Stefan Schulte	Director	Sebastian Strasser
Copywriters	Marian Götz	Producers	Boris Schepker
	Kai Abd El-Salam		Janet Fox
	David Oswald		Patrick Scharf
		Client	Volkswagen, "Made in Germany" Campaign

This campaign manages to both praise and tease the Germans. In the first spot, we see a group of Volkswagen technicians staging some kind of impromptu cabaret. Armed with an acoustic guitar, one of them sings the lamest folk song imaginable, which involves unconvincing animal impressions. Another makes balloon animals and a grim-faced clown with rabbit ears briefly appears. Then the singer abandons his guitar for a sock puppet. The Germans are not humorous – but who wants a funny car?

A middle-aged disco dancing teacher is trying to show a bunch of VW tech guys how to be "funky". The first one tries to imitate the teacher's loose-hipped moves – with dramatic lack of success. A group dance session is even worse: the VW geeks are as rigid as frozen boards. Sure, the Germans are stiff – but who wants a shaky car? Fortunately, Volkswagens are made in Germany.

Touareg

Agency	Publicis, Bucharest	Agency	Pristop, Ljubljana
Creative Director	Razvan Capanescu	Creative Director	Aljosa Bagola
Copywriter	Dan Frinculescu	Copywriter	Aljosa Bagola
Art Director	Bogdan Nestor	Art Director	Robert Krizmancic
Photographer	Bogdan Nestor	Photographer	Sasa Hes
Client	Nissan Tiida	Client	Volkswagen Touareg

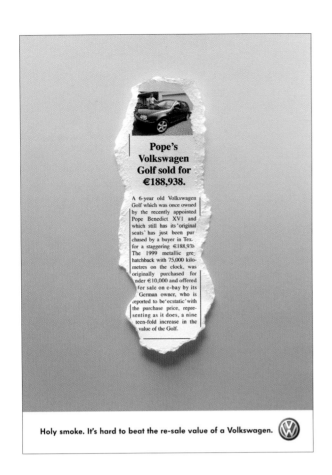

Just 5.9 kilograms per horsepower. The Golf GTI® Edition 30.

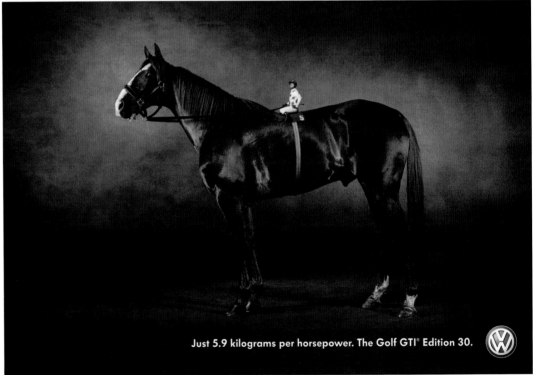

Just 5.9 kilograms per horsepower. The Golf GTI® Edition 30.

Agency	Owens DDB, Dublin
Creative Directors	Colin Murphy
	Donald O'Dea
Copywriter	Colin Murphy
Art Director	Donal O'Dea
Photographer	Neil McDougald
Client	Volkswagen Golf

Agency	DDB Germany, Berlin
Executive CD	Amir Kassaei
Creative Directors	Stefan Schulte
	Bert Peulecke
Copywriter	Sebastian Kainz
Art Director	Marc Wientzek
Photographers	Yann Arthus-Bertrand
	Sven Schrader
Graphic Design	Wulf Rechtacek
Client	Volkswagen Golf GTI

Overtake faster. New Golf R32 with 250 hp and launch control.

Overtake faster. New Golf R32 with 250 hp and launch control.

Agency	DDB Germany, Düsseldorf
Executive CD	Amir Kassaei
Creative Directors	Heiko Freyland
	Raphael Milczarek
	Eric Schoeffler
Copywriters	Heiko Freyland
	Felix Lemcke
	Jan Propach
Art Directors	Raphael Milczarek
	Fabian Kirner
	Michael Kittel
Photographer	Eberhard Sauer
Client	Volkswagen Golf R32

No 25,000,000th Golf without the 2,936,182nd Golf.

Thanks.

No 25,000,000th Golf without the 3,114,873rd Golf.

Thanks. VW

No 25,000,000th Golf without the 9,921,283rd Golf.

Thanks. VW

No 25,000,000th Golf without the 16,993,208th Golf.

Thanks. VW

No 25,000,000th Golf without the 19,901,557th Golf.

Thanks. VW

NO SCHOOL RUN, NO COMMUTER ON THE HANDS-FREE, NO BUS BROKEN DOWN, NO TAXI DOING U-TURN, NO BIKE IN YOUR BLINDSPOT, NO MAN SELLING ROSES, NO SUN IN YOUR EYES, NO SWEAT ON YOUR BACK, NO TIME TO READ THIS POSTER.

Night Driving by Golf
night-driving.com

212 **Automobiles**

Agency	DDB Amsterdam
Creative Directors	Dylan de Backer
	Joris Kuijpers
Copywriter	Erik Falke
Art Director	Dennis Baars
Photographer	Edith Paol
Client	Volkswagen Golf

Agency	DDB London
Creative Director	Jeremy Craigen
Copywriter	Sam Oliver
Art Director	Shishir Patel
Photographer	Ernst Fischer
Client	Volkswagen Golf

The new Touareg

In advertising, you're allowed to exaggerate.
(that explains the caravan)

Our Touareg is towing a Boeing 747. Seriously. We tested it. 155,000 kilos altogether, no exaggeration. Of course, the necessary adjustments were made. After all, a Boeing doesn't fit on a normal towing hook. And we never would have gotten a proper grip without 4,300 kilos of extra ballast in the car.

But aside from that it's a normal Volkswagen Touareg. In other words, the same Touareg you'll find at the dealer. Because of course it's anything but 'normal', a car that can tow a gigantic Boeing.

That's why we want to advertise it. We're so proud, and some-

times we get a little carried away. See, to be honest, the photo was retouched. The caravan was added later. So yes, those 360 kilos are a tad exaggerated.

The powerful Touareg by Volkswagen. Who else?

Agency	DDB London	Agency	DDB Amsterdam
Creative Director	Jeremy Craigen	Creative Directors	Dylan de Backer
			Joris Kuijpers
Copywriter	Matt Lee	Copywriter	Dylan de Backer
Art Director	Peter Heyes	Art Director	Joris Kuijpers
Photographer	David Harriman	Client	Volkswagen Touareg
Client	Volkswagen Touareg		

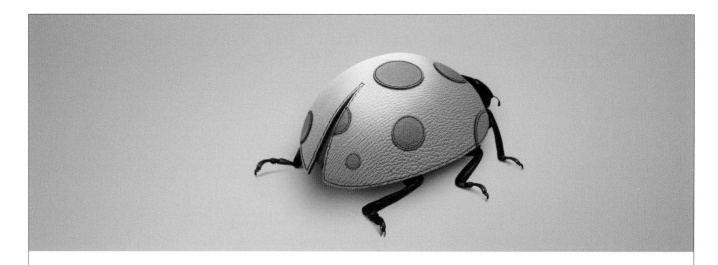

New Beetle, now with leather as standard.

A bit wilder. The CrossGolf.

214 **Automobiles**

Agency	DDB Milan		**Agency**	DDB Germany, Berlin
Creative Director	Vicky Gitto		**Executive CD**	Amir Kassaei
Copywriter	Davide Valenti		**Creative Directors**	Bert Peulecke
Art Director	Francesco Vigorelli			Stefan Schulte
Client	Volkswagen Beetle		**Copywriter**	Birgit van den Valentyn
			Art Director	Tim Stübane
			Photographer	Matthias Koslik
			Client	Volkswagen CrossGolf

 Don't let the winter sky pass by.

EOS. A cabriolet with glassroof.

For the love of the automobile

Agency	Kryn, Minsk	Agency	Medina Turgul DDB, Istanbul
Creative Director	Alexander Shevelevich	Creative Director	Kurtcebe Turgul
Copywriter	Vlad Saveliev	Copywriters	Erdem Koksal
Art Director	Sergey Tishkov		Ali Bozkurt
Photographer	Sergey Tishkov	Art Directors	Ferit Yantur
Illustrator	Sergey Tishkov		Arda Albayraktar
Client	Volkswagen	Photographer	Hasan Deniz
		Client	Volkswagen EOS

Agency	Leagas Delaney, Rome		**Agency**	Lowe Brindfors, Stockholm
Creative Directors	Stefano Campora		**Creative Director**	Magnus Wretblad
	Stefano Rosselli		**Copywriter**	Per Sundin
Copywriter	Valeria Villari		**Art Director**	Carl-Johan Ekberg
Art Director	Guido Bonarelli		**Photographer**	Frederik Lieberath
Photographer	Davide Bodini		**Client**	Saab BioPower
Client	Saab BioPower			

Agency	McCann Erickson, Madrid
Creative Director	David Moure
Copywriter	David Moure
Art Director	Gustavo Marioni
Client	Saab 93 Cabrio

Agency McCann Erickson, Tel Aviv
Creative Director Eldad Weinberger
Copywriter Yrmi Nir
Art Director Assaf Levy
Director Shahar Segal
Producer Orly Vilensky
Client Volvo S80, "Wife"

A man drives his wife to an elegant soirée in their Volvo S80. When his concentration wanders for a moment, she warns him that another car is braking in front of him by exclaiming: "Beep beep!" A few moments later, she repeats the trick when a motorcycle appears from a blind spot just as her husband is about to pull out: "Toot toot!" She needn't have worried, however, because the S80 is equipped with pre-emptive accident technology. Just like the man's wife, apparently.

218   Automobiles

Agency TBWA\Paris
Creative Directors Erik Vervroegen
Chris Garbutt
Copywriter Xander Smith
Art Directors Bjoern Ruehmann
Joakim Reveman
Production The Gang Films, Paris
Director Joaquin Baca-Asay
Client Nissan Qashqai, "Skateboard"

A giant weaves through the urban streets using a Nissan Qashqai car as a skateboard. We only ever see the giant's sneaker-shod feet as he flips and turns the car, zooming it up walls and along rooftops, thus demonstrating the Qashqai's suspension and manoeuvrability. With a final expert flick of his heel, he tucks the car neatly into a parking space. The Nissan Qashqai: urban proof.

Agency TBWA\Paris
Creative Directors Erik Vervroegen
Chris Garbutt
Copywriter Benoit Leroux
Art Director Philippe Taroux
Production Paranoid Projects, Paris
Director Blue Source
Client Nissan Note, "Burst"

Vacation season, and this man is about to set off with his family. But when he slams the boot of his luggage-packed car, the vehicle bursts like a balloon, scattering belongings everywhere. In fact, all along the street, over-stuffed cars are exploding with the strain. A younger man hesitates for a split second before closing the trunk of his Nissan Note. Needless to say, nothing happens, because the Nissan Note is roomier than most automobiles. He drives away with his family, while over-filled cars burst all around them.

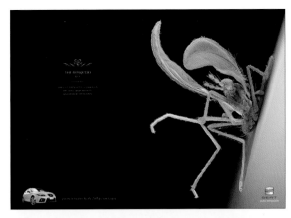

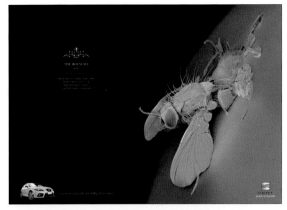

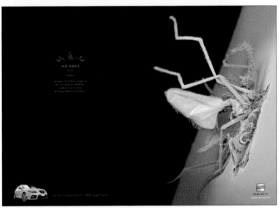

Agency	Atletico International Advertising, Barcelona	- The Mosquito: The last things to go through his mind were his nose followed by his behind.	- The Housefly: Not even lightning reactions nor compound vision was enough to avoid this inevitable collision.
Creative Director	Arndt Dallmann		
Copywriter	Jonny Biggins		
Art Director	Jason Bramley	- The Midge: Heard the turbocharger but heeded no warnings, woke up alive but was dead by mid-morning.	- The Moth: Met her demise on a cool winter's night, by the irresistible lure of Bi-Xenon light.
Photographer	Volker Steger		
Client	Seat Leon Cupra		

Agency	Fallon London
Executive CD	Richard Flintham
Copywriters	Chris Bovill
	John Allison
Art Directors	Chris Bovill
	John Allison
Production	Gorgeous Enterprises
Director	Chris Palmer
Producers	Rupert Smythe
	Nicky Barnes
Client	Skoda Fabia, "Cake"

Eggs are cracked into a mixing bowl. We see some whisking, and what appear to be cakes being placed in an oven. We're clearly in some kind of kitchen: but what dish are the cooks preparing? Oddly, we begin to recognise a few of the objects: isn't that an engine? To our surprise, we see that the cooks are assembling a giant cake in the shape of a car. With a wobble, a rear light made out of jelly is lifted into place. The new Skoda Fabia is "full of lovely stuff".

Agency	Publicis Conseil, Paris
Creative Directors	Olivier Altmann
	Hervé Plumet
Copywriter	Marc Rosier
Art Director	Jean-Marc Tramoni
Production	Wanda
Director	David Shane
Producer	Pierre Marcus
Client	Renault Megane Olympic, "Fosbury" & "Football"

These two spots for a car commemorating the Olympics feature unlikely sporting feats. In the first execution, a smartly-dressed young businessman appears to be warming up on the sidewalk. He begins to jog purposefully across the road. Then, with a hop, skip and jump, he performs a faultless "Fosbury flop" straight through the side window of his car. The Megane Olympic: for sports addicts.

The protagonist of the second spot is slightly more hapless. Outside his home, he places a plastic bottle of mineral water on the ground. Measuring distances, he then kicks the bottle with pinpoint accuracy through the open rear of his Megane hatchback. Goal! Looking pleased with himself, he gets into the car. Unfortunately, he had forgotten that his girlfriend was waiting in the passenger seat. The drenched woman wordlessly hands him the dented plastic bottle.

Je rijbewijs kwijt in 11,3 sec.

De nieuwe 911 GT3 RS van 0 - 200 km/u in 11,3 seconden

PORSCHE

SCENIC Special Edition Exclusive, with panoramic glass roof.

Agency	AGH & Friends, 's-Hertogenbosch	Lose your license in 11,3 seconds.	**Agency**	Publicis, Lisbon
Copywriter	Jeroen Tebbe		**Creative Director**	Paulo Monteiro
Art Director	Patrick van der Heijden		**Copywriter**	Márcio Martins
Client	Porsche 911 GT3 RS		**Art Director**	Federico Barbato
			Photographer	Hugo Gonçalves
			Client	Renault Scenic

Agency	BBDO, Düsseldorf
Creative Directors	Toygar Bazarkaya
	Sebastian Hardieck
	Matthias Eickmeyer
	Stefan Meske
Art Directors	Szymon Rose
	Florian Barthelmess
	Jonathan Schupp
Production	Cobblestone,
	Hamburg
Directors	Markus Walter
	Malte Hagemeister
Producers	Nicolas Mirbach
	Tanja Bruhns
	Annette Berkenbusch
	Mareike Ceranna
	Steffen Gentis
Client	Smart Fortwo,
	"Back Seat"

In a selection of scenes from old B-movies, we see various characters come to a sticky end at the hand of assassins sitting on the back seat of their cars. Whether it's in the form of a plastic bag over the head, chloroform, a karate chop or simply a bullet, bad news always seems to come from behind. We then see the words: "No back seats. The new Smart Fortwo." The little runabout is shown parked – perfectly safely – in a sinister underground car park.

Agency	Nordpol+ Hamburg
Creative Director	Lars Ruehmann
Copywriter	Sebastian Behrendt
Art Directors	Tim Schierwater
	Christoph Bielefeldt
Production	Element e, Hamburg
Director	Silvio Helbig
Producer	Juergen Joppen
Client	Renault, "Ballet"

Different models of Renault are performing a complex vehicular ballet in the desert. But then something goes wrong – one car slices off the wing mirror of another. The action swiftly escalates as cars begin colliding all over the place, with four head-on crunches, a side-on smash and a highly dramatic roll. As a finale, two cars collide in mid air. The whole troupe then performs a curtain call – battered but still around to drive another day. Following tests, these Renault models have been voted among the safest on the planet.

Agency	Nordpol+ Hamburg
Creative Director	Lars Ruehmann
Copywriter	Ingmar Bartels
Art Directors	Bertrand Kirschenhofer
	Christoph Bielefeldt
Production	Element e, Hamburg
Director	Thorsten Kirves
Producer	Patrick Dettenbach
Client	Renault, "Collision"

People from various nationalities are involved in "collisions", the symbol usually associated with crash-test dummies stencilled on their faces. Sumo wrestlers, maypole dancers and Germans in lederhosen all enter a world of pain when they bash into one another. However, a French couple, instead of colliding head on, lock lips in a passionate kiss. Is it any wonder that the best protection against head-on collisions comes from France? Renault: créateur d'automobiles.

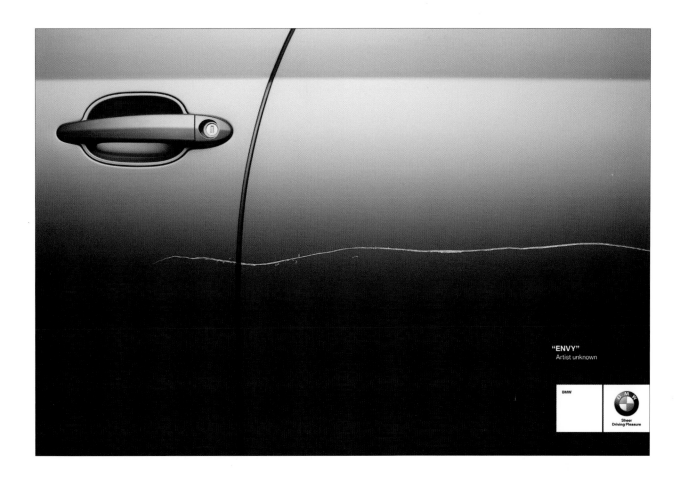

"ENVY"
Artist unknown

BMW
BMW
Sheer
Driving Pleasure

Vorsprung durch Technik www.audi-me.com

The new Audi TT Coupé

Agency	Jung von Matt, Stockholm	Agency	Grey Worldwide, Dubai
Copywriter	Fredric Thunholm	Creative Director	Alisdair Miller
Art Directors	Johan Jäger	Copywriter	R.S. Murugan
	Max Larsson von Reybekiel	Art Director	Prasad Pradhan
Photographer	Pekka Stålnacke	Client	Audi TT
Client	BMW		

NEW 4x4 CITROËN C-CROSSER.

NEW 4x4 CITROËN C-CROSSER. 16.07.07.

Automobiles

Agency	Euro RSCG, London	Agency	SMFB, Oslo
Executive CD	Mark Hunter	Creative Director	Erik Heisholt
Creative Director	Justin Hooper	Copywriter	Erik Heisholt
Copywriter	Ryan Petie	Art Director	Torgrim Nærland
Art Director	Dave Herse	Photographer	Torgrim Nærland
Illustrator	Mark Osborne	Client	Land Rover
Client	Citroën C-Crosser		

Agency	Ogilvy, Stockholm
Creative Directors	Björn Ståhl
	Andy Dibb
Copywriters	Mikael Ström
	Björn Persson
Art Directors	Attila Kiraly
	Hans Elander
Photographer	Glassworks
Client	Ford Flexifuel

Better choose genuine parts.

So your Volkswagen will stay a Volkswagen.

226 **Automotive & Accessories**

Agency	DDB Germany, Berlin	Production	Mob Film, London	
Executive CD	Amir Kassaei	Director	Vadim Jean	
Creative Directors	Bert Peulecke	Producers	Shaun Nickless	
	Stefan Schulte		John Brecklehurst	
Copywriters	Sebastian Kainz		Boris Schepker	
	Marc Wientzek	Client	Volkswagen Service,	
Art Directors	Marc Wientzek		"Cuckoo Clock"	
	Sebastian Kainz			

An elderly couple eat lunch in their sedate dining room, an ornate cuckoo clock on the wall above them. As the time hits one o'clock, a figurine in the shape of a gangsta rapper in sunglasses springs out of the cuckoo clock and chants, "Yo motherfucker! Yo motherfucker! Yo!" before recoiling on his spring. The couple look resigned. When you're repairing something, buy genuine parts. And that especially goes for your Volkswagen.

New F350. The world's highest horsepower outboard. ⊛YAMAHA

 Automotive & Accessories **227**

Agency	1861 United (Red Cell), Milan
Creative Directors	Pino Rozzi
	Roberto Battaglia
Copywriter	Laura Cattaneo
Art Director	Giorgio Cignoni
Client	Yamaha Marine

Agency	Duval Guillaume Brussels	A jogger runs through the woods. We hear a buzzing sound, and suddenly the man has accidentally swallowed a fly. He coughs, gulps, and then runs on. By the time he gets home, he's forgotten about the incident. He moves into the bathroom and takes off his sweaty clothes. As he lowers his jogging pants, we see the fly emerge from between his buttocks. It flies off. But surely it can't have popped out of his...? The insect clearly has a knack of finding its way out of tight corners: just like the Mio DigiWalker GPS navigator
Creative Directors	Katrien Bottez Peter Ampe	
Copywriters	Virginie Lepère Wilfrid Morin	
Art Directors	Fred Van Hoof Jean-Marc Wachsmann	
Production	Lovo Films, Brussels	
Director	Serdar	
Producers	Bert Brulez François Mercier Dieter Lebbe	
Client	Mio DigiWalker, "The Fly"	

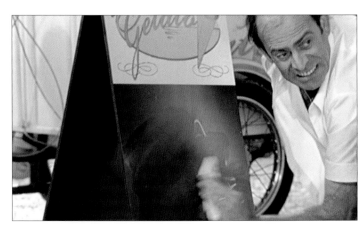

228   **Automotive & Accessories**

Agency	BBDO, Stuttgart	Sitting in his office, a man spots a traffic warden who's about to ticket a parked Mercedes. He leaves his desk and walks up to her. She is blonde and quite attractive. At first she ignores him, but then she notices him smiling at her. He has an imploring look on his face. We see her beginning to thaw, a smile forming on her own lips. Just then, another man appears and drives off in the Mercedes. Confused, the traffic warden then notices the logo on the man's sweater: he works for Mercedes Service, and has just helped out a customer.
Creative Directors	Armin Jochum Thomas Bruns Oliver Froehnel	
Production	Hager Moss Commercial, Munich	
Director	Joergen Lööf	
Producers	Juergen Kraus Mirjam Thole	
Client	Mercedes-Benz, "Traffic Warden"	

Agency	DDB Amsterdam	An Italian ice-cream vendor has just set up his stall when he notices a VW van across the way. It's decorated with a picture of an ice-cream and the words "50c". Furious, the man gestures at the van and defiantly cuts his price to "40c". An elderly couple roll up and buy two ice-creams. But the vendor is amazed when he sees them getting into the VW van. Then he realises that their old VW hasn't been selling ice-creams for many years now: they are retired. Volkswagens carry on working long after you've stopped.
Creative Directors	Joris Kuijpers Dylan de Backer	
Copywriter	Jakko Achterberg	
Art Director	Niels Westra	
Production	Hazazah, Amsterdam	
Director	Wim van der Aar	
Producers	Bianca Licher Yuka Kambayashi	
Client	Volkswagen Commercial Vehicles, "Gelato"	

Sticky tyres.

Agency	Grey, Oslo	Agency	1861 United (Red Cell), Milan
Client	Continental Tyres	Creative Directors	Pino Rozzi
			Roberto Battaglia
		Copywriter	Vincenzo Celli
		Art Director	Giorgio Cignoni
		Photographer	Giovanni Pirajno
		Client	Yamaha Marine

ACCESSORIES COLLECTION 2007.

Agency   ON, Milan
Creative Director Enrico Bonomini
Copywriters   Enrico Bonomini
                  Eleonora Mandelli
Art Director   Mariangela Vomero
Photographer   Simone Galbusera
Client   Mini Accessories

I'll just put this part back and then I'm off...
What's the problem?

Some oil... yes...

OK, I did cut the cables, that's true...

...I panicked, Jimmy.

We'll take a little here...

Dad, something gushes from the engine!

Book at www.okq8.se
Boka på www.okq8.se
OKQ8

There, Jocke... it got some oil now.

"Gas stations with do-it-yourself"
Macken med
Gör-Det-Själv-hallar
OKQ8
No. No tasting the oil.

230   **Automotive & Accessories**

Agency   DraftFCB, Stockholm
Creative Director Lars Hansson
Copywriter   Jesper Eronn
Art Director   Andreas Englund
Production   Mister Krister,
                  Stockholm
Director   Jens Sjögren
Producers   Cornelia Opitz
                  Marcus Sundquist
Client   OK Q8 Garages,
                  "The Well Equipped
                  Gas Station"
                  & "Oil Refill"

"I took out the master spark plug and there are some chords hanging there," a man is saying to his friend on the phone, as he stands in a service station forecourt. He explains: "I'm like – checking for errors." A few seconds later, he's pulled another part out of the car. In fact, he seems determined to wreck the engine. "OK, I did cut the cables...I panicked, Jimmy," he tells his friend. Just then, his little son dashes out of the garage: "Dad...something gushes from the engine!" Q8 garages have rental cars, as well as do-it-yourself service facilities.

In the second spot, the inexperienced driver is "putting some oil" in his car. Not knowing how to do so, he treats the engine a bit like a plant: a few drops here, a splash there, a bigger splash to finish things off. Pleased with his handy work, he says to his son: "There, Jocke, it's got some oil now." The little boy doesn't look convinced.

Agency   Kolle Rebbe, Hamburg
Creative Director   Ulrich Zuenkeler
Copywriter   Verena Schneider
Art Director   Joerg Dittmann
Photographers   Stephan Jouhoff
      Pim Vuik
Client   Volkswagen Parts

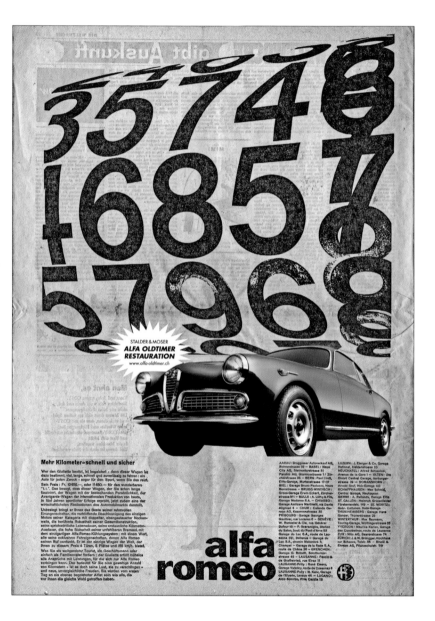

Automotive & Accessories

Agency	Owens DDB, Dublin	This page was published in the	Agency	Publicis, Zurich	Stalder & Moser recycled genuine Alfa

Agency — Owens DDB, Dublin
Creative Directors — Colin Murphy
Donald O'Dea
Copywriter — Colin Murphy
Art Director — Donal O'Dea
Client — Volkswagen Ireland

This page was published in the entertainment section of the same newspaper it originally appeared in 57 years ago, printed with a 60-dot screen for authenticity.

Agency — Publicis, Zurich
Creative Director — Florian Beck
Art Directors — Florian Beck
Denis Schwarz
Matthias Günter
Client — Stalder & Moser

Stalder & Moser recycled genuine Alfa ads from the early 1960s with the original black and white images of the cars being replaced with newly restored models in colour.

New big Viano.

YAMAHA
Deep passion

Agency	Zapping/M&C Saatchi, Madrid	Agency	1861 United (Red Cell), Milan
Creative Directors	Uschi Henkes	**Creative Directors**	Pino Rozzi
	Manolo Moreno		Roberto Battaglia
	David Palacios	**Copywriter**	Vincenzo Celli
	Urs Frick	**Art Director**	Giorgio Cignoni
Copywriter	David Palacios	**Photographer**	Joan Garrigosa
Art Director	José Carlos Gómez	**Client**	Yamaha Marine
Client	Mercedes-Benz Viano		

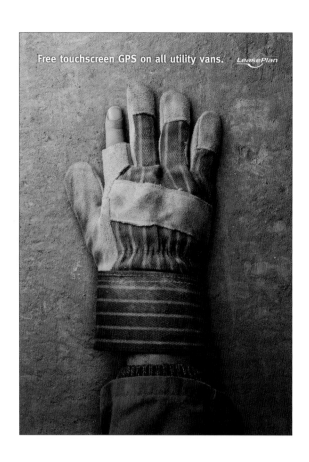

Free touchscreen GPS on all utility vans. *LeasePlan*

Why take unnecessary risks at work ?
ABS, airbags and cruise control as standard on Crafter.

Why take unnecessary risks at work ?
ABS, airbags and cruise control as standard on Crafter.

234 **Automotive & Accessories**

Agency	Duval Guillaume Brussels	**Agency**	DDB Paris
Creative Directors	Katrien Bottez	**Creative Directors**	Alexandre Hervé
	Peter Ampe		Sylvain Thirache
Copywriters	Raoul Maris	**Copywriter**	Edouard Pérarnaud
	Hugues Vanden Steen	**Art Director**	Martin Darfeuille
Art Director	Christian Loos	**Photographer**	Garry Simpson
Photographer	Kris Van Beek	**Client**	Volkswagen Crafter
Client	LeasePlan		

Agency	Uncle Grey, Aarhus
Creative Director	Per Pedersen
Copywriter	Kristian Eilertsen
Art Director	Jonas Nørregaard
Client	Peugeot Boxer

IT'S ALL IN YOUR HEAD.

AND ON 13TH STREET
THE ACTION & SUSPENSE CHANNEL
13thstreet.de

Agency	Jung von Matt, Berlin	Accompanied by eerie music, the camera closes in on a spooky suburban house. An ethereal young woman sits alone. The doorbell rings. The woman opens the door to a boy scout, who is selling cookies for charity. With a brief glance to see if anybody is looking, she invites him in. Cut to dinner time, and the woman and her husband are eating. "Tastes a bit different than usual," comments the man. The woman smiles mysteriously as she cuts the meat. Don't worry – the horror is all in your head. And on 13th Street, the action and suspense channel.
Creative Directors	Mathias Stiller	
	Wolfgang Schneider	
	Jan Harbeck	
	David Mously	
Copywriter	Maximilan Millies	
Art Director	Andreas Boehm	
Production	Frisbee Film, Berlin	
Director	Till Franzen	
Producers	Alexander Bickenbach	
	Nadja Catana	
Client	13th Street, "Sunday Roast"	

▲ Media **237**

Agency   Marcel, Paris
Creative Directors Frédéric Témin
                  Anne de Maupeou
Copywriter   Eric Jannon
Art Director   Dimitri Guerassimov
Client   France 24

Agency	Publicis, Zurich
Creative Directors	Florian Beck
	Markus Gut
Copywriters	Tom Zürcher
	Mario Nelson
Art Director	Florian Beck
Production	Pumpkin Film, Zurich
Director	Caroline Büchel
Producers	Tolga Dilsiz
	Suzana Kovacevic
Client	3+ TV Network, "Supernanny"

Kids are not what they were. Take this one for instance: although she looks innocent, it seems she's not entirely happy with her birthday present. "I wanted a pony, not a fucking dog. First I'm going to cut off his tail. Then I'm going to shove some nails up his ass. Then I'm going to put him in the microwave and watch him explode." She clearly needs some more wholesome entertainment. Fortunately there's Supernanny on 3+.

Agency	BETC Euro RSCG, Paris
Creative Director	Stéphane Xiberras
Copywriter	Olivier Couradjut
Art Director	Rémy Tricot
Production	Partizan, Paris
Director	Dominic Murphy
Producer	David Green
Client	Canal+, "Double Meaning"

This spot shows how the media can manipulate images to give a false impression of the news. In Iraq, we hear distant gunshots and see sprawled limbs through a doorway. Shot, or sleeping? When an army unit bursts in to check, they see a family struggling to their feet. Now the images are re-edited and played again. The soldiers burst into the home, the family get to their feet. We hear gunshots. Then we see sprawled limbs in a doorway. When images are this easy to manipulate, best watch a channel you can trust.

Agency	BETC Euro RSCG, Paris
Creative Director	Michèle Cohen
Copywriter	Luc Rouzier
Art Director	Eric Astorgue
Production	Bollywood, Paris
Director	Eric Valette
Client	Le Parisien, "Elections"

Parisians are a smart but nasty bunch. Take this guy: standing in line to vote, he notices that the man in front of him has broken wind in the tiny screened booth containing the ballot box. Thinking fast, the man in the queue politely cedes his place to the elderly lady behind him. The woman gratefully accepts, steps into the booth – and is subjected to the full force of the ripe fart. Le Parisien: better to read one than to meet one.

Agency	BETC Euro RSCG, Paris
Creative Director	Stéphane Xiberras
Copywriter	Olivier Couradjut
Art Director	Rémy Tricot
Production	Big Productions, Paris
Director	Terri Timely
Producer	Isabelle Menard
Client	13th Street (13éme Rue), "Gali"

We settle down to watch an apparently harmless kiddies' puppet show called Gali the Alligator. But when Gali greets his "friends", the birds, he crunches one of them in his huge jaws, spraying blood everywhere. He then proceeds to decimate the furry citizens of the forest, pulling off their arms and squeezing them until their eyes pop. "Better stay out of his path, if you want to escape his wrath," sings the chirpy theme tune. If 13th Street had to make a kids' show, it would look like this. In fact the channel is devoted to crime and suspense.

Agency	BETC Euro RSCG, Paris
Creative Director	Stéphane Xiberras
Copywriter	Benjamin Sanial
Art Director	Raphael Halin
Production	Les Télécreateurs, Dak Tirak, Paris
Directors	Didier Barcelo Nicolas Benamou Nicolas Marie
Producers	David Green Michel Teicher
Client	Canalsat, "Blur TV"

We're watching a channel called Blur TV. As its name suggests, it broadcasts only blurred images. The camera pulls back to reveal a group of Canalsat employees, who are discussing "the concept" of the new channel. "Rubbish," one of them sums up succinctly. The television experts at Canalsat watch the worst before selecting the best.

Agency	BETC Euro RSCG, Paris
Creative Director	Stéphane Xiberras
Copywriter	Benjamin Sanial
Art Director	Raphael Halin
Production	Les Télécreateurs, Dak Tirak, Paris
Directors	Didier Barcelo Nicolas Benamou Nicolas Marie
Producers	David Green Michel Teicher
Client	Canalsat, "Starkers TV"

In the second spot, the Canalsat experts tune into another television concept called Starkers TV. This time they see a bike race in which all the competitors are stark naked. The experts sit there aghast with their mouths hanging open in disbelief. They watch the worst before selecting the best.

Agency	BETC Euro RSCG, Paris
Creative Director	Stéphane Xiberras
Production	Partizan, Paris
Directors	Les Elvis
Producer	David Green
Client	Canal+, "Brokeback Mountain"

In a canteen, a woman explains the story of a film she's just seen: "Brokeback Mountain". Unfortunately, at the start of the tale her friend imagines that it is about a rollercoaster. As the woman continues, the images in the friend's head become more confused. A cowboy takes his sheep onto the rollercoaster. He falls in love with one of them. And "the terrible accident" of the real film now involves the beloved sheep plunging from the amusement park ride. If you really want to catch up with hit movies, it's better to watch them on Canal Plus.

Agency	DDB Paris
Creative Directors	Alexandre Hervé Sylvain Thirache
Copywriter	Céline Landa
Art Director	Benjamin Marchal
Production	Les Télécréateurs
Director	Didier Barcelo
Producers	Dominique Porte Amélie Talpaert
Client	France Football, "The Cliff"

Two men are discussing the merits of the four-four-two formation in soccer. One of them is perched on a wall. Suddenly, he falls off it, plunging down a cliff. Even more shockingly, his friend jumps after him. They hit a steep hill and roll down it – while continuing their football conversation. After rolling and tumbling for what seems like an eternity, they arrive at the bottom of the hill and dust themselves off. They stroll away, still talking football. Like soccer newspaper France Football, the men are obsessed with the sport.

Agency	DDB Paris
Creative Directors	Alexandre Hervé Sylvain Thirache
Copywriter	Céline Landa
Art Director	Benjamin Marchal
Production	Les Télécréateurs
Director	Didier Barcelo
Producer	Agathe Michaux Terrier
Client	L'Equipe, "Souvenirs"

At an outdoor cocktail party, a man walks around with a barbecue fork stuck in his shoulder. He bumps into a man who has a pizza wheel embedded in his forehead. Comparing notes, they discover that both mishaps occurred during great French sporting triumphs: as they raised their arms to cheer the victory, they forgot that they were holding dangerous cooking utensils. Then they see a man who has the blade of a revolving fan planted in his skull. When France won the World Cup in 1998, he jumped for joy.

YOU CAN'T
KNOW EVERYTHING
ABOUT EVERYTHING

The Economist

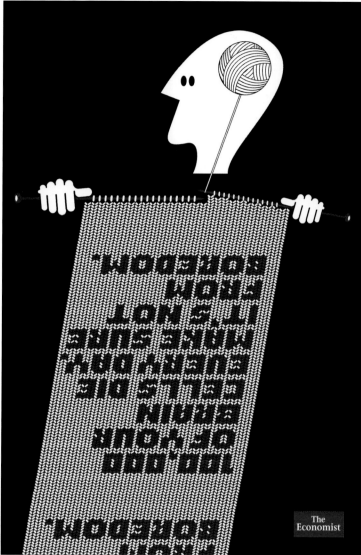

The Economist

The
world
revolves
around
the
sun.
Not
the
British
Isles.

The Economist

The Economist

WHAT'S THE WORST THING TO LOSE AS WE GET OLDER? OUR HAIR OUR TEETH OUR CURIOSITY

The Economist

Agency Abbott Mead Vickers BBDO, London
Creative Director Paul Brazier
Copywriter Mark Fairbanks
Art Director Paul Cohen
Illustrators Fine 'N' Dandy
Mick Marston
Geoff McFetridge
Client The Economist

Agency	Freud Communications, London
Creative Director	Dave Waters
Copywriter	Brendan Wilkins
Art Director	Rod Kavanagh
Production	Red Bee Media, London
Director	Steve Cope
Producer	Edel Erickson
Client	BBC Radio 2, "Elvis"

On stage, Elvis Presley introduces his phenomenal line-up of musicians. On vocals we have the Sugababes and Marvin Gaye, on guitar there's Jimmy Page and Noel Gallagher, on drums there's Keith Moon, on bass guitar Sheryl Crow, and on piano, none other than Stevie Wonder. Wow! Of course, this line-up is only possible thanks to film trickery: but on BBC Radio 2, you can easily come across these music legends at any time of the day.

Agency	Grey, Oslo
Production	Moland Film
Director	Hans Petter Moland
Producer	Mone Mikkelsen
Client	Canal Digital, "Our World"

A series of vignettes captures the hypnotic power of television. Walking in front of an electrical store window, a little girl is captivated by an image. Returning to pull her away, the girl's mother is also drawn to the screen. A man pauses in the middle of cleaning his teeth, riveted by something on his TV. Sports fans, lovers, a woman doing her ironing...they're all hooked by the images in front of them. And although we hardly ever see what they're watching, we understand their fascination. Canal Digital has so much to show its audience.

Agency	Jung von Matt, Berlin
Creative Directors	Mazhias Stiller
	Wolfgang Schneider
Copywriter	Maximilan Millies
Art Director	Andreas Boehm
Production	Frisbee Film, Berlin
Director	Till Franzen
Producers	Alexander Bickenbach
	Nadja Catana
Client	13th Street, "Birthday Surprise"

An untrustworthy-looking trucker picks up a young hitchhiker. As the truck accelerates away, we see a shot of a chainsaw in the back of the pick-up. The young man informs the trucker he's off to surprise his grandmother for her birthday. The trucker replies that he's taking the same route. Cut to the next morning, and a shot of the grandmother descending the steps of her home. A parcel sits there. But what's the red stuff oozing out of it? And where did all those flies come from? Don't worry – it's all in your head. And on 13th Street.

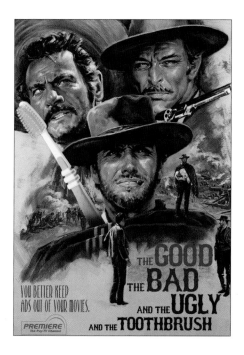

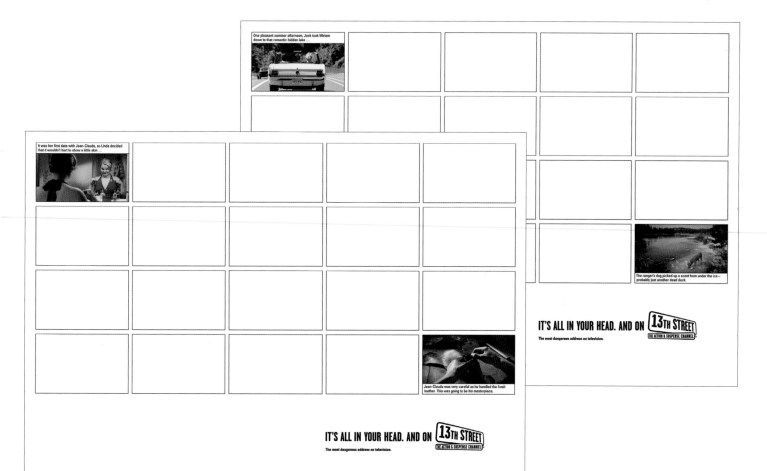

Agency	DDB Germany, Düsseldorf	Agency	Jung von Matt, Berlin
Execuctive CDs	Amir Kassaei	Creative Directors	Mathias Stiller
	Eric Schoeffler		Wolfgang Schneider
Creative Directors	Tim Jacobs		David Mously
	Thomas Schwarz		Jan Harbeck
Copywriter	Dennis May	Copywriter	Maximilian Millies
Art Director	Kristine Holzhausen	Art Director	Andreas Boehm
Client	Premiere	Photographer	Cornelius Zoch
		Client	13th Street

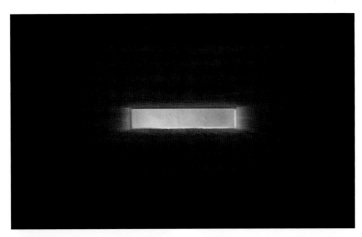

Agency	Concept, Istanbul
Creative Director	Niyal Akmanalp
Copywriter	Taygun Dombekcioglu
Art Director	Omer Durgut
Production	Torpido Istanbul
Director	Murat Senoy
Client	Cumhuriyet, "Vote for a Secular Turkey"

We're inside a ballot box, staring up at the slot in the top. A woman's face hovers over the gap, then closes in, until we can only see her eyes through the slit. It's as if she's wearing a veil. "Vote for a secular Turkey," says the voiceover, referring to recent fears that a Muslim fundamentalist party would be elected to run the country. The advice is given by newspaper Cumhuriyet.

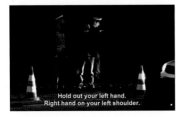

Agency	Kempertrautmann, Hamburg
Creative Directors	Frank Bannöhr Daniel Ernsting
Copywriter	Daniel Ernsting
Art Director	Frank Bannöhr
Production	F+P Commercial Filmproduction, Hamburg
Director	Alex Feil
Client	MTV Comedy Central, "Turk"

A roadside cop has flagged down a car and asked the driver to step out. The cop instructs the man to stick out his left arm. Then his right. "Now put your hands behind your head. Now bend your knees," says the cop. Confused, the man complies. "Now repeat," commands the cop. As the man does so, we hear a couple of hidden policemen giggling. Then one of them switches on some music. The "suspect" now appears to be dancing. MTV Comedy Central: not a moment without comedy.

Agency	Selmore, Amsterdam
Copywriters	Poppe van Pelt Tomas Minken
Art Directors	Diederick Hillenius Albert Vegers
Production	Bonkers, Amsterdam
Director	Jonathan Herman
Producers	Paul Harting Suzanne Van Den Bouwhuijsen
Client	Sky Radio, "Poolboy"

A man arrives home unexpectedly early, clutching some flowers. Marching into the house, he shouts his wife's name. Nothing – but then he hears the sound of music upstairs, and a thumping noise. He charges up the stairs and into the bedroom, where he finds his wife is in bed. But where's her lover? The man looks everywhere, to no avail. Furious, he switches off the radio. But the song continues. Aha! Whipping open a cupboard, the man discovers the naked pool boy – who just couldn't resist singing along with Sky Radio.

Agency   Family, Helsinki
Copywriter   Markku Uusitalo
Art Director   Marko Muona
Photographer   Kimmo Virtanen
Client   Canal Digital

Agency   SMFB, Oslo
Copywriters   André Koot
                Hans Martin Rønneseth
Art Directors   André Koot
                Hans Martin Rønneseth
Photographer   Philip Karlberg
Client   Hjemmet Mortensen
                Publishers

The pages of life.

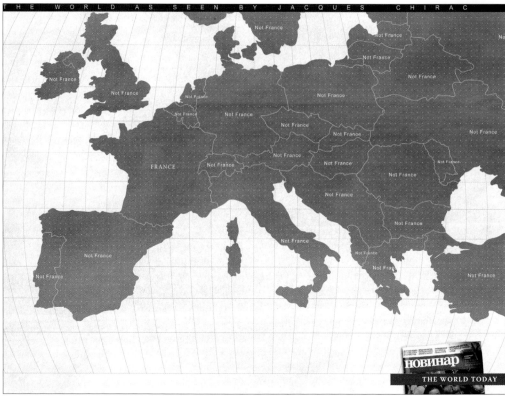

Agency	BETC Euro RSCG, Paris	**Agency**	Leo Burnett, Kiev
Creative Director	Stéphane Xiberras	**Creative Director**	Jarek Wiewiorski
Copywriter	Arnaud Assouline	**Copywriter**	Tania Fedorenko
Art Director	Benjamin Le Breton	**Art Director**	Pasha Klubnikin
Client	Canal+	**Client**	Novynar

What if our town has a budget surplus? Will they finally pay someone to cut this bush?

Stay informed. Tages-Anzeiger

What if wheat prices keep rising? Will the restaurant here still sell spaghetti for only 12 francs?

Stay informed. Tages-Anzeiger

What if Internet TV gets more popular? Will the ugly satellite dish on the house opposite here vanish?

Stay informed. Tages-Anzeiger

What if soft drugs are legalized? Will they plant different grass down here?

Stay informed. Tages-Anzeiger

What if everybody has a mobile phone? Will children have no idea what this thing to the right is?

Stay informed. Tages-Anzeiger

What if Switzerland wins the Euro08? Will these football fields see more action?

Stay informed. Tages-Anzeiger

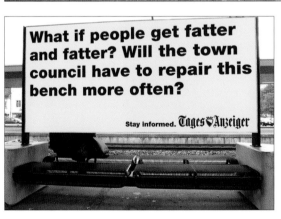

What if people get fatter and fatter? Will the town council have to repair this bench more often?

Stay informed. Tages-Anzeiger

What if the Green Party gets into the Federal Council? Will they forbid these lit-up billboards?

Stay informed. Tages-Anzeiger

Agency   Spillmann/Felser/Leo Burnett, Zurich
Creative Director Martin Spillmann
Copywriter   Peter Brönnimann
Art Director   Katja Puccio
Client   Tages-Anzeiger

248   Media

Agency	BETC Euro RSCG, Paris
Creative Director	Stéphane Xiberras
Copywriter	Arnaud Assouline
Art Director	Benjamin Le Breton
Photographer	Philippe Gueguen
Client	Canal+

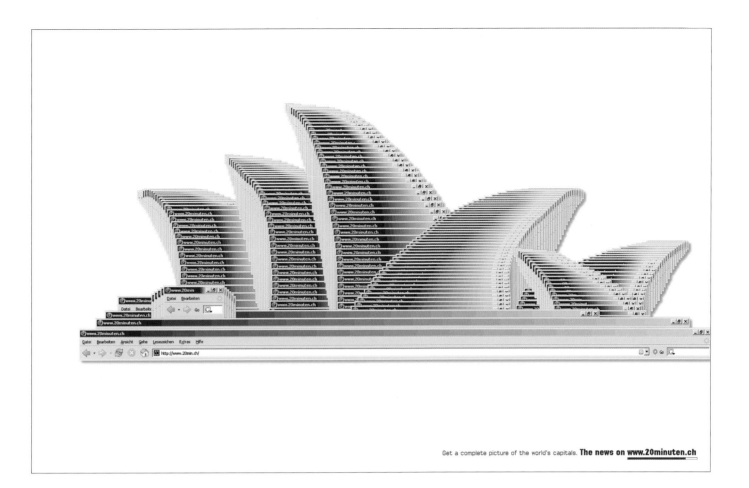

Get a complete picture of the world's capitals. **The news on** <u>**www.20minuten.ch**</u>

The Economist

Agency	Euro RSCG Group Switzerland,Zurich	**Agency**	Abbott Mead Vickers BBDO, London
Executive CD	Frank Bodin	**Creative Director**	Paul Brazier
Creative Directors	Petra Bottignole Juerg Aemmer	**Copywriter**	Mark Fairbanks
		Art Director	Paul Cohen
Copywriter	Serge Deville	**Illustrators**	Paul Cohen
Art Director	Dominik Oberwiler		Neil Craddock
Illustrator	Rahel Boesinger	**Client**	The Economist
Client	20Minuten.ch		

Media

Agency	Duval Guillaume, Antwerp	Agency	FCB, Cape Town
Creative Directors	Geoffrey Hantson	Creative Director	Francois de Villiers
	Dirk Domen	Copywriter	Marius Van Rensburg
Copywriter	Sam De Vriendt	Art Director	Anthony de Klerk
Art Director	Bart Gielen	Photographer	Chad Henning
Photographer	Kris Van Beek	Client	Die Burger
Client	Utopolis		

JUSTIN TIMBERLAKE

~~RED KALE IN YUS TJIM~~
~~IN SU TIMST MLE KJBER~~

I'M A JURK BUT LISTEN

BRITNEY SPEARS
~~ENIBTNY SPESAR~~
~~IESPT NB SPYERA~~

PRESBYTERIAN

AXL ROSE
~~ARO SLEX~~
~~OSE LARX~~

ORAL SEX

**GOING AWAY PARTY
SUNDAY 6TH OF MAY 8PM**

canalplus.fr

CANAL+

Agency	Y&R, Prague	
Creative Director	Daniel Ruzicka	
Copywriter	Ondrej Klima	
Art Directors	Martin Paur	
	Alex McReynolds	
Client	Report	

Agency	BETC Euro RSCG, Paris
Creative Director	Stéphane Xiberras
Copywriter	Benjamin Sanial
Art Director	Raphael Halin
Client	Canal+

This Jacques Chirac puppet was a popular satirical character on Canal+ during his years in office. At 8pm on May 6th, 2007 the French election results were announced.

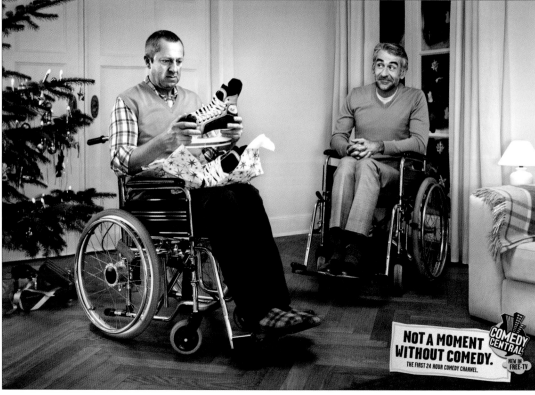

Agency	Duval Guillaume, Antwerp		**Agency**	Kempertrautmann, Hamburg
Creative Directors	Geoffrey Hantson		**Creative Directors**	Frank Bannöhr
	Dirk Domen			Daniel Ernsting
Copywriter	Kristof Snels		**Copywriters**	Daniel Ernsting
Art Director	Sebastien De Valck			Christian Soldatke
Photographer	Evert Thiry		**Art Directors**	Frank Bannöhr
Client	Ché Magazine			Axel Schilling
			Photographer	Arthur Mebius
			Illustrator	Tim Belser
			Graphic	Marita Locmele
			Client	MTV Comedy Central

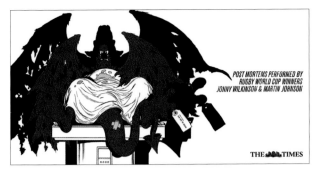

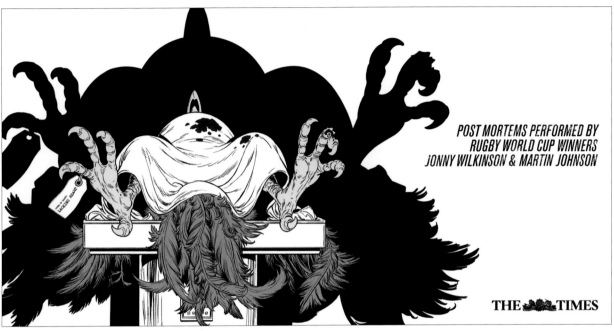

Agency	RKCR/Y&R, London	Agency	DDB London
Creative Directors	Mike Boles	Creative Director	Adam Tucker
	Jerry Hollens	Copywriter	Will Lowe
Copywriters	Jolyon Finch	Art Director	Victor Monclus
	Steve Moss	Illustrator	Dennis Scott
Art Directors	Jolyon Finch	Client	Financial Times
	Steve Moss		
Illustrator	Glenn Fabry		
Client	The Times		

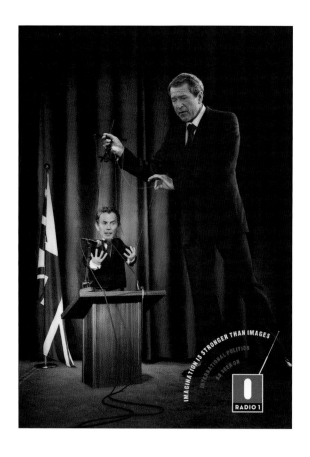

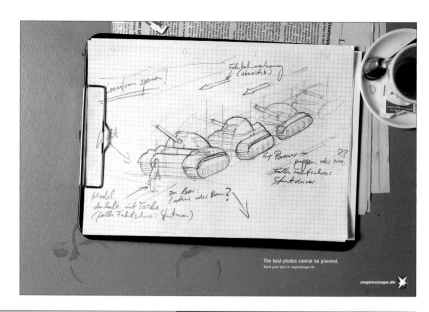

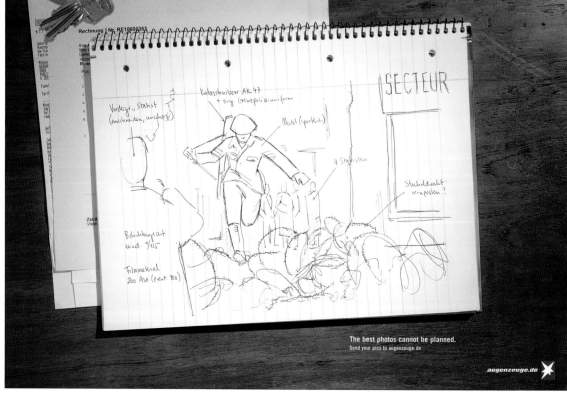

Agency	Duval Guillaume Brussels	Agency	Grabarz & Partner, Hamburg
Creative Directors	Katrien Bottez	Executive CD	Ralf Heuel
	Peter Ampe	Creative Directors	Patricia Pätzold
Copywriter	Tom Berth		Ralf Nolting
Art Directors	Alexander Cha'ban	Copywriter	Martin Grass
	Vanessa Hendrickx	Art Directors	Tomas Tulinius
	Geert De Rocker		Djik Ouchiian
Photographer	Gregor Collienne		Alexandra Marzoll
Client	Radio 1	Photographer	Sven Berghäuser
		Client	Augenzeuge.de

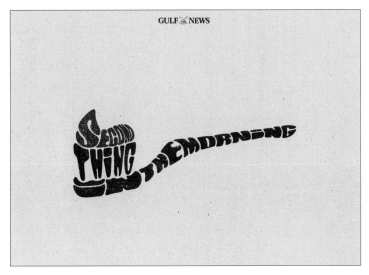
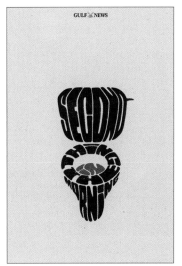

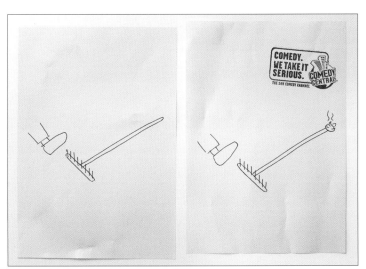
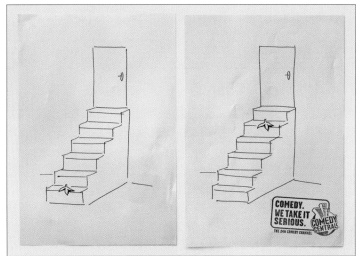

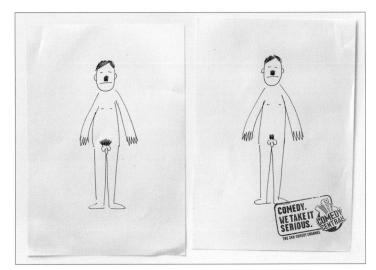

Agency	Team Y&R, Dubai
Creative Director	Shahir Ahmed
Copywriter	Vikram Divecha
Art Director	Vikram Divecha
Illustrator	Vikram Divecha
Client	Gulf News

Agency	Kempertrautmann, Hamburg
Creative Director	Mathias Lamken
Copywriter	Mathias Lamken
Art Director	Mathias Lamken
Illustrator	Mathias Lamken
Client	MTV Comedy Central

SEE FILMS DIFFERENTLY

Volkswagen supports independent cinema.

Agency	DDB London	A cinema usher explains the subtext of Toy
Creative Director	Jeremy Craigen	Story, which is apparently about "the trials
Copywriters	Graeme Hall	of puberty and sexuality". After all, how else
	Gavin Siakimotu	do you explain the fact that the young hero
Art Directors	Gavin Siakimotu	has a "Woody" that comes to life when his
	Graeme Hall	parents have left the room? Unfortunately, this
Production	Rattling Stick	Woody is limp and ineffectual most of the time,
Director	Andy McLeod	"especially around Bo Peep". And then he
Producers	Kirsty Burns	feels threatened by Buzz: "a ten-inch battery
	Sarah Browell	operated toy". In the end, the usher adds, at
Client	Volkswagen /	least Woody provides a bit of variety, just like
	Independent Cinema,	a real man. See movies differently, thanks to
	"Toy Story"	Volkswagen's support of independent cinema.

Agency	KNSK Werbeagentur, Hamburg
Creative Director	Claudia Bach
Copywriter	Fabian Tritsch
Art Director	Lisa Port
Client	Hansapark

Agency	Advico Young & Rubicam, Zurich	**Agency**	DDB London
Creative Director	Urs Schrepfer	**Creative Director**	Jeremy Craigen
Copywriter	Martin Stulz	**Copywriters & ADs**	Graeme Hall Gavin Siakimotu
Art Director	Marietta Albinus	**Production**	Rattling Stick
Photographer	Markus Weber	**Director**	Andy McLeod
Client	Head Snowboards	**Producers**	Kirsty Burns Sarah Browell
		Client	Volkswagen / Independent Cinema, "Lord of the Rings" & "Ghostbusters"

Two nerdy cinema employees give alternative interpretations of hit movies. First of all, we learn that Lord of the Rings is a film about "responsibility". Yet Gandalf relinquishes all responsibility by sending "little kids" to deliver the ring. Then he wastes time talking to giant moths, stealing horses and generally hindering rather than helping. "The guy's a bad role model – and he's lazy," adds our self-appointed critic.

A projectionist treats us to a critique of Ghostbusters, which is apparently about the obesity crisis. "New Yorkers are trying to get rid of these blobby bodies that are taking over their city," he suggests. "When Sigourney Weaver is possessed, the hounds of hell come out of her fridge." See movies differently; Volkswagen supports independent cinema.

Agency	Ogilvy & Mather, Copenhagen	Agency	Jung von Matt, Hamburg
Art Director	Claus Collstrup	Creative Directors	Arno Lindemann
Client	Matchbox Toys		Bernhard Lukas
		Copywriter	Daniel Schaefer
		Art Director	Szymon Rose
		Photographer	Achim Lippoth
		Client	Lego

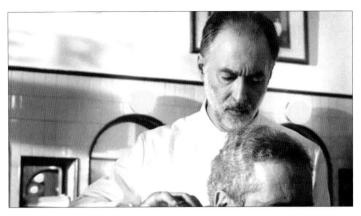

In a quiet hairdresser, a barber is snipping efficiently away, his scissors gnashing like steel teeth. But suddenly the rhythm of his cutting slows, and then stops altogether. The customers stare at him. The barber is oblivious, a look of delighted realisation on his face. A penny of some kind has clearly dropped. The slogan reads: "20 years since David Lynch's Blue Velvet premieres. Time enough to get it." The snipping recommences. Catch up on all your favourite fantasy movies at the Sitges festival.

260 Recreation & Leisure

A golf course appears to have become a battle zone. It's absolutely packed with golfers, and the balls fly like bullets. A new club member is forced to venture onto the perilous fairway in an armoured golf cart. When he emerges from the vehicle, he's dressed like all the other golfers in a crash helmet and padding, recalling an American footballer. He needn't have bothered: there's not enough room on the green to take a putt. The lotto has created so many millionaires that the golf club is way oversubscribed.

A well-dressed man is frustrated while waiting for a group of Downs Syndrome people to settle the bill in a restaurant. He assumes they will take ages and makes no attempt to hide his frustration. "How hard can it be to split 49 by 5?" he snorts, loudly. Meanwhile, thanks to a nearby TV screen, one of the group realises that they have just won the lottery. With a meaningful glance at the intolerant man, he says: "Hey guys: how hard can it be to split 10 million by five?"

One **World**
One **Cup**
One **Beer**

Simply come back tomorrow.

Simply come back tomorrow.

Simply come back tomorrow.

Agency	McCann Erickson, Dublin	Agency	Scholz & Friends, Berlin
Creative Directors	Jonathan Stanistreet	Creative Directors	Matthias Spaetgens
	Shay Madden		Jan Leube
Copywriter	Jonathan Stanistreet		Martin Pross
Art Director	Shay Madden	Copywriter	Florian Schwalme
Photographer	Kevin Griffen	Art Director	Mathias Rebmann
Client	Heineken World Cup	Photographer	Matthias Koslik
		Graphic	Heidrun Kleingries
			Felix Pfannmueller
		Client	Berlin Zoo

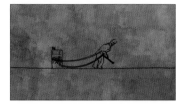

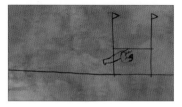

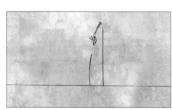

262   Recreation & Leisure

Agency	180 Amsterdam	In this campaign, famous sports men and women recount their stories – with the help of a few cartoons. First up is soccer star David Beckham, who recalls the long depression he went through after a temper tantrum led to him being sent off during the 1998 World Cup. But when he scored a goal against Greece, three years later, he was welcomed back into the fold. Next we hear from rugby star Jonah Lomu, who continued to play despite a chronic kidney disorder. He was finally cured by a kidney transplant.	Meanwhile, top pole-vaulter Yelena Isinbayeva explains that she originally wanted to be a gymnast, but she grew too tall. She was depressed until her coach suggested pole-vaulting. Right away, she was a natural. Finally, the All-Blacks talk us through an animated version of their legendary battle dance, the Hakka. Ancient New Zealand spirits entering a rugby team? Impossible is nothing.
Creative Directors	Sean Thompson		
	Dean Maryon		
Copywriter	Sean Thompson		
Art Director	Dean Maryon		
Production	Passion Pictures		
Directors	Sean Thompson		
	Dean Maryon		
Producers	Russel McLean		
	Kate Morrison		
	Tony Stearns		
Client	Adidas, "Impossible is Nothing" Campaign		

TRIBUTE TO ALFRED HITCHCOCK.

SPONSOR OF ROME FILM FEST.

TRIBUTE TO LARS VON TRIER.

SPONSOR OF ROME FILM FEST.

TRIBUTE TO SERGIO LEONE.

SPONSOR OF ROME FILM FEST.

TRIBUTE TO QUENTIN TARANTINO.

SPONSOR OF ROME FILM FEST.

Agency	D'Adda, Lorenzini, Vigorelli, BBDO, Milan
Creative Directors	Luca Scotto di Carlo
	Giuseppe Mastromatteo
Copywriter	Sonia Cosentino
Art Directors	Velia Mastropietro
	Pietro Mandelli
Client	Mini / Rome Film Festival

Veterans Basket Festival, Novi Grad 27- 30. jul 2007.

GET RID OF THE GUY WHO ISN'T CROUCHING WHEN PASSING BY.

NATIONAL MOVIE ARCHIVE
Selected movies, selected audience.

GET RID OF THE GUY TALKING ON THE PHONE.

NATIONAL MOVIE ARCHIVE
Selected movies, selected audience.

Agency	New Moment New Ideas Company, Belgrade		**Agency**	McCann Erickson, Bucharest
Creative Directors	Dragan Sakan Svetlana Copic		**Creative Directors**	Adrian Botan Alexandru Dumitrescu
Copywriter	Ana Cvejic		**Copywriter**	Catalin Dobre
Art Director	Ana Cvejic		**Art Director**	Razvan Chifu
Client	Veterans Basketball Festival		**Photographer**	Ionut Macri
			Client	Romanian National Movie Archive

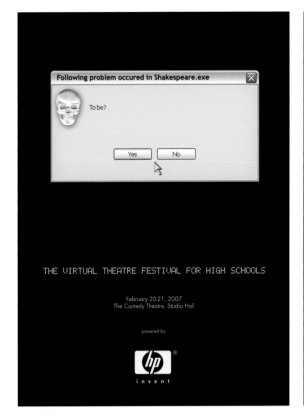

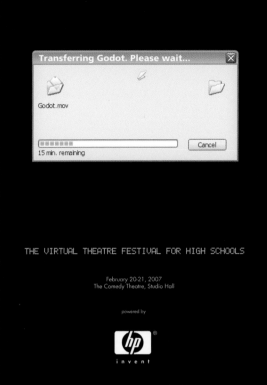

Agency	Publicis, Bucharest
Creative Director	Razvan Capanescu
Copywriter	Marian Enache
Art Director	Catalin Rulea
Client	HP / Virtual Theatre Festival

Agency	Publicis, Zurich
Creative Director	Philipp Skrabal
Copywriter	Livio Dainese
Art Director	Simon Staub
Photographer	Felix Streuli
Client	Pastorini

266   Recreation & Leisure

Agency	King James, Cape Town	**Agency**	& Co., Copenhagen
Creative Director	Alistair King	**Creative Director**	Thomas Hoffmann
Copywriter	Jacques Shalom	**Art Directors**	Thomas Hoffmann
Art Director	Wallace Seggie		Martin Storegaard
Illustrators	Haydn Fairman	**Photographer**	Casper Sejersen
	Anthony Murray	**Client**	Go Golf
Client	Maglite		

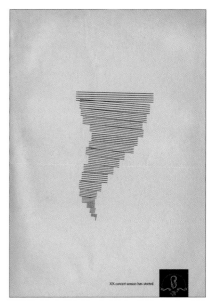

Agency	Milk, Vilnius	**Agency**	Storåkers McCann, Stockholm
Creative Director	Rimantas Stanevicius	**Copywriter**	Christian Sundgren
Copywriter	Rimantas Stanevicius	**Art Director**	Jonas Frank
Art Director	Marius Kneipferavicius	**Photographers**	Bisse / Adamsky
Illustrator	Marius Kneipferavicius	**Client**	Wetterling Gallery
Client	Lithuanian State Symphony Orchestra		

268   Recreation & Leisure

Agency	Wieden+Kennedy, Amsterdam	
Creative Directors	Alvaro Sotomayor Sue Anderson	
Copywriter	David Smith	
Art Director	Sezay Altinok	
Photographer	Carlos Serrao	
Client	Nike South Africa	

Agency	Wieden+Kennedy, Amsterdam
Creative Directors	Alvaro Sotomayor Sue Anderson
Copywriter	David Smith
Art Director	Sezay Altinok
Production	Park Pictures
Director	Joaquin Baca–Asay
Producers	Lalou Dammond Neil Henry
Client	Nike South Africa, "How I Fight"

South African sportsmen are captured in a series of graceful, inspiring shots. "This is my weapon...this is how I win my war," says the voiceover. The commercial is part of a "Just Do It" campaign for the South African market; responding to the problems of urban violence that afflict the country. The campaign demonstrates that beating opponents through sports can change lives in a positive way and is a real alternative to mindless violence. The TV campaign was supported with outdoor media (shown above).

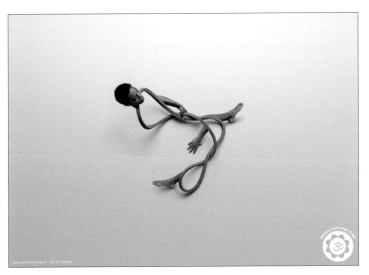

Agency	Leagas Delaney, Rome	Agency	Compagnie 360 Euro RSCG,
Creative Directors	Stefano Campora		Suresnes
	Stefano Rosselli	**Creative Director**	Jean-François Goize
Copywriter	Francesco Poletti	**Copywriter**	Antoine Colin
Art Director	Selmi Bali Barissever	**Art Director**	Jean-Philippe Magnaval
Photographer	LSD	**Photographer**	Alexandre Roberdet
Client	Ashtanga Milano Yoga	**Client**	Joupi Toys

15,000 TONS OF STEEL
DEFY THE SEA.
AND A FEW MINERAL
PARTICLES TOO.

A CABLE CAR PROVIDES
THE MOST INCREDIBLE
CONNECTIONS.
ON ITS HOUSING,
FOR EXAMPLE.

FUNCTIONAL FILLERS FOR CORROSION PROTECTION.

SOMETIMES THE
MOST FASCINATING
WORLDS ARE NOT IN
FRONT OF THE DIVING
MASK, BUT IN IT.

FUNCTIONAL FILLERS FOR RUBBER

What is absolutely waterproof at all depths and provides a clear view? Not least our Neuburg siliceous earth. Shown here at a scale of 15,000:1. As a natural agglomerate of corpuscular quartz and lamellar kaolinite it offers enormous advantages and innumerable application options for industry. As functional filler, for example, for elastomers in diving masks, full rubber tyres, fitness equipment and cable insulation.

270 **Industrial & Agricultural Products**

Agency	Serviceplan Munich/Hamburg
Creative Director	Christoph Everke
Copywriter	Tim Strathus
Art Director	Matthias Mittermüller
Photographer	Peter Schober
Graphic Design	Andrea Gärtner
	Basma Attalla
Client	Hoffmann Minerals

Agency	The Jupiter Drawing Room, Johannesburg	**Agency**	BBDO, Düsseldorf
Creative Directors	Michael Blore	**Creative Directors**	Carsten Bolk
	Tom Cullinan		Helmut Bienfuss
			Toygar Bazarkaya
Copywriter	Paola Mastrogiuseppe	**Copywriters**	Dennis Tjoeng
Art Directors	Lida Fourie		Andreas Walter
	Dana Cohen	**Art Directors**	Milena Hirschochs
Photographer	Clive Stewart		Jacques Pense
Client	PPC Cement	**Illustrator**	Stefan Kranefeld
		Client	Cemex Cement

WE PROTECT EVERY PIG AS IF IT WERE THE LAST ONE

Pfizer Animal Health

WE PROTECT EVERY PIG AS IF IT WERE THE LAST ONE.

Pfizer Animal Health

272 **Industrial & Agricultural Products**

Agency	BBDO, Düsseldorf	Agency	D'Adda, Lorenzini, Vigorelli, BBDO, Milan
Creative Directors	Carsten Bolk		
	Helmut Bienfuss	Creative Director	Luca Scotto di Carlo
Copywriter	Silke Hartmann	Copywriter	Alessandro Fruscella
Art Directors	Joerg Sachtleben	Art Director	Sara Portello
	Lisa Weller	Photographer	LSD
Client	Cemex Cement	Client	Pfizer Animal Health

Pfizer BRD treatment program. Business solutions for the cattle breeding.

Agency	D'Adda, Lorenzini, Vigorelli, BBDO, Milan	Agency	Çözüm, Istanbul
Creative Director	Luca Scotto di Carlo	Creative Director	Mithat Aksuyek
Copywriter	Alessandro Fruscella	Copywriter	Tugrul Mengi
Art Director	Sara Portello	Art Director	Volkan Turkkan
Photographer	LSD	Client	Jon-Stone Cleaning Services
Client	Pfizer Animal Health		

Come on boys! Let's hurry.

There are many young engineers.
We can't wait till they grow up.

HYDRO

274   **Professional Equipment & Services**

Agency	DDB, Oslo	
Copywriter	Torbjørn Kvien Madsen	
Art Director	Martin Thorsen	
Production	Motion Blur	
Director	Roenberg	
Producers	Richard Patterson	
	Cyril Boije	
Client	Hydro, "Train"	

This terrific little spot shows a bunch of youngsters messing around with steel girders and welding equipment somewhere in the countryside. One of them is filming the amateur construction project. But what the hell are they building? Then one of them shouts: "The train is coming! The train is coming!" The kids crouch down by the railway lines – and we see the speeding train whiz around the vertical loop they've constructed, rollercoaster-style. One day, these young engineers will work for Hydro.

POLICE MEGAPHONE
SOFT FOOTSTEPS
LOUD PARTY MUSIC

THE SOUND MAKES THE FILM. NJP TONSTUDIO

MACHINE GUN
SCREECHING BIRDS
ROCK MUSIC

THE SOUND MAKES THE FILM. NJP TONSTUDIO

"WE'LL GET THAT REDSKIN TOMORROW"
"I SMELL OIL, J.R., AND LOTS OF IT"
"DO YOU STILL LOVE ME?"

Use the power of sound for your TV advert or film: www.njp.ch

THE SOUND MAKES THE FILM. **NJP TONSTUDIO**

Professional Equipment & Services   **275**

Agency	Advico Young & Rubicam, Zurich
Creative Directors	Urs Schrepfer
	Christian Bobst
Copywriter	Johannes Raggio
Art Directors	Christian Bobst
	Isabelle Hauser
Photographer	Serge Hoeltschi
Client	NJP Sound Studio

Turn around!

HYDRO

Agency   DDB Oslo
Copywriter   Torbjørn Kvien Madsen
Art Director   Martin Thorsen
Production   Motion Blur
Director   Roenberg
Producers   Richard Patterson
                Cyril Boije
Client   Hydro, "Car"

The small engineers are at it again. This time they're rewiring a car engine. What mayhem are they about to cause? Suddenly they abandon the car and rush off into hiding. The father of one of the kids gets into the vehicle. "Fire it up!" whispers one of the young geniuses. The man is astonished when the car starts of its own accord and zooms off down the drive. Then it performs a series of death-defying stunts. We see that the kids are controlling it with a powerful remote control device. One day, they'll work for Hydro.

- I am now Nordic Region Executive Manager In Systems Integration Of Technology Infrastucture Outsourcing.

-Do you realize that you son is Nordic Region Executive Manager

- Oh well son. We'd love you even if you were SENIOR Nordic Region

Executive Manager In Systems Integration Of Technology Infrastucture Outsourcing.

carrot
OIKEITA TÖITÄ.

Carrot. Real jobs.

Look, "Sanfrost" equals vegetarian food

And the Panda is an endangered, vegetarian animal

And what's more appropriate than a...

Recycle

McCann Erickson

Agency   Dynamo Advertising,
                Helsinki
Copywriter   Timo Silvennoinen
Art Director   Jyrki Poutanen
Production   Filmiteollisuus Fine, Helsinki
Director   Johanna Vuoksenmaa
Producer   Marko Talli
Client   Carrot.fi, "Confession"

A no-nonsense husband and wife with a vaguely hippie tinge get home from work. Their yuppie son has a confession to make: "I am now Nordic Region Executive Manager in Systems Integration of Technology Infrastucture Outsourcing." His parents don't seem too happy about this. After a long silence, his mother sighs: "Oh well, son, we'd love you even if you were SENIOR Nordic Region Executive Manager in Systems Integration of Technology Infrastucture Outsourcing." Get a real job, with Carrot.fi.

Agency   McCann Erickson,
                Tel Aviv
Creative Director Yaniv Melinarsky
Copywriter   Ido Ben Dor
Art Director   Maya Kerman
Director   Liat Dahan
Producer   Hadas Yosifun
Client   McCann Erickson,
                "Panda"

A couple of McCann creatives pitch the same idea to a variety of clients. They tell makers of vegetarian food that their ideal brand spokesman would be a panda – "a vegetarian animal". Next, they reassure makers of diapers that the panda would make a terrific logo because "it's soft". Clients from Volvo are not convinced that "an endangered species" is right for a car that "protects people". Bizarrely, though, financial newspaper Marker loves the panda pitch. McCann encourages its staff to recycle – but maybe not ideas.

Agency	DDB Germany, Düsseldorf	Good advertising from sound. (The word
Executive CD	Amir Kassaei	'ton' means both 'sound' and 'clay' in
Creative Directors	Tim Jacobs	German, which explains why this audio
	Thomas Schwarz	production studio has reconstructed
	Eric Schoeffler	some well known award-winning print
Copywriter	Dennis May	ads - in clay).
Art Director	Kristine Holzhausen	
Photographer	Ongart Photography	
Illustrator	Albert Radl	
Client	Hastings Audio Network	

Eleonora Giovanardi.
2nd year student.

Paolo Grassi Acting School.
Registrations are open.

Agency — Leo Burnett, Milan
Creative Directors — Sergio Rodriguez
Enrico Dorizza
Copywriter — Sergio Rodriguez
Art Director — Sergio Rodriguez
Production — Bedeschi Film
Director — Andrea Cecchi
Producers — Giovanni Bedeschi
Antonello Filosa
Client — Paolo Grassi
Acting School,
"Registrations are Open"

In a grim part of town, a young woman finds a thief trying to hack through the lock of her scooter. The thief turns to confront her, perhaps even to assault her. But something makes him hesitate. Seizing her advantage, the girl movingly describes how she took a trip on that scooter with her father, shortly before he died. The scooter and that precious memory of her dead father are linked in her mind. Her imploring eyes are full of tears. Relenting, the thief shuffles off. The endline reveals that the girl is a student of the Paolo Grassi Acting School.

Agency — DDB Germany, Berlin
Executive CD — Amir Kassaei
Creative Directors — Bert Peulecke
Stefan Schulte
Copywriters — Kai Abd El-Salam
Marian Götz
Art Directors — Marc Isken
Christian Jakimowitsch
Production — DDB Berlin
Producer — Hendrik Raufmann
Illustrator — Andreas Barhainski
Client — Berlitz,
"Ken" & "Camelia"

Hilariously bad translations of famous pop song lyrics drive this campaign for a language school. In the first version, MC Hammer's "Can't Touch This" becomes "Ken Touched This", complete with an animation featuring Ken (as in Barbie's boyfriend) molesting a gay action figure. Other notable lyrics include: "That's how we're living in your nose" and "Paul is on a mission so fall on back". Somebody needs to sign up with Berlitz.

In the second spot, Culture Club's "Karma Chameleon" gets the treatment. Or should we say "Cama Camelia", which is how the translator puts it. "You come and go" becomes "You come in gold", while things get even more surreal with "wrapped goat in green" and "you stream alone". Every song tells a story. After a couple of Berlitz classes, you may get it.

Agency	Lemon Scented Tea, Amsterdam	Agency	Serviceplan Munich/Hamburg	Serviceplan Hamburg urgently requires a
Creative Directors	Bastiaan Rijkers	**Creative Directors**	Alexander Schill	graphic designer with IT skills. (The ads
	Rogier Heijning		Axel Thomsen	were made from wood, wool, Lego blocks
Copywriter	Kamiel van Zutphen	**Copywriter**	Christoph Nann	and drawing pins; they were displayed on
Art Directors	Bastiaan Rijkers	**Art Director**	Maik Kähler	notice boards in design colleges).
	Rogier Heijning	**Client**	Serviceplan Recruitment	
Illustrators	Saddington & Baynes			
Client	Amsterdam School of Technology			

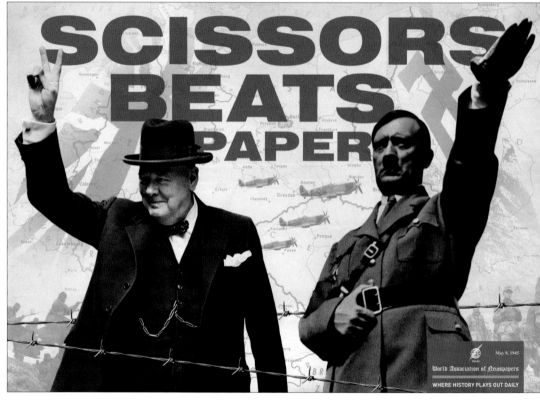

Agency	Euro RSCG, Prague
Creative Directors	Dejan Stajnberger
	Ana Vehauc
Copywriter	Ana Vehauc
Art Directors	Dejan Stajnberger
	Juraj Dudas
Photographer	Juraj Dudas
Client	Belécole

Agency	The Dukes of Urbino.Com Global,
	Johannesburg
Creative Directors	Graham Warsop
	Michael Blore
	Liam Wielopolski
Copywriters	Michael Blore
	Gavin Stradi
	Darren Kilfoil
Art Directors	Liam Wielopolski
	Heath Geddes
Illustrator	Joseph Makwela
Client	World Association of Newspapers

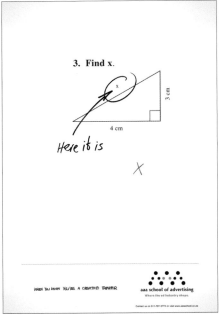

3. Find x.

x

3 cm

4 cm

Here it is

X

WHEN YOU KNOW YOU'RE A CREATIVE THINKER

aaa school of advertising
Where the ad industry shops.

Contact us on 011-781 2772 or visit www.aaaschool.co.za

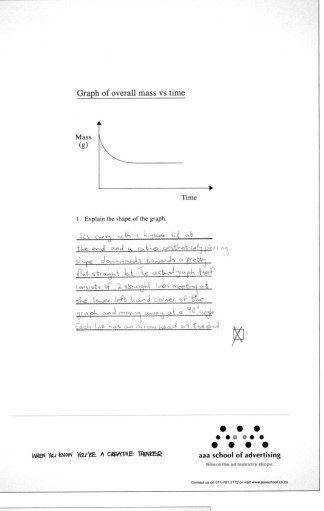

Graph of overall mass vs time

Mass (g)

Time

1. Explain the shape of the graph.

It's curvy, with a higher bit at the end and a rather aesthetically pleasing slope downwards towards a pretty flat straight bit. The actual graph itself consists of 2 straight lines meeting at the lower left hand corner of the graph and moving away at a 90° angle. Each line has an arrow head on the end.

WHEN YOU KNOW YOU'RE A CREATIVE THINKER

aaa school of advertising
Where the ad industry shops.

Contact us on 011-781 2772 or visit www.aaaschool.co.za

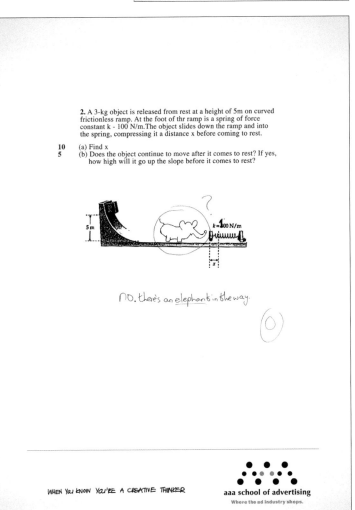

2. A 3-kg object is released from rest at a height of 5m on curved frictionless ramp. At the foot of thr ramp is a spring of force constant k - 100 N/m. The object slides down the ramp and into the spring, compressing it a distance x before coming to rest.

10 (a) Find x
5 (b) Does the object continue to move after it comes to rest? If yes, how high will it go up the slope before it comes to rest?

5 m

$k = 100 \text{ N/m}$

NO. there's an elephant in the way.

(0)

WHEN YOU KNOW YOU'RE A CREATIVE THINKER

aaa school of advertising
Where the ad industry shops.

Contact us on 011-781 2772 or visit www.aaaschool.co.za

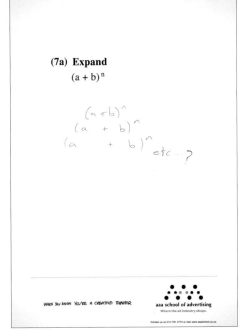

(7a) Expand
$(a + b)^n$

$(a + b)^n$
$(a + b)^n$
$(a + b)^n$ etc...?

WHEN YOU KNOW YOU'RE A CREATIVE THINKER

aaa school of advertising
Where the ad industry shops.

Contact us on 011-781 2772 or visit www.aaaschool.co.za

Professional Equipment & Services 281

Agency	The Jupiter Drawing Room, Johannesburg
Creative Directors	Graham Warsop
	Michael Blore
Copywriter	Lwazi Mkhize
Art Director	Saki Piliso
Illustrator	Saki Piliso
Client	AAA School of Advertising

282　**Professional Equipment & Services**

Agency	Stenström Red Cell, Stockholm	Agency	Scholz & Friends, Berlin
Creative Director	Patrik Bruckner	Creative Directors	Matthias Spaetgens
Copywriter	Sylvia Ziemski		Jan Leube
Art Director	Kajsa Pontén	Copywriters	Daniel Boedeker
Client	Post-it Super Sticky		Axel Tischer
		Art Director	David Fischer
		Photographer	Hans Starck
		Graphic	Robert Bilz
			Steffen Kreft
			Tabea Rauscher
		Client	Jobsintown.de

Get rid of your German accent: Inlingua Business-English

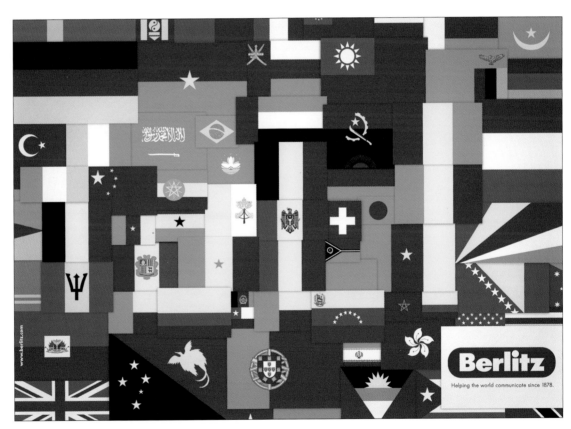

Agency	Kolle Rebbe Werbeagentur, Hamburg		**Agency**	Scholz & Friends, Berlin
Creative Directors	Sven Klohk		**Creative Directors**	Jan Leube
	Ulrich Zuenkeler			Matthias Spaetgens
Copywriters	Florian Ludwig		**Copywriter**	Edgar Linscheid
	Constantin Sossidi		**Art Director**	Fabian Esslinger
Art Directors	Pia Kortemeier		**Graphic**	Cindy Huchatz
	Kay-Owe Tiedemann		**Client**	Berlitz Language School
Client	Inlingua Language School			

BUSINESS ENGLISH COURSES

GREAT THOUGHTS SHOULD NEVER GET STUCK. *Double A*, NO JAM. NO STRESS.

Double A
Double Quality Paper

GREAT THOUGHTS SHOULD NEVER GET STUCK. *Double A*, NO JAM. NO STRESS.

Double A
Double Quality Paper

284 **Professional Equipment & Services**

Agency	BBDO, Athens
Creative Directors	Theodosis Papanikolaou
Copywriter	Daphne Patrikiou
Art Director	David Kaneen
Client	Business English Courses

Agency	JWT, Dubai
Creative Director	Chafic Haddad
Copywriters	Moaiad Khaiti
	Tushar Kadam
Art Director	Firas Medrows
Illustrators	Nabil Kamara
	Firas Medrows
Client	Double A Paper

GREAT FILMS WITH LOW BUDGET?
BIG IDEAS ARE PRODUCED EVEN WITH SMALL BUDGETS. ASK TO CENTRAL GROUCHO. WWW.CENTRALGROUCHO.IT
CENTRAL GROUCHO

Agency	Maxima, Moscow
Creative Director	Piotr Jagielski
Copywriter	Alexander Ovsiankin
Art Directors	Oleg Panov
	Denis Popenkov
Client	MTA, Moscow Translation Agency

Agency	Arnold Worldwide, Milan
Creative Directors	Maurizio Maresca
	Alessandro Sabini
	Paolo Troilo
Copywriter	Alessandro Sabini
Art Director	Aureliano Fontana
Photographer	Paolo Troilo
Client	Central Groucho

In-crease comfort with

Canesten® HC

1% hydrocortisone and 1% clotrimazole

Nothing beats Canesten HC for treating a wide range of inflamed fungal skin infections, including sweat rash (candidal intertrigo), jock itch (tinea cruris) and athlete's foot (tinea pedis). The unique combination of clotrimazole and hydrocortisone rapidly relieves symptoms and helps eliminate inflammation and infection. Prescribe Canesten HC and help your patients feel comfortable again.

Anti-Inflammatory. Anti-Fungal. Anti-Bacterial*

*exhibits activity against *Trichomonas*, staphylococci, streptococci and *Bacteroides*

286 **Prescription Products**

Agency	Paling Walters, London
Creative Director	Frank Walters
Copywriter	Carmel Thompson
Art Director	Dorran Wajsman
Photographer	Tim Platt
Client	Canesten HC

Agency	Sudler & Hennessey, Milan		Agency	Heart Reklambyrå, Stockholm
Creative Directors	Mike Batik		Creative Director	Jonas Svedberg
	Nathalie Garcia		Copywriter	Mats Lindborg
Copywriter	Mike Batik		Art Director	Mark Schlobohm
Art Director	Nathalie Garcia		Photographer	Christer Carlson
Client	Daylong Actinica		Client	Xenical

Hard sex.

Don't let one risk hide another.
We worry about meningitis. What about otitis media ? Streptococcus pneumoniæ and non-typable Hæmophilus influenzæ cause otitis media or meningitis. Both diseases can slow down children's development. This is why remedial solutions should cover both bacteria. Let's protect children from both Sp and NTHi.*
*Streptococcus pneumoniæ and Non Typeable Hæmophilus influenzæ

Don't let one risk hide another.
We worry about meningitis. What about otitis media ? Streptococcus pneumoniæ and non-typable Hæmophilus influenzæ cause otitis media or meningitis. Both diseases can slow down children's development. This is why remedial solutions should cover both bacteria. Let's protect children from both Sp and NTHi.*
*Streptococcus pneumoniæ and Non Typeable Hæmophilus influenzæ

288   **Prescription Products**

Agency	Sudler & Hennessey, Milan	**Agency**	Air, Brussels
Creative Directors	Angelo Ghidotti	**Creative Directors**	Eric Hollander
	Bruno Stucchi		Michel Van Dyck
Copywriter	Angelo Ghidotti	**Copywriters**	Nam Simonis
Art Directors	Massimiliano Luzzani		Anthony Hirschfeld
	Alessandro Radaelli	**Art Directors**	Nam Simonis
Client	Viagra		Anthony Hirschfeld
		Photographer	Paul Ruigrok
		Client	Synflorix

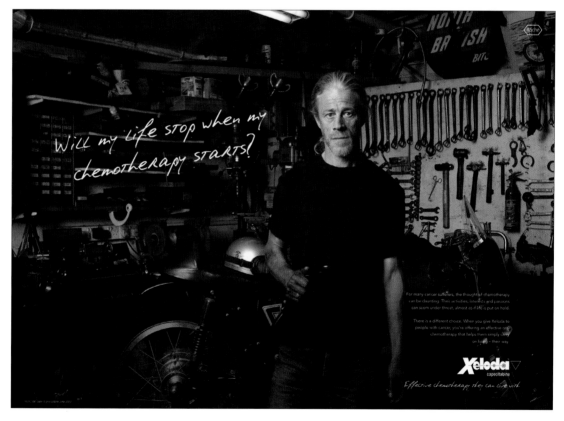

Agency	Paling Walters, London	Agency	Paling Walters, London
Creative Director	Frank Walters	**Creative Director**	Frank Walters
Copywriter	Carmel Thompson	**Copywriter**	Carmel Thompson
Art Director	Adrian Parr	**Art Director**	Adrian Parr
Photographer	Andy Mac	**Photographer**	Chris Holland
Client	Xenical	**Client**	Xeloda

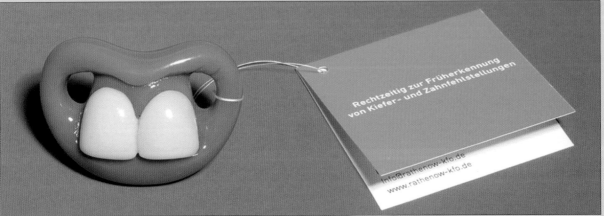

Consumer Direct

Agency	Leo Burnett, Frankfurt	In Germany, advertising for doctors is subject to strict restrictions, with bans on print ads, TV and radio commercials. But legally speaking, giving away gifts or business cards is fine. To promote the service of Dr. Rathenow without breaking the law, specially designed pacifiers were handed out to parents of small children. The pacifiers gave the parents a funny but striking impression of how their kids could look with uncorrected teeth. The doctor's business card was attached to the pacifiers.
Creative Directors	Andreas Heinzel Peter Steger	
Copywriter	Florian Kroeber	
Art Director	Claudia Böckler	
Client	Dr. Rathenow, Orthodontist	

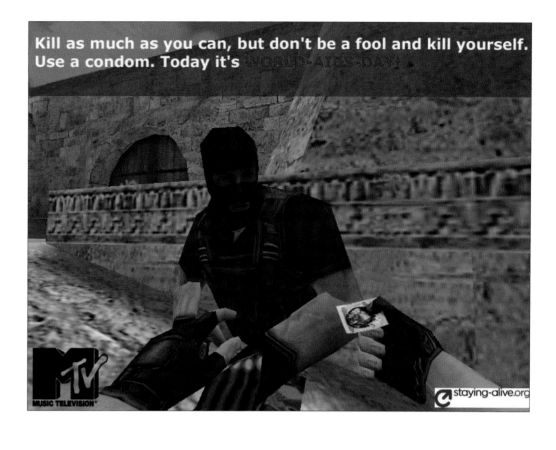

Kill as much as you can, but don't be a fool and kill yourself. Use a condom. Today it's WORLD-AIDS-DAY!

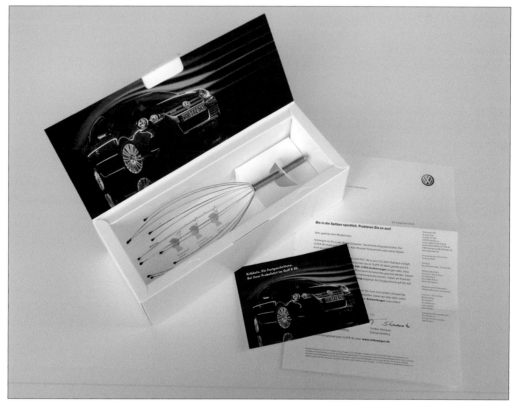

Agency	Ogilvy, Frankfurt	Counterstrike is the most popular online
Creative Director	Christian Seifert	"shooter" game worldwide. In Germany
Copywriter	Christian Seifert	alone, 2.2 million people play daily on more
Art Director	Christian Seifert	than 20,000 servers. And 80% of these
Client	MTV, Anti-AIDS	are aged between 16 and 26. As part of

Counterstrike is the most popular online "shooter" game worldwide. In Germany alone, 2.2 million people play daily on more than 20,000 servers. And 80% of these are aged between 16 and 26. As part of the MTV anti-AIDS campaign "Staying Alive", a graphics file was installed on more than 12,000 Counterstrike servers to warn players about the dangers of AIDS. When players accessed the server on world AIDS day, they were confronted with the anti-AIDS message before they could start playing the game.

Agency	Tribal DDB, Hamburg
Creative Directors	Martin Drust
	Friedrich von Zitzewitz
Copywriter	Angela Gillmann
Art Director	Andrea Schlaffer
Client	Volkswagen Golf R 32

It's not possible to describe driving the new Golf R 32: you have to experience it. That's why the agency mailed out this special device that stimulates the goose-bumps you get when you accelerate from 0-100 in 6.2 seconds. Judging by the number of test-drive requests that followed, many recipients tried the device and decided they wanted to experience the same sensation behind the wheel.

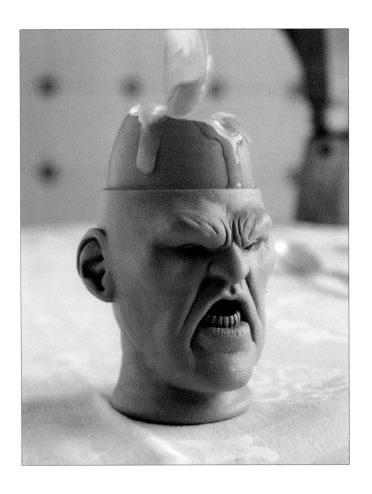

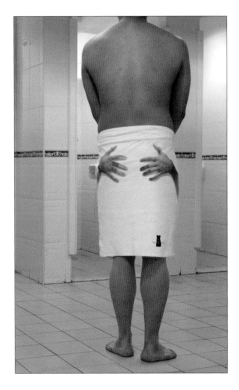

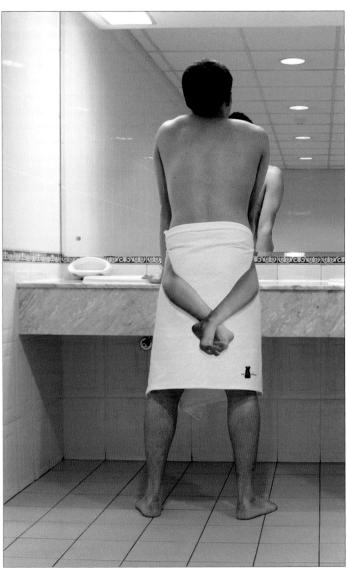

Agency	Nordpol+ Hamburg	Right-wing radicalism is a problem in Germany.
Copywriter	Sebastian Behrendt	So this anti-Nazi charity encouraged citizens
Art Director	Tim Schierwater	to do a good deed at breakfast time by using
Client	Loud Against Nazis	these eggcups.

Agency	Lowe MENA, Dubai	To communicate that Axe is now available
Creative Directors	Dominic Stallard	as a shower gel, these 'Axe Effect' towels
	Clinton Manson	were handed out in men's gyms. They
Copywriters	Clinton Manson	became very popular amongst male
	Ma'n Abutaleb	teenagers in the UAE.
Art Director	Dominic Stallard	
Client	Axe Shower Gel	

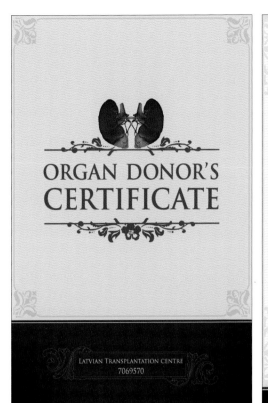

ORGAN DONOR'S CERTIFICATE

LATVIAN TRANSPLANTATION CENTRE
7069570

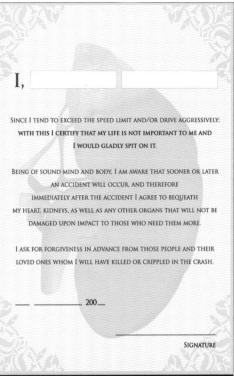

I, _____ _____

SINCE I TEND TO EXCEED THE SPEED LIMIT AND/OR DRIVE AGGRESSIVELY:
WITH THIS I CERTIFY THAT MY LIFE IS NOT IMPORTANT TO ME AND
I WOULD GLADLY SPIT ON IT.

BEING OF SOUND MIND AND BODY, I AM AWARE THAT SOONER OR LATER
AN ACCIDENT WILL OCCUR, AND THEREFORE
IMMEDIATELY AFTER THE ACCIDENT I AGREE TO BEQUEATH
MY HEART, KIDNEYS, AS WELL AS ANY OTHER ORGANS THAT WILL NOT BE
DAMAGED UPON IMPACT TO THOSE WHO NEED THEM MORE.

I ASK FOR FORGIVENESS IN ADVANCE FROM THOSE PEOPLE AND THEIR
LOVED ONES WHOM I WILL HAVE KILLED OR CRIPPLED IN THE CRASH.

_____ 200_

_____
SIGNATURE

Agency	Mooz!, Riga	These organ donation certificates were
Creative Director	Eriks Stendzenieks	handed out to aggressive drivers by the
Copywriter	Eriks Stendzenieks	Latvian traffic police.
Art Director	Maris Upenieks	
Client	Latvian Road Traffic Safety Department	

Agency	Lowe Brindfors, Stockholm	Zarah is a new opera based on the life of the Swedish actress Zarah Leander who
Creative Director	Tove Langseth	accepted an invitation from Herman Göring
Copywriter	Ulrika Eriksson	to become one of the greatest stars of the
Art Directors	Kalle dos Santos	Third Reich. She became persona non
	Petter Lublin	grata when she returned to Sweden in
Client	Folkoperan	1943 and did not perform again until the

1950s. The VIP invitation used recordings from the opera on an old-fashioned vinyl record with the text: Revered and Reviled. Each Hitler mustache on the artist's portrait was hand-drawn.

Wael Khalife
Shiite _____

Lebanon&Co. L Center Badaro P.O. Box 478 Beirut Lebanon
Telephone: (961) I 05 05 05   E-mail: wkhalife@lebanonco.net.lb

Jad Saleh
Sunni _____

Lebanon&Co. L Center Badaro P.O. Box 478 Beirut Lebanon
Telephone: (961) I 05 05 05   E-mail: jsaleh@lebanonco.net.lb

Yasmina Homsi
Greek Catholic _____

Lebanon&Co. L Center Badaro P.O. Box 478 Beirut Lebanon
Telephone: (961) I 05 05 05   E-mail: yhomsi@lebanonco.net.lb

Marwan Younes
Druze _____

Lebanon&Co. L Center Badaro P.O. Box 478 Beirut Lebanon
Telephone: (961) I 05 05 05   E-mail: myounes@lebanonco.net.lb

Karim Daher
Maronite _____

Lebanon&Co. L Center Badaro P.O. Box 478 Beirut Lebanon
Telephone: (961) I 05 05 05   E-mail: kdaher@lebanonco.net.lb

Manal Mansour
Greek Orthodox _____

Lebanon&Co. L Center Badaro P.O. Box 478 Beirut Lebanon
Telephone: (961) I 05 05 05   E-mail: mmansour@lebanonco.net.lb

STOP SECTARIANISM BEFORE IT STOPS US.

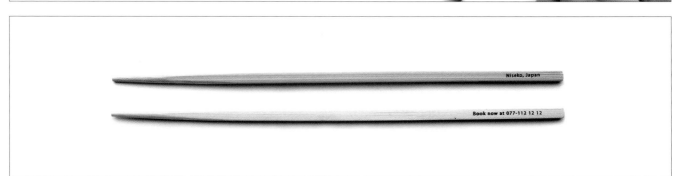

Agency	H&C Leo Burnett, Beirut
Creative Director	Bechara Mouzannar
Copywriter	Omar Boustany
Art Directors	Reem Kotob
	Yasmina Baz
	Manal Nagi
Client	Amam

This operation was a comment on religious sectarianism in Lebanon. Fake business cards were left behind in restaurants, bars and nightclubs. In each case, the person's job position was replaced by their religion. The message on the back of each card read: Stop sectarianism before it stops us.

Agency	Goss, Gothenburg
Copywriters	Micke Schultz
	Ulrika Good
	Elisabeth Berlander
Art Directors	Mattias Frendberg
	Gunnar Skarland
	Jan Eneroth
	Mimmi Andersson
	Albin Larsson
Client	Langley Travel

Every year, ski travel specialist Langley Travel arranges a trip to an exotic skiing destination like Africa, Iran or Siberia. This has become a tradition well known to clients and the press, with the announcement of each year's destination hotly anticipated. This mailing was sent out to the press and Langley's most intrepid customers. Chopsticks in a ski case clearly equalled: skiing in Japan! Printed on the chopsticks were the destination (Niseko, Japan), the departure date and the phone number where you could book the trip.

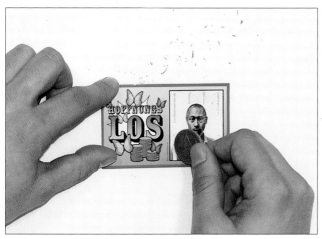

Agency	Mark BBDO, Prague	Chinese restaurants often give away "fortune cookies" after a meal. These usually contain a message: ancient Chinese wisdom or a proverb. In this case, the cookies reminded guests to chew gum after every meal. The message (presumably written by Yoda from Star Wars) reads: "He who chews Orbit after every meal, healthy teeth will have."	**Agency**	DraftFCB Kobza, Vienna
Creative Directors	Leon Sverdlin		**Creative Director**	Patrik Partl
	Martin Charvat		**Copywriters**	Florian Schwab
Copywriter	Pavel Sobek			Eva Sommeregger
Art Director	Dan Kurz		**Art Directors**	Andreas Gesierich
Client	Orbit			Daniel Senitschnig
			Graphic Design	Kerstin Schudo
			Client	Amnesty International

Agency Mark BBDO, Prague
Creative Directors Leon Sverdlin
 Martin Charvat
Copywriter Pavel Sobek
Art Director Dan Kurz
Client Orbit

Chinese restaurants often give away "fortune cookies" after a meal. These usually contain a message: ancient Chinese wisdom or a proverb. In this case, the cookies reminded guests to chew gum after every meal. The message (presumably written by Yoda from Star Wars) reads: "He who chews Orbit after every meal, healthy teeth will have."

Agency DraftFCB Kobza, Vienna
Creative Director Patrik Partl
Copywriters Florian Schwab
 Eva Sommeregger
Art Directors Andreas Gesierich
 Daniel Senitschnig
Graphic Design Kerstin Schudo
Client Amnesty International

The charity produced lottery scratch cards showing a political prisoner behind bars. By scratching the bars with a coin you could rub them out and set the prisoner free. Beneath the bars were printed the words: "A single coin can have a great effect, if you use it wisely." In a related mailing, prison bars were printed on the windows of standard business envelopes. By taking the letter out of the envelope, recipients could 'liberate' the prisoner who's face appeared behind the bars.

Consumer Direct

Agency	Mayer McCann, Ljubljana	Vale Novak's "SmartCovers" allowed its customers to disguise their trashy vacation novels as more intellectual subject matter. Readers could thereby avoid embarrassment and appear to have more sophisticated literary tastes.
Creative Director	Vera Stankovic	
Copywriter	Barbara Brodnik	
Art Director	Tina Brezovnik	
Photographer	Tina Brezovnik	
Client	Vale Novak Bookstore	

Agency	Skadialog, Frankfurt	In Germany, cellulite is known as 'orange-peel skin'. This mailing promoted cellulite reduction sessions at the Fitness Company.
Creative Directors	Jeanette Bouffier	
	Ralf Dulisch	
Copywriter	Judith Schneider	
Art Director	Carmen Fischer	
Client	The Fitness Company	

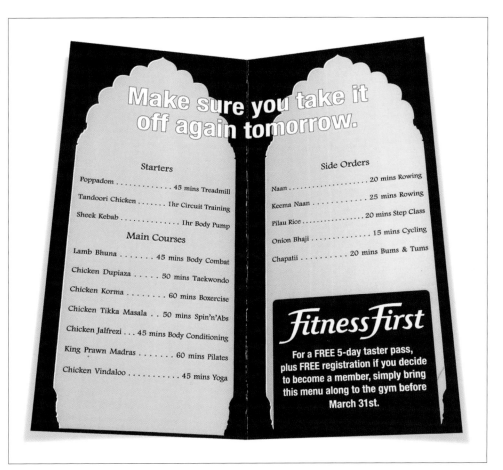

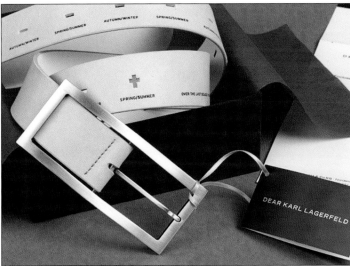

OVER THE LAST DECADES THE FASHION INDUSTRY CREATED A TREND. WITH 63,000 DEDICATED FOLLOWERS.

Consumer Direct 297

Agency	Wunderman, London
Creative Director	Steve Harrison
Copywriter	Iain Hunter
Art Director	Jamie Bell
Illustrator	Jamie Bell
Client	Fitness First

This operation aimed to recruit new members for the Fitness First gym. Most gym advertising features people with perfect bodies. Fitness First took a different approach by suggesting that it was okay to indulge occasionally, as long as you burned off the extra calories. It did this by creating its own version of the flyers normally posted through letterboxes by takeaway food joints. The leaflets showed those who might be tempted to indulge in a takeaway how much exercise would be required to "take away" the extra pounds.

Agency	Ogilvy, Frankfurt
Creative Directors	Christian Mommertz
	Dr. Stephan Vogel
Copywriter	Eva Bender
Art Director	Catrin Farrenschon
Client	Magersucht.de

Hundreds of thousands of women suffer from anorexia. Many die as a result of their illness. And yet the fashion industry insists on using skeletally thin models. Self-help internet forum www.magersucht.de wanted to bring this callousness to the attention of the public. The charity sent Karl Lagerfeld, Heidi Klum and other fashion industry figures a belt representing the shocking consequences of anorexia. The last hole on the belt, at the point where its wearer would be at her thinnest, was a cross. The operation generated considerable media coverage, but was not popular amongst the recipients.

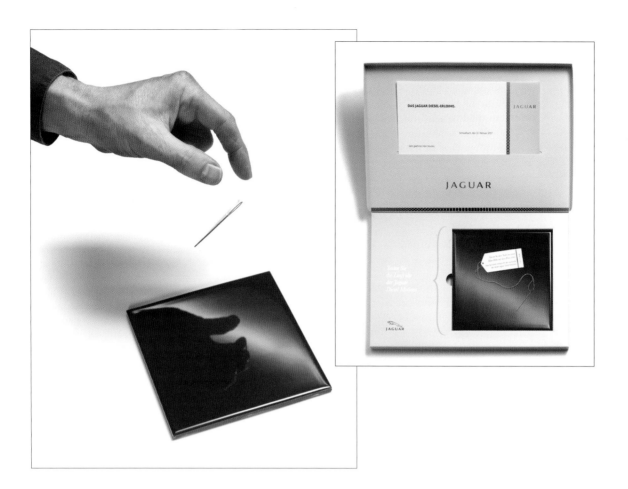

Agency	Wunderman, Frankfurt	The new Jaguar 2.7 litre diesel engine is so
Creative Directors	Bernd Fliesser	quiet one can hear a pin falling. Recipients
	Stephan Beier	of this mailing were able to experience this
Copywriter	Gregor Burk	sound themselves.
Art Director	Markus Renner	
Client	Jaguar Germany	

Agency	Chemistry, Dublin	When somebody has dropped their key
Creative Director	Mike Garner	in the street, your first inclination is to pick
Copywriter	Ann Fleming	it up in the hope that you can return it.
Art Director	Nicole Sykes	Homeless charity Focus Ireland used this
Client	Focus Ireland	instinct to draw attention to the plight of
		those who have nowhere to live. Hundreds
		of keys were scattered all over Dublin.
		On one side of the key-ring was printed:
		"Thousands of people in Ireland are missing
		their keys." And on the other: "Help us help
		the homeless: Focus Ireland."

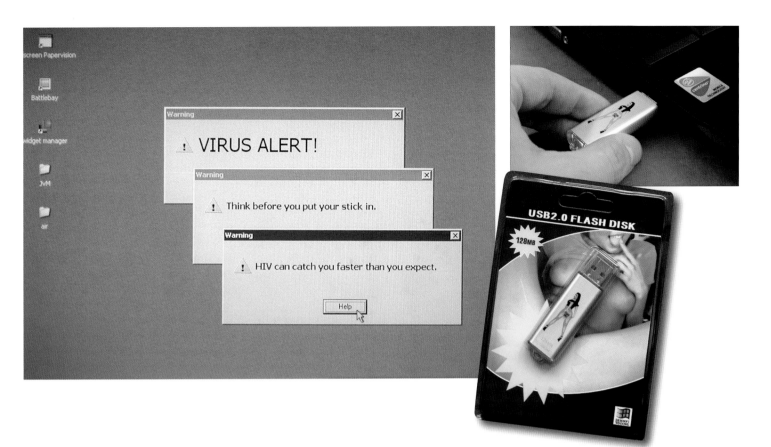

Agency	Jung von Matt, Hamburg	Female teams handed out USB sticks at erotica trade fairs. With racy pictures and the text "Cum on!" the sticks' packaging suggested sexy content. But instead of porn, the USB sticks were loaded with an auto-start file which automatically opened a virus alarm when the stick was plugged in. This virus alarm was a dramatic way of demonstrating how quickly people can be infected with HIV. When users clicked on "help" or "close", the stick's submenu opened, including a link to the official website of the AIDS charity.	**Agency**	Nordpol+ Hamburg	Travel is more efficient by taxi, was the message of this operation. Das Taxi sent out its own version of the official public transport timetable. It described in great detail exactly how long it would take to get from A to B if you booked a taxi at a certain time of the day. The mailing coincided with the release of taxi route map posters mimicking the public transport maps seen in stations and bus shelters all over the city.
Creative Directors	Bernhard Lukas Arno Lindemann		**Creative Director**	Lars Ruehmann	
Copywriters	Ole Kleinhans Markus Kremer		**Copywriters**	Ingmar Bartels Sebastian Behrendt	
Art Directors	Ole Kleinhans Markus Kremer		**Art Directors**	Tim Schierwater Bertrand Kirschenhofer	
Client	Regenbogen		**Illustrators**	Christoph Bielefeldt Stephanie Schneider Barbara Schirner	
			Client	Das Taxi, Hamburg	

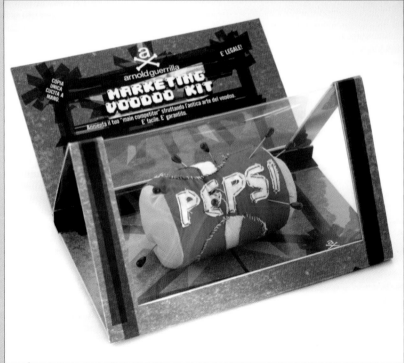

Agency	Arnold Worldwide, Milan
Creative Directors	Maurizio Maresca
	Alessandro Sabini
	Paolo Troilo
Copywriter	Alessandro Sabini
Art Director	Paolo Troilo
Client	Arnold Guerrilla

The agency Arnold Worldwide Italy opened a guerrilla marketing department. It wanted to create a guerrilla operation that would attract the attention of marketing managers. So it sent them these "voodoo dolls" representing their brands' biggest rivals.

Agency	Young & Rubicam, Frankfurt	Germany's largest association for protection of nature and the environment, NABU, wanted to alert opinion leaders, journalists and editors to the threat of climate change and encourage them to subscribe to its newsletters. The "Earth Memory" game shows all the things that are changing on planet earth. The game consists of before-and-after photos showing glaciers past and present, lakes that have vanished and mountain peaks that have long ceased to be snow-capped. It tackles the issue of climate change without the wagging of an admonishing finger.
Creative Directors	Uwe Marquardt	
	Christian Daul	
Art Director	Harald Schumacher	
Client	NABU	
	Naturschutzbund	
	Deutschland	

Agency	Ester, Stockholm	Cities often issue souvenir plates. This is one with a twist, designed to promote a crime novel called The German Child. The author, Camilla Läckberg, always sets her mysteries in the same town. And so on the back of the plate there was a message from her: "With a population of 1000 people in Fjällbacka and an average of two murders a book, I can write a least 500 books before I have run out of victims." The souvenir plates were sent to 150 key members of the Swedish media. They generated good buzz for Camilla Läckberg and her new book.
Creative Director	Lotta Mellgren	
Copywriter	Nils-Gustav Tollman	
Art Directors	Annika Mellgren	
	Lotta Mellgren	
Illustrator	Agnes Miski Török	
Client	Camilla Läckberg,	
	"Tyskungen"	
	("The German Child")	

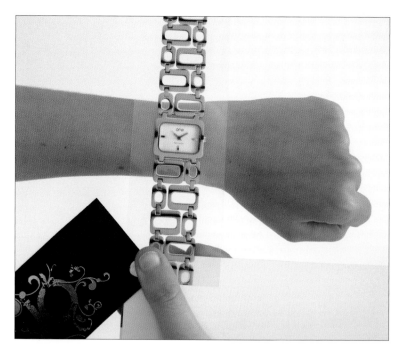

Agency	Etcetera, Amsterdam	LogicaCMG offers ICT solutions and
Creative Director	Ben Imhoff	services. To help arrange meetings with
Copywriter	Jan Willem Vergouwen	hard-to-reach CEOs, all ardent golfers,
Art Director	Maarten Reijnen	these 'Big Big Bertha' clubs echoed the
Client	LogicaCMG	new campaign promise: Releasing your
		potential. The oversize golf clubs proved
		too big to ignore.

Agency	Leo Burnett, Lisbon	Local Portuguese watch brand Planet
Creative Directors	Chacho Puebla	One needed a new way of presenting
	Joao Roque	their collection to retailers. Instead of a
Copywriter	Pedro Ribeiro	traditional catalogue the agency created
Art Director	Pedro Roque	Pantone-like transparent swatches that
Client	Planet One	could be wrapped around the wrist.

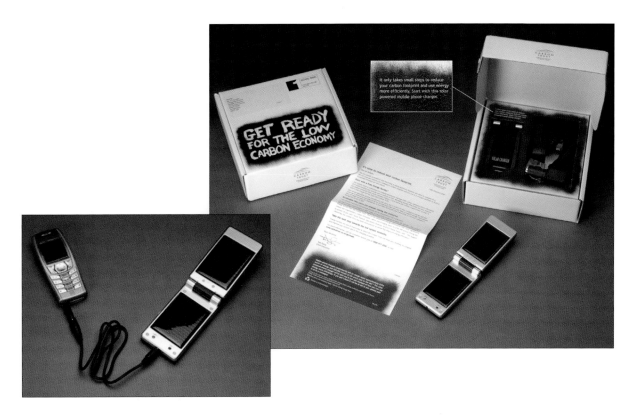

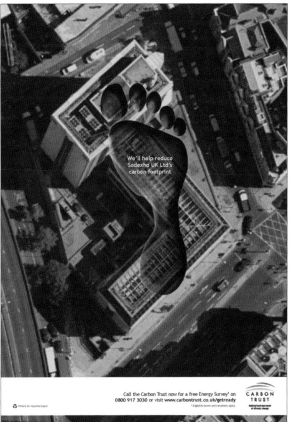

Agency	Tequila\London	For some companies, climate change is perceived as something too big and too complex and is therefore not a priority on their agendas. Surveys by the Carbon Trust, however, cut energy bills by up to 20% via a series of minor adjustments; hence the solar powered mobile phone charger used in this mailing.
Creative Director	Cordell Burke	
Copywriter	Anna Jewes	
Art Director	Claus Larsen	
Client	The Carbon Trust	

Agency	Tequila\London	The Carbon Trust aimed to reduce carbon emissions among medium-sized companies with this 'Footprint Mailing' that used Google Earth images of the individually targeted firms.
Creative Director	Cordell Burke	
Copywriter	Anna Jewes	
Art Directors	Cordell Burke	
	Claus Larsen	
Client	The Carbon Trust	

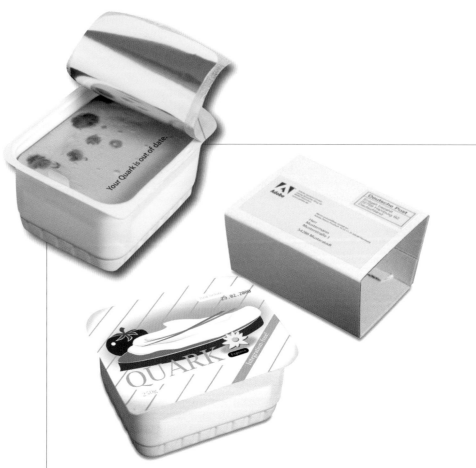

Agency	OgilvyOne Worldwide, Frankfurt	This children's mobile, 'Sofia Model', was sent to German companies doing	**Agency**	Rapp Collins, Hamburg
Creative Directors	Michael Koch Christine Abbel	business in Bulgaria to help raise money for homeless children living in the capital.	**Executice CD**	Olaf Klumski
Copywriter	Markus Toepper	The mobile was anything but child-friendly,	**Creative Director**	Ute Lange
Art Director	Thomas Knopf	it consisted of a broken bottle, a syringe, a	**Art Director**	Anne Kathrin Lüders
Photographer	Thomas Abbel	condom and a tube of glue - all everyday	**Client**	Adobe
Client	Prijateli	items in the lives of these abandoned children.		InDesign Software

Agency OgilvyOne Worldwide, Frankfurt
Creative Directors Michael Koch / Christine Abbel
Copywriter Markus Toepper
Art Director Thomas Knopf
Photographer Thomas Abbel
Client Prijateli

This children's mobile, 'Sofia Model', was sent to German companies doing business in Bulgaria to help raise money for homeless children living in the capital. The mobile was anything but child-friendly, it consisted of a broken bottle, a syringe, a condom and a tube of glue - all everyday items in the lives of these abandoned children.

Agency Rapp Collins, Hamburg
Executice CD Olaf Klumski
Creative Director Ute Lange
Art Director Anne Kathrin Lüders
Client Adobe / InDesign Software

In German, "Quark", Adobe's principal competitor, is also the name for "curd cheese", a popular dairy product sold in every German supermarket. Playing on this double meaning, the agency created a "mouldy Quark" mailing. Targets received a tub of Quark cheese that was well past its expiration date. Under a layer of "mould", a flyer resembling a recipe book showcased Adobe InDesign's superior freshness and offered recipients a free trial download.

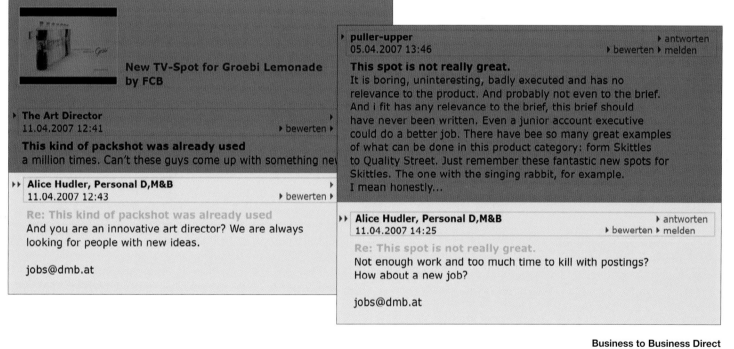

Agency	Arc Worldwide, London	Van drivers buy their vehicles based on dimensions; choosing the model that best suits their daily needs. This mailing for the full range of Fiat commercial vehicles therefore included a Fiat Professional tape measure that showed the sizes of various items the van driver might want to carry, as well as key dimensions of the different Fiat models.	**Agency**	Demner, Merlicek & Bergmann, Vienna	Austrian advertising agencies promote their latest work on a popular industry website called www.etat.de. Needless to say, everyone goes online to comment and criticise the work, often in the frankest terms. The agency Demner, Merlicek & Bergmann took advantage of this situation for an online recruitment campaign. Head of human resources Alice Hudler would reply to the wittiest or most caustic criticisms offering the writer an interview.
Creative Directors	Aaron Martin Garry Munns		**Creative Director**	Francesco Bestagno	
Copywriter	Kevin Travis		**Copywriter**	Alexander Hofmann	
Art Director	Ian Mitchell		**Art Director**	Francesco Bestagno	
Client	Fiat Commercial Vehicles		**Client**	Demner, Merlicek & Bergmann, Recruitment	

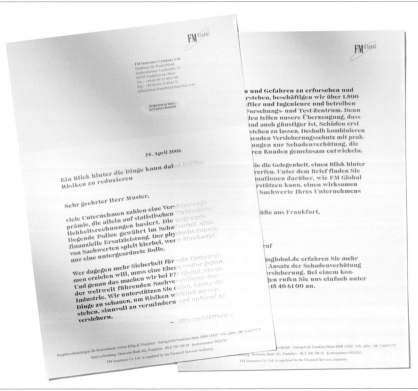

Agency	Skadialog, Frankfurt	Delphi Advisors assist American firms
Creative Directors	Jeanette Bouffier	invest in Germany. To win new clients,
	Ralf Dulisch	prospects were sent a real German
Copywriter	Nils Netheler	cuckoo clock to make the point that this
Art Director	Susanne Bock	is the right time to invest in Germany. But
Client	Delphi Advisors	it's not a cuckoo that pops out on the

Delphi Advisors assist American firms invest in Germany. To win new clients, prospects were sent a real German cuckoo clock to make the point that this is the right time to invest in Germany. But it's not a cuckoo that pops out on the hour, it's an American bald eagle singing the US national anthem!

Agency	OgilvyOne Worldwide,
	Frankfurt
Creative Director	Christine Blum-Heuser
Copywriter	Michael Buss
Art Director	Dajana Reichel
Client	FM Global

FM Global insures the assets of large industrial companies with a unique concept that pinpoints possible dangers. To demonstrate the need for detailed background information to identify potential losses, the mailing uses punched-out letters that can only be read "behind the scenes".

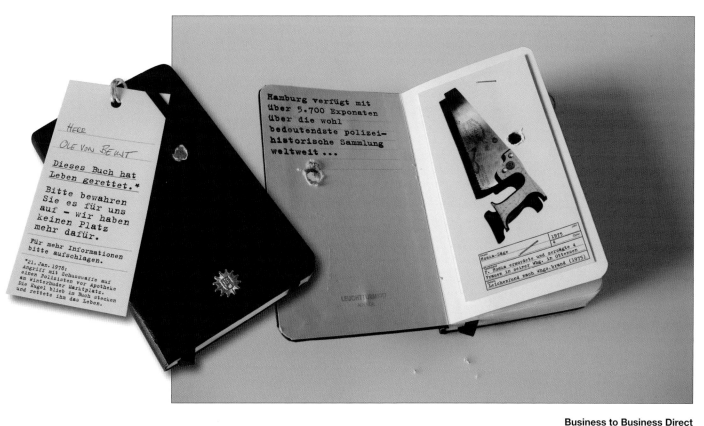

Agencies	Claydon Heeley, London	A small book highlighting infamous business mistakes was sent to prospective buyers to make the point that they too would be making a big mistake not to consider the Viano. Several Post-it notes point the reader to particular pages and suggest that others had already read and learned from the book, giving it an important, business-like feel.
	Zulu, London	
Executive CD	Peter Harle	
Creative Director	Dave Woods	
Copywriter	Tim Noble	
Art Director	Gem Hagan	
Designer	Andrew Carlisle	
Client	Mercedes-Benz Viano	

Agency	TöpferGrenvilleCrone, Hamburg	The idea is based on a true story. German police officers always carry a thick "pocket book" for taking notes. A police officer's life was once saved by such a book, which stopped a bullet. To encourage members of the Hamburg Senate to provide funding for a new police museum the agency manufactured police pocket books featuring the kind of artefacts that would be placed on display (various murder weapons etc.). The expected cost of the museum took the form of a cash register receipt. A bullet hole added authencity and the evidence was mailed to the target group in plastic bags marked "Exhibit A".
Creative Director	Dirk Wäger	
Copywriter	Oliver Grenville	
Art Director	Jörg Crone	
Photographer	Christian Lohfink	
Client	Hamburg Police Museum	

Media Innovation

Agency	Euro RSCG, Düsseldorf
Creative Directors	Felix Glauner
	Harald Wittig
	Martin Breuer
Copywriter	Kajo Titus Strauch
Art Director	Ingmar Krannich
Producer	Detlef Stuhldreier
Client	Dulcolax Laxative

Agency	Jung von Matt, Hamburg	**Agency**	JWT, Cairo
Creative Directors	Doerte Spengler-Ahrens	**Creative Director**	Fady Chamaa
	Jan Rexhausen	**Art Director**	Shady Abdellatif
Copywriter	Sergio Penzo	**Client**	Lipton Tea
Art Director	Pablo Schencke		
Client	Mondo Pasta		

Agency   Jung von Matt,
                      Berlin
Creative Directors   Wolfgang Schneider
                      Mathias Stiller
                      Jan Harbeck
                      David Mously
Copywriter   Jan Harbeck
Art Director   David Mously
Production   Entspannt Film,
                      Berlin
Director   Nicolai Niemann
Producer   Nicolai Niemann
Client   DHL,
                      "Commercial Break"

This idea involved the co-operation of all the other brands involved in the same commercial break: Ferrero, Rama, Tui and Ricola. DHL wanted to express the idea that it delivers rapidly around the world. At the start of the break, the DHL man gets into his van and sets off to make a delivery. Then, to our surprise, he is seen in the background, driving through all the other spots in the break. Finally, he stops to drop off his parcel. Anywhere in record time: DHL.

310   **Media Innovation**

Agency   Lunar BBDO,
                      London
Creative Directors   Ben Kay
                      Daryl Corps
Client   Muscleworks Gym

Agency   Publicis, Frankfurt
Creative Directors   Stephan Ganser
                      Nico Juenger
                      Peter Kaim
Copywriter   Konstantinos Manikas
Art Directors   Hendrik Frey
                      Evelyne Werner
Photographer   Johannes Krzeslack
Client   Rubin Freshness Bags

Agency	Saatchi & Saatchi, Frankfurt	
Executive CD	Burkhart von Scheven	
Creative Director	Florian Pagel	
Copywriter	Manuel Rentz	
Art Director	Philipp Böttcher	
Producers	Thomas Breen	
	Erwin Endlich-Frey	
Client	Wonderbra	

Agency	Saatchi & Saatchi, Frankfurt
Creative Director	Eberhard Kirchhoff
Copywriter	William John
Art Director	Patrick Ackmann
Producer	Amandus Platt
Client	Wonderbra

To illustrate the Wonderbra effect, the agency placed a simple branded billboard in front of the Weimar Hills: two concealed but perfectly formed water containers, situated next to a busy stretch of motorway.

312 **Media Innovation**

Agency	Duval Guillaume, Antwerp
Creative Directors	Geoffrey Hantson
	Dirk Domen
Copywriter	Eric Becker
Art Director	Gilles de Boncourt
Client	Ché Men's Magazine

Agency	Garbergs Reklambyrå, Stockholm
Copywriter	David Orlic
Art Directors	Johan Wilde
	Mattias Dahlqvist
Illustrators	Johan Wilde
	Mattias Dahlqvist
Client	Stockholm International
	Jazz & Blues Festival

Agency	Istropolitana D'Arcy, Bratislava	How do you get beer bottles into a hockey match when it's being broadcast on TV, even though they're banned in the stadium? Topvar made plastic trumpets in the shape of its beer bottles and handed them out to fans. As the fans blew into the trumpets to encourage their team, it looked as if they were swigging from bottles of beer. And, of course, the results were visible on TV screens.	**Agency**	Scholz & Friends, Berlin	To promote Germany as a land of creativity and invention these sculptures representing some of the country's best ideas were placed in prominent locations in Berlin. A football boot represented the Dassler family, creators of Adidas. Of course there was a giant car, invented by Mr. Daimler and Mr. Benz. A giant pill represented milestones in medicine, while a pile of books paid homage to German literature.
Creative Director	Peter Darovec		**Creative Directors**	Wolf Schneider	
Copywriter	Katarina Popravcova			Tobias Wolff	
Art Director	Vladimir Durajka			Sebastian Turner	
Client	Topvar		**Copywriter**	Mirko Derpmann	
			Art Directors	Juergen Krugsperger	
				Danielle Sellin	
				Alf Speidel	
			Client	Germany, "Land of Ideas"	

Agencies	TBWA\Germany, Berlin Stream, Hamburg	**Agency**	Storåkers McCann, Stockholm
Creative Directors	Gerti Eisele Catrin Florenz Stephanie Krink Dietrich Zastrow	**Copywriter** **Art Director** **Client**	Christian Heinig Ola Von Bahr SEB Bank
Copywriter	Anna Lena Garde		
Art Director	Gerti Eisele		
Production	Loft Tonstudios, Hamburg		
Client	Arena Opera, "Nabucco"		

In 2007, a giant staging of Verdi's opera Nabucco was taken to sports stadiums in Hamburg and Mannheim. The opera is famous for the song "The Prisoners' Chorus". As part of an integrated campaign, the agency got bus passengers singing! On Hamburg buses, instead of being announced in the normal way, the names of stops were sung by a professional tenor to the tune of "The Prisoners' Chorus". Passengers could get more information on the opera via monitors and advertising spaces on the bus.

To promote SEB's sponsorship of the renowned Solheim Cup, the agency built a 9-hole street golf course in the town centre. Bus shelters provided the infrastructure for the course, as well as advertising messages to go alongside it. Golfing equipment could be borrowed from a nearby SEB office. By treating the public to some street golf, the bank succeeded in making the tournament more accessible. It also underlined SEB's commitment to golf and showed off its official green colour.

**Disability can hit anyone.
But everyone can help.**

Disability can hit anyone.
But everyone can help.

Disability can hit anyone.
But everyone can help.

KEEP PLAYING

KEEP PLAYING

CASINO DI VENEZIA
AN INFINITE

Media Innovation 315

Agency	Demner, Merlicek & Bergmann, Vienna	The original poster simply shows three children standing next to one another. However, the poster is "badly" pasted onto billboards intentionally. This is done in such a way that, each time, a different child is "disfigured" by the clumsy placement. It is pure chance which of the three children is affected, because as the headline points out: "Disability can hit anyone".	
Creative Director	Francesco Bestagno		
Art Director	Francesco Bestagno		
Photographer	Stefan Badegruber		
Graphic	Daniela Schabernak		
Client	Disability Awareness Initiative		

Agency	AdmCom, Bologna	The baggage conveyor belts at Venice's Marco Polo airport were decorated to resemble a giant roulette wheel and passengers were given free entry tickets for the casino. As a result casino visitors increased 60%.
Creative Director	Maurizio Cinti	
Copywriters	Rebecca Rossi	
	Silva Fedrigo	
Art Directors	Andrea Ligi	
	Sergio Lelli	
Producer	Alessandra Bigatti	
Client	Casinò di Venezia	

Agency	KNSK Werbeagentur, Hamburg	**Agency**	DraftFCB, Hamburg
Creative Directors	Tim Krink	**Creative Director**	Alexander Gutt
	Niels Holle	**Copywriter**	Tobias Schneider
	Ulrike Wegert	**Art Director**	Behnaz Pakravesh
Copywriter	Steffen Steffens	**Photographers**	Matthias Klages
Art Director	Gabor Zador		Hayo Heye
Client	WMF Knives	**Client**	Weight Watchers

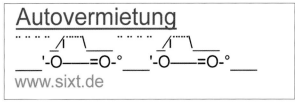

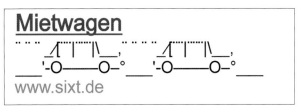

Agency	Jung von Matt, Stuttgart	Entering 'car rental' into Google returns approximately 30 million results – and all of them look pretty much alike. Sixt, one of the largest car rental and leasing companies in Germany, wanted to stand out from the crowd. And with its agency it found a simple but very effective way to meet the challenge: ASCII art – or pictures made out of letters. This was a low budget solution with high impact. In a 'word only' environment, Sixt's ads were highly visible and clearly distinguishable. And they received 47% more clicks than before.	**Agency**	The Bridge, Glasgow
Creative Director	Holger Oehrlich		**Creative Director**	Jonathan d'Aguilar
Art Director	Matthias Erb		**Copywriter**	Gregor Stevenson
Production	Daniel Bretzmanner		**Art Director**	Simon Parker
Client	Sixt		**Client**	Rock Radio

Agency	Ogilvy Group, London	Agency	Saatchi & Saatchi Simko, Geneva
Executive CD	Malcolm Poynton	Creative Director	Olivier Girard
Creative Director	Colin Nimick	Copywriter	Sandrine Llopis
Copywriter	Emma de La Fosse	Art Directors	Frédéric Doms
Art Director	Charlie Wilson		Gabriel Mauron
Client	Cancer Research UK	Client	Groupe e, Energy Supplier

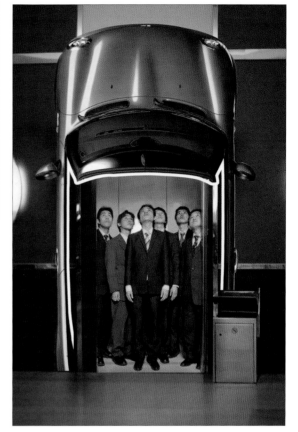

Agency	D'Adda, Lorenzini, Vigorelli, BBDO, Milan	**Agency**	Saatchi & Saatchi, Beirut
Creative Directors	Luca Scotto di Carlo	**Creative Director**	Samer Younes
	Giuseppe Mastromatteo	**Art Director**	Rajaa Khalifé
Copywriter	Cristino Battista	**Client**	Sebamed Anti Acne Foam
Art Director	Dario Agnello		
Client	Mini Cabriolet		

To illustrate the way that acne can disfigure even the most attractive faces, posters featuring good-looking models were pasted onto rough and pitted walls. Their formerly smooth skin looked roughened and blemished: but Sebamed is there to help.

Dar el primer beso del año con la boca llena no tiene precio

Agency	The Jupiter Drawing Room, Cape Town	
Executive CD	Ross Chowles	
Creative Director	Livio Tronchin	
Copywriter	Johnathan Commerford	
Art Director	Jamie Mietz	
Typographer	Joanne Thomas	
Client	Mont Blanc	

Pen & Art is a retail chain that stocks high-end writing instruments. Lately, the use of fountain pens has declined dramatically. The agency was briefed to increase the sales of these premium quality pens. It chose to reach its audience through a daily newspaper read by professionals in Cape Town. The agency convinced the newspaper to a let it hand write an entire page. The paper provided the articles and the agency rewrote them by hand and set them in the style of a newspaper layout.

Agency	Universal McCann, Madrid
Creative Director	José Antonio Nogales
Client	MasterCard

At midnight on New Year's Eve in Spain, everyone eats a grape for each chime of the clock. The clock-tower at Madrid's Puerta del Sol is broadcast live on all TV channels at that moment. As the bells tolled, two "Pac-Man" characters munched grapes from each side of the clock, finally meeting with a kiss. The MasterCard logo then appeared with the message: "The first kiss of the year with your mouth full. Priceless".

Agency	BBDO, Düsseldorf	**Agency**	Goss, Gothenburg
Creative Directors	Toygar Bazarkaya	**Copywriters**	Micke Schults
	Sebastian Hardieck		Ulrika Good
	Ton Hollander		Elisabeth Berlander
	Matthias Eickmeyer	**Art Directors**	Emil Jonsson
Copywriter	Stephan Schaefer		Mattias Frendberg
Art Director	Jake Shaw		Gunnar Skarland
Photographer	Rainer Rudolf		Jan Eneroth
Production	Jack Liberties, Amsterdam		Mimmi Andersson
Directors	Jake Shaw		Albin Larsson
	Stephan Schaefer	**Client**	Onsala Sausages
Producer	Steffen Gentis		
Client	Smart Brabus, "Bridge Jump"		

After more than 50 years on the Swedish market, Onsala sausages are now available ready-sliced.

Agency	The Jupiter Drawing Room, Johannesburg	Drunk driving causes 46% of deaths on South African roads, with the accidents mainly involving drivers between 18 and 30. To target young drinkers, realistic decals of drunks were stuck in nightclub or bar toilets and parking areas. The life-sized drunks' T-shirts spouted clichés like: "I just need to get it out of my system" or "I'll sober up when I'm behind the wheel." The operation was an effective way of dramatising the message without lecturing the target group.
Creative Directors	Graham Warsop	
	Michael Blore	
	Tom Cullinan	
Copywriter	Gavin Stradi	
Art Directors	Frank Van Rooijen	
	Chantelle Dos Santos	
Photographer	Graham Kietzmann	
Client	Arrive Alive	

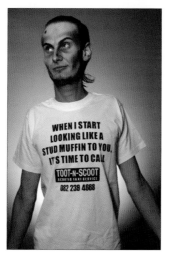

Agency	Zoom Advertising, Cape Town	Feedback provides food for many South African communities were hunger and malnourishment is a way of life. To support this programme the everyday, common blue dustbins in South African cities were transformed into beautifully designed food packaging, but with a twist. Expecting wholesome goodness, passersby were revolted by the descriptions of the contents. All the information on the label echoed the unpalatable scavengings which many of the homeless survive on.	
Executive CD	Graeme Taylor-Warne		
Copywriter	Stu Macwheel		
Art Director	Graeme Taylor-Warne		
Photographer	Pete Maltbie		
Client	Feedback		

Agency	TBWA Tequila\ Johannesburg	The brief was to persuade people not to drink and drive, but to try a new scooter taxi service instead (the clients are driven home in their own cars with a scooter stored in the back for the driver to return on). The campaign was launched over the Christmas season in pubs and clubs. A team of ugly – well, let's say aesthetically challenged – people spread the word by wearing T-shirts that read: "When I start looking like a supermodel to you, it's time to call Toot-n-Scoot." These walking, talking sobriety tests were, in fact, paid actors made-up to look as unappealing as possible.
Creative Directors	Gary Steele
	Hagan de Villiers
Copywriter	Hagan de Villiers
Art Director	Gary Steele
Photographers	Janyon Boschoff
	Brian Gibbs
Producer	Craig Walker
Client	Toot-n-Scoot

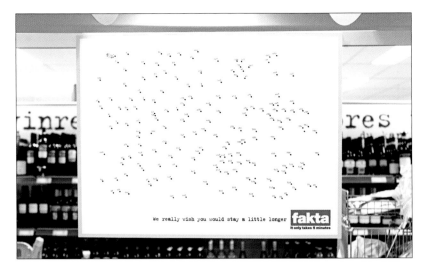

Agency	Young & Rubicam, Frankfurt	On a midtown Frankfurt office tower, a large illuminated display with the Colgate tube was installed. It was arranged for the lights in an adjacent row of offices to be left on at night. The result: a sparkling row of teeth that could be seen for miles around.	**Agency**	Uncle Grey, Aarhus
Creative Director	Uwe Marquardt		**Creative Director**	Per Pedersen
Copywriter	Andreas Richter		**Copywriters**	Ulrik Juul
Art Director	Helge Kniess			Kristian Eilertsen
Photographers	Daniel Tripp		**Art Directors**	Jesper Hansen
	Helge Kniess			Jon Goltsche
Producer	Marion Lakatos		**Client**	Fakta Supermarkets
Client	Colgate Total Whitening			

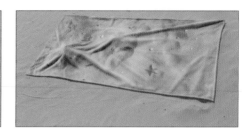

Agency	DDB Amsterdam	Take an ordinary white beach towel, then print a very realistic image of the beach on the other side. What do you get? The Sand Towel; the perfect way of covering your belongings – and camouflaging their presence – while you go and take a dip in the sea. Do-it-yourself insurance from FBTO.	
Creative Director	Martin Cornelissen		
Copywriter	Daniel Snelders		
Art Director	Niels de Wit		
Photographer	Ernst Yperlaan		
Client	FBTO Travel Insurance		

Agency	Young & Rubicam, Frankfurt	Zwilling knives are advertised on the cropped edges of popular cookbooks to demonstrate their ability to slice paper-thin.
Creative Directors	Christian Daul Uwe Marquardt	
Copywriter	Andreas Richter	
Art Director	Helge Kniess	
Producer	Marion Lakatos	
Client	Zwilling Knives	

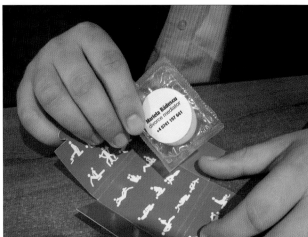

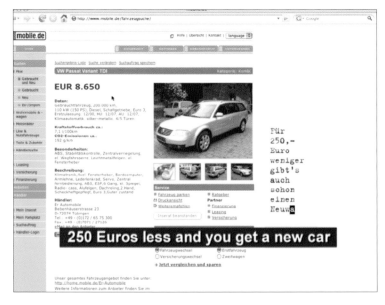

Agency	Propaganda, Bucharest	In a country where lawyers are banned from advertising, a divorce lawyer had problems attracting new clients. Coming to her aid, the agency placed the lawyer's contact details on a specially-designed condom pack. The free condoms were left in motels where adulterous couples were likely to spend some time. The stunt created buzz for the lawyer – and maybe got some people out of unhappy marriages.
Creative Director	Dan Moldovan	
Copywriter	Adrian Albu	
Art Director	Bogdan Moraru	
Client	Marieta Bădescu, Divorce Lawyer	

Agency	Nordpol+ Hamburg	The modestly-priced Dacia estate car (€ 8,400) cropped up in all the places where potential customers make decisions about spending money. In up-market shopping areas, billboards on top of the car compared the price of the Dacia to those of certain luxury goods (Do you prefer the watch or the car?). Online spots showed how much car you can normally expect to get for € 8,400 and internet banners compared the price of a new Dacia to advertisements for second hand vehicles.
Creative Director	Lars Ruehmann	
Copywriter	Sebastian Behrendt	
Art Directors	Tim Schierwater	
	Dominik Anweiler	
Client	Dacia Logan MCV	

Agency	Saatchi & Saatchi Simko, Geneva	Agency	Philipp und Keuntje, Hamburg	The new Audi A3 comes complete with an "open sky" roof system that gives drivers
Creative Director	Olivier Girard	Creative Directors	Diether Kerner	and their passengers a panoramic view.
Art Director	Gabriel Mauron		Oliver Ramm	The agency dramatized this at an exhibition
Photographer	Yann Gross	Copywriter	Rene Ewert	of the artist Casper David Friedrich in
Client	Accessorize	Art Director	Sönke Schmidt	Hamburg. It "extended" some of the
		Client	Audi A3,	paintings upwards by adding an additional
			Open Sky System	view, which might have been enjoyed by
				Friedrich had he been driving the Audi.

Agency	Euro RSCG, Düsseldorf	With the help of a small specially designed pimple sticker, the cover of a popular youth magazine was transformed into a Clearasil ad. The sticker could be peeled off to reveal the brand name and web address on the back.
Creative Directors	Felix Glauner Harald Wittig Markus Daubenbuechel	
Art Director	Jean-Pierre Gregor	
Photographer	Stefan Minder	
Producer	Detlef Stuhldreier	
Client	Clearasil Ultra	

Agency	King, Stockholm	Swedish divers were astonished to discover this illuminated billboard five meters below the surface at a popular dive location in the murky waters of the Stockholm Archipelago.
Creative Director	Frank Hollingworth	
Copywriters	Christian Karlsson Pontus Ekström	
Art Director	Tommy Carlsson	
Photographer	Christian Karlsson	
Production	Fasadpartners	
Producer	Anna Magnusson	
Client	Ving Travel	

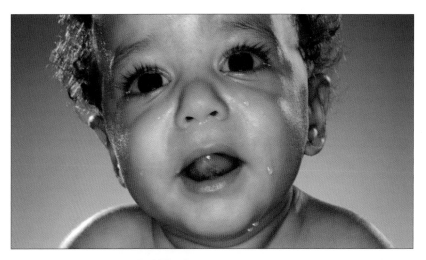

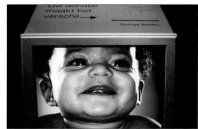

Agency	Ogilvy, Amsterdam
Creative Director	Carl Le Blond
Copywriters	Tim Den Heijer
	Maxim Van Wijk
Art Director	Deborah Bosboom
Photographer	Jonathan Weyland
Producer	Jaap Hoogerdijk
Client	Orange Babies

Visitors approaching the Orange Babies stand at the Millionaire Fair in Amsterdam received a picture of a crying baby on their mobiles, with the line: "Do you hear a baby crying? Let her smile again." The stand featured an interactive video screen showing the same baby. Above the image was a slot for money. When a visitor inserted coins or notes, the baby stopped crying and started giggling. The instant response immediately gave the donor a warm feeling about giving the money. Everything hinged on the slogan: "Your donation makes the difference."

Agency	Forsman & Bodenfors, Gothenburg
Client	Music Box

Agency	Memac Ogilvy, Tunis	Violin lessons – beginners and
Creative Director	Nicolas Courant	advanced classes.
Art Director	Wilfrid Guérin	
Photographer	Anis Cherif	
Client	Conservatoire de	
	Musique Ilyes Jaryan	

Agency	DraftFCB/Lowe Group,	Artesanos Camiseros is a tailor that can
	Zurich	make shirts for people of all shapes and
Creative Director	Keith Loell	sizes. To prove the point, the agency
Copywriter	Juerg Waeber	challenged the tailor to make shirts for
Art Director	Fernando Perez	people-shaped objects all over town.
Client	Artesanos Camiseros	Public spaces outside financial institutions
		and other businesses likely to provide
		potential clients were selected. The result
		was a highly successful Christmas season
		for the tailor.

Agency	Serviceplan Munich/Hamburg	These glass-lung ashtrays were installed outside swimming pools, public buildings, hospitals, and restaurants. The web address (www-I-will-become-a-nonsmoker.de) linked to the AOK website.	**Agency**	Åkestam Holst, Stockholm
Creative Directors	Ekkehard Frenkler Christoph Everke		**Copywriter**	Göran Åkestam
Copywriter	Cosimo Möller		**Art Directors**	Lars Holthe Johan Baettig
Art Director	Alexander Nagel		**Illustrator**	Ylva Krantz
Client	AOK Health Insurance		**Client**	Playground

These glass-lung ashtrays were installed outside swimming pools, public buildings, hospitals, and restaurants. The web address (www-I-will-become-a-nonsmoker.de) linked to the AOK website.

Playground is an outdoor equipment store. To reassure customers that its clothing could withstand freezing conditions, the store constructed the coldest-ever fitting room. With ten cubic metres of snow and 200 kilos of dry ice, the temperature in the room plunged to -25°C (-13°F). Images were beamed online via webcam and the media quickly picked up on the stunt. Visits to the store increased by 400% during the promotion – and sales of warm coats doubled.

Advertising Photography

Agency	TBWA\Paris
Creative Director	Erik Vervroegen
Copywriters	Veronique Sels
	Daniel Perez
Art Directors	Ingrid Varetz
	Javier Rodriguez
Photographer	Michael Lewis
Client	Amnesty International

Is there any greater journey than love? Steffi Graf, Andre Agassi. Room 27. Late June. New York.

LOUIS VUITTON

NikeParis
67 avenue des Champs-Elysées

Agency	Ogilvy & Mather, Paris	Agency	DDB Paris
Creative Director	Christian Reuilly	Creative Directors	Alexandre Hervé
Copywriter	Edgard Montjean		Sylvain Thirache
Art Director	Antoaneta Metchanova	Copywriter	Matthieu Elkaïm
Photographer	Annie Leibovitz	Art Director	Pierrette Diaz
Client	Louis Vuitton	Photographer	Diego Alborghetti
		Client	Nike France

334 **Advertising Photography**

<table>
<tr><td>Agency</td><td>Abbott Mead Vickers BBDO, London</td><td>Agency</td><td>Smith Reklambyrå, Stockholm</td></tr>
<tr><td>Creative Director</td><td>Paul Brazier</td><td>Copywriter</td><td>Gustaf Grapengiesser</td></tr>
<tr><td>Copywriter</td><td>Bern Hunter</td><td>Art Director</td><td>Christopher Barnekow</td></tr>
<tr><td>Art Director</td><td>Mike Bond</td><td>Photographer</td><td>Tomas Monka</td></tr>
<tr><td>Photographer</td><td>Spike Watson</td><td>Client</td><td>Cordon-Bleu Cookware Stores</td></tr>
<tr><td>Client</td><td>Focus 12</td><td></td><td></td></tr>
</table>

Agency	& Co., Copenhagen	Agency	SMFB, Oslo
Creative Director	Thomas Hoffmann	Creative Director	Erik Heisholt
Art Directors	Thomas Hoffmann	Copywriter	Erik Heisholt
	Martin Storegaard	Art Director	Torgrim Nærland
Photographer	Casper Sejersen	Photographer	Torgrim Nærland
Client	Ichi Jeans	Client	Land Rover

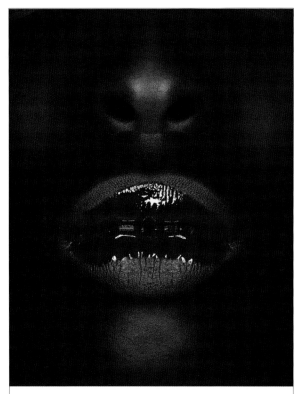

Black with red leather. The New Beetle Limited Edition.

336   **Advertising Photography**

Agency	DDB, Milan	Agency	Agent Provocateur (In-House),
Creative Director	Vicky Gitto		London
Copywriter	Vicky Gitto	**Creative Directors**	Serena Rees
Art Director	Massimo Valeri		Joseph Corre
Photographers	Winkler & Noah		Tim Bret-Day
Client	Volkswagen Beetle	**Photographer**	Tim Bret-Day
	Limited Edition	**Client**	Agent Provocateur

Human after all

Agency	Marcel, Paris	Agency	Tim Bret-Day Photography, London
Creative Directors	Frédéric Témin	Creative Director	Tim Bret-Day
	Anne de Maupeou	Copywriter	Tim Bret-Day
Copywriters	Eric Jannon	Photographer	Tim Bret-Day
	Dimitri Guerassimov	Logo Design	David Bray
Art Directors	Romin Favre	Client	Harvey Nichols
	Nicolas Chauvin		
Photographer	Johan Renck		
Client	Diesel		

www.kiss-my-ash.fi

338 **Advertising Photography**

Agency	Bob Helsinki	Agency	180 Amsterdam
Copywriter	Iina Merikallio	Creative Director	Sean Thompson
Art Directors	Joni Kukkohovi	Copywriter	Dario Nucci
	Anu Igoni	Art Director	Sam Coleman
Photographer	Jussi Hyttinen	Photographer	Nadav Kander
Client	Kiss-My-Ash.fi	Client	Adidas Originals

SUNGLASSES € 24.-
Access to water: €8.-

Text 'aid' to 2255 and donate € 1.50   ◉ People in Need
                                                  Cordaid

Just 5.9 kilograms per horsepower. The Golf GTI® Edition 30.

Agency	Saatchi & Saatchi, Amsterdam		**Agency**	DDB Germany, Berlin
Creative Director	Magnus Olsson		**Executive CD**	Amir Kassaei
Art Director	Tim Bishop		**Creative Directors**	Bert Peulecke
Photographer	Carl Stolze			Stefan Schulte
Client	Cordaid/People in Need		**Copywriter**	Sebastian Kainz
			Art Director	Marc Wientzek
			Photographers	Yann Arthus-Bertrand
				Sven Schrader
			Client	Volkswagen Golf GTI

Illustration & Graphics

Agency	McCann Erickson, London
Creative Directors	Brian Fraser
	Simon Learman
Copywriters	Neil Clarke
	Jay Phillips
Art Directors	Neil Clarke
	Jay Phillips
Illustrator	John Martin
Typographer	Gary Todd
Client	Heinz Salad Cream

Agency	BeetRoot, Thessaloniki	The walls of this upmarket hotel were
Creative Directors	Yiannis Haralambopoulos	enlivened with graphics depicting scenes
	Alexis Nikou	from Aesop's Fables. In these famous
	Vagelis Liakos	stories, the actions of animal characters
Illustrators	Alexis Nikou	illustrate a moral truth. Each room depicts
	Ilias Pantikakis	a different story.
Client	Ekies Hotel & Resort	

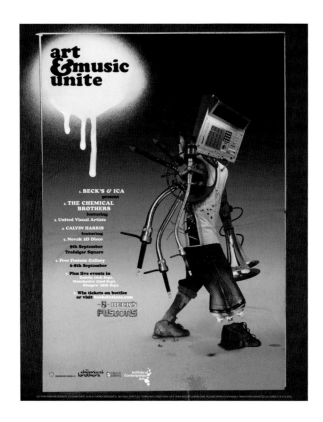

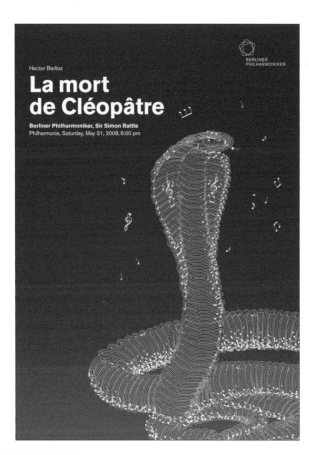

342   **Illustration & Graphics**

Agency	Leo Burnett, London	Agency	Scholz & Friends, Berlin
Executive CD	Jim Thornton	Creative Director	Michael Winterhagen
Creative Director	Dave Beverley	Copywriter	Nils Busche
Copywriters	Nick Pringle	Art Director	Philipp Weber
	Clark Edwards	Illustrators	Philipp Weber, Tina Kron
Art Directors	Nick Pringle	Graphic	Friederike Hamann
	Clark Edwards	Client	Berliner Philharmoniker
Illustrator	Village Green		
Typographer	Lance Crozier		
Client	Becks Fusions		

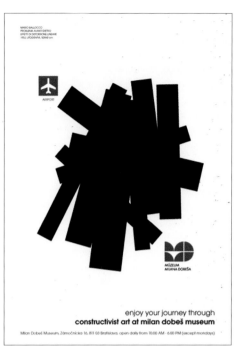

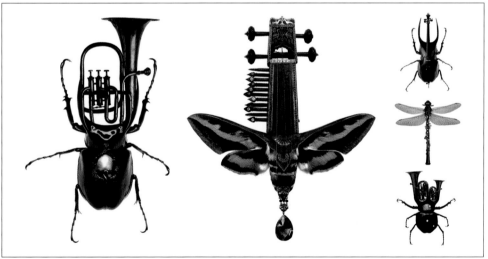

Agency	Vaculik Advertising, Bratislava	Agency	Scandinavian DesignLab,
Creative Directors	Juraj Vaculik		Copenhagen
	Milan Hladky	Creative Director	Per Madsen
Copywriter	Zuzana Hasanova	Art Directors	Per Madsen
Art Director	Dejan Galovic		Robert Daniel Nagy
Client	Milan Dobeš Museum	Client	ParisTexas Fashion Store

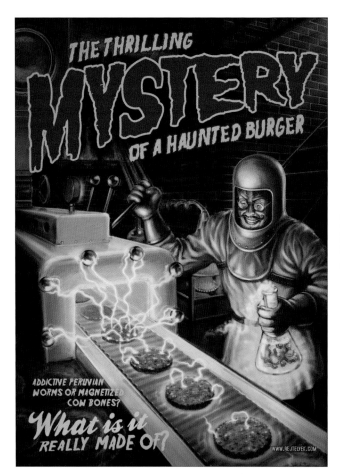

Agency	DDB Budapest	Agency	Hundra Advertising Agency, Gothenburg
Creative Director	Milos Ilic	Copywriters	Johan Brink
Copywriter	László Hevesi		Andrea Tureson
Art Director	Rodrigo Fernandes	Art Director	Torbjörn Briggert
Illustrator	6B Estudio	Illustrator	Torbjörn Briggert
Client	McDonald's	Client	Kultur & Näringsliv,
			Chatwalk Lectures

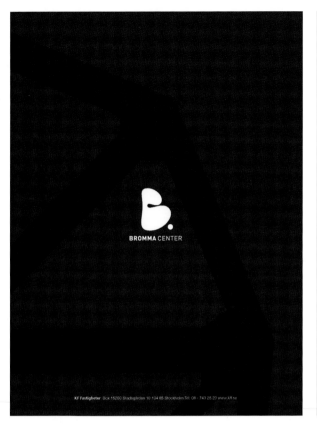

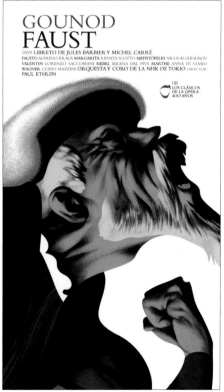

Agency	Identityworks, Stockholm	**Agency**	Silva! Designers, Lisbon
Creative Director	Helena Stendahl Hägg	**Art Directors**	Jorge Silva
Art Directors	Adam Dahlstedt		Sílvia Pacheco
	Robert Gardfors	**Illustrators**	Alain Corbel
Client	Bromma Center		Alex Gozblau
			André Carrilho
			Miguel Rocha
		Client	Classics of the Opera, Book & CD Collection

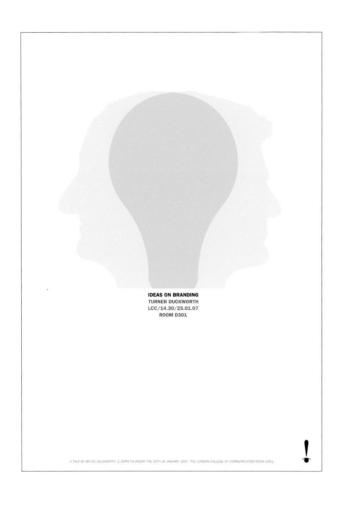

346 **Illustration & Graphics**

Agency	Turner Duckworth,	Agency	MAB, Berlin
	London & San Francisco	Creative Directors	Nils Haseborg
Creative Directors	David Turner		Sven Sorgatz
	Bruce Duckworth		Christian Jakimowitsch
Art Director	Sam Lachlan	Copywriter	Ilja Schmuschkowitsch
Artworker	Reuben James	Art Director	Michael Janke
Client	London College of Comunication	Illustrators	Alexander Tibelius
			Jutta Kuss
		Client	BMW

Agency	Kaffeine Communications, Kiev	Agency	BeetRoot, Thessaloniki
Creative Director	Jovan Rocanov	**Creative Directors**	Yiannis Haralambopoulos
Art Director	Jovan Rocanov		Alexis Nikou
Designer	Anna Timkov		Vagelis Liakos
Client	Consumer Society &	**Art Director**	Ilias Pantikakis
	Citizen Networks Logo	**Illustrator**	Ilias Pantikakis
		Client	Zen Mascaro Fashions

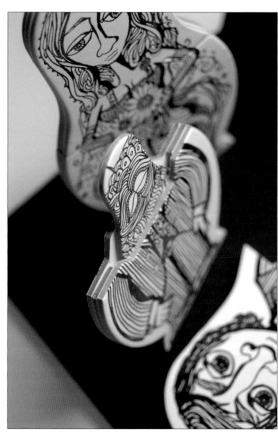

348   **Illustration & Graphics**

Agency	Bittersuite, Cape Town		**Agency**	BeetRoot, Thessaloniki
Creative Director	Andrew Hofmeyr		**Creative Director**	Alexis Nikou
Copywriter	Marcelle Lang		**Illustrator**	Alexis Nikou
Art Director	Michel Brink		**Client**	Wedding Invitation
Illustrators	Toby Newsome			
	Heath Nash			
	Saskia de Jong			
	Michel Brink			
Client	Bittersuite Corporate Identity			

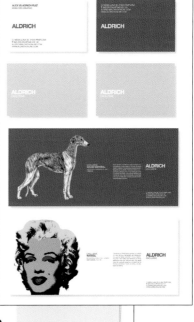

Agency	Euro RSCG Group Switzerland, Zurich	Agency	Comunicacion Aldrich, Pamplona
Executive CD	Frank Bodin	Creative Director	Alex Viladrich
Creative Directors	Dominik Oberwiler	Art Director	Andoni Egúzkiza
	Juerg Aemmer	Client	Aldrich Brand Identity
	Petra Bottignole		
Illustrator	Rahel Boesinger		
Client	Team Tibet		

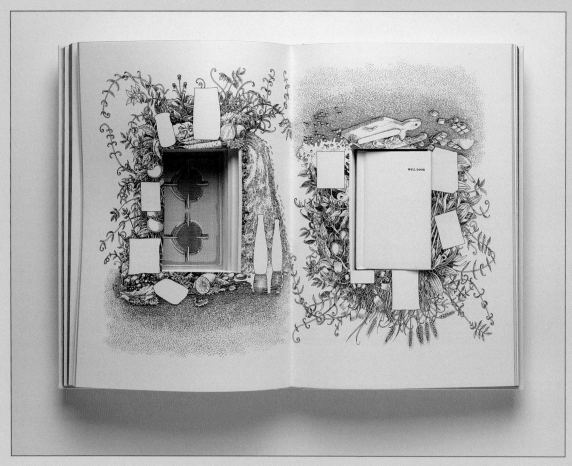

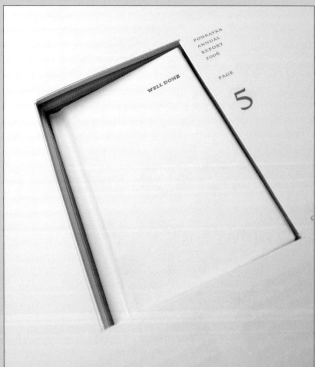

Agency	Bruketa & Zinic, Zagreb	This unusual annual report for a food
Creative Directors	Davor Bruketa	company came complete with a small
	Nikola Zinic	booklet titled "Well done". Recipients were
Copywriters	Teo Tarabaric	instructed to wrap this in foil and bake it!
	Lana Cavar	After 25 minutes at 100°C, illustrations
Art Directors	Imelda Ramovic	of empty plates were magically filled with
	Mirel Hadzijusufovic	food, and empty pages were filled with
Photographer	Nikola Wolf	recipes, advice and stories about food. It's
Illustrator	Tomislav Tomic	the world's first cookable annual report..
Client	Podravka Annual Report	
	"Well Done"	

Agency	Atelier 004, Lisbon	Egoista contains regular contributions from leading Portuguese and international photographers, journalists, artists and authors.	
Editor	Patricia Reis		
Design	Henrique Cayatte		
	Filipa Gregorio		
	Rita Salgueiro		
	Rodrigo Saias		
Producers	Francisco Ponciano		
	Claudio Garrudo		
Client	Egoista Magazine		

Agency	Kolle Rebbe Werbeagentur (KOREFE), Hamburg	Polyplaypylene was an unusual gift to Lego's partners and the press to mark the brand's 50th anniversary in Germany.
Creative Director	Katrin Oeding	
Copywriter	Alexander Baron	
Art Director	Reginald Wagner	
Photographer	Reginald Wagner	
Typographer	Reginald Wagner	
Client	Lego	

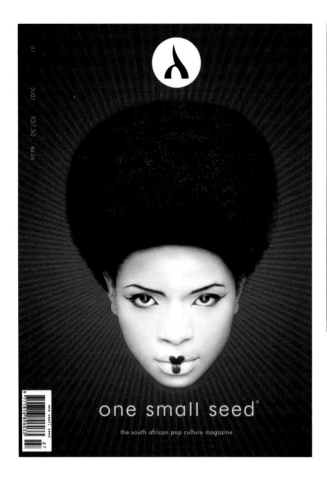

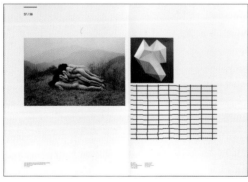

Agency	Designed04, Cape Town	One Small Seed is the definitive South African pop culture magazine. It encompasses the essence of cosmopolitan lifestyle through stylish design and features. Spreads on local bands, DJs and even graphic designers are given a treatment that launches what could be rather conventional words and pictures into a different sphere.
Editor-in-Chief	Giuseppe Russo	
Sub-Editor	Amelia Burgertor	
Graphic Designer	Tracey-Lee Scully	
Client	One Small Seed Magazine	

Agency	Section.D Design. Communication, Vienna	Parabol SE, The Recollection Issue, curated by Philipp Kaiser, is a special edition of the art magazine Parabol to mark the 35th anniversary of the Essl Collection in Austria. Agnes and Karlheinz Essl's love of innovation and interest in unconventional methods of communicating art were the key factors that led to this extraordinary insight into the collection. Philipp Kaiser's very personal view of the collection gave rise to a special exhibition of contemporary art in a two-dimensional space.
Creative Director	Chris Goennawein	
Curator	Philipp Kaiser	
Publisher	Max Haupt-Stummer Katharina Boesch	
Client	Parabol SE Special Edition	

THINK INSIDE THE BOX

tHINK

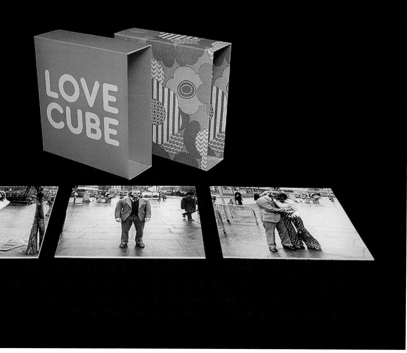

Agency	Dragster Communication, Gothenburg
Creative Director	Martin Johansson
Copywriter	Maria Melkersson
Art Directors	Caspar Ekwall
	Christoffer Persson
Photographer	Jonatan Fernström
Client	Cramo

Cramo rents out movable, flexible modular units with the same standards as permanent premises. The most typical uses are for temporary office space and educational facilities. Aimed at architects, "Think Inside the Box" shows the wide range of possibilities offered by modular space.

Agency	SWE Advertising, Stockholm
Creative Director	Björn Schumacher
Copywriter	Johan Skogh
Art Director	Greger Ulf Nilson
Photographer	Martin Parr
Client	Love Cube

In 1972, Martin Parr studied photography at Manchester Polytechnic. With one year to go, he created Love Cube on the streets of Manchester. Nine men, nine women, nine couples. After 35 years, it has finally been published in its original format, as a board game.

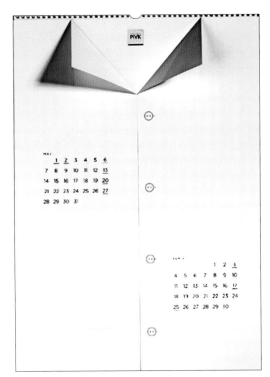

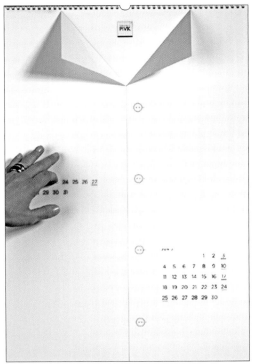

Agency	Futura DDB, Ljubljana	This calendar for a dry cleaning service is as simple and elegant as your favourite white shirt. A sheet of paper symbolizes a shirt, and the dates on it can be scratched out with every day that passes.
Creative Director	Žare Kerin	
Art Director	Andraž Filač	
Client	Pivk Dry Cleaner	

Agency	GRP, Glasgow	Mimicking the 1950s-style "Ladybird" books that helped many British kids learn to read, these "Be Books" are designed to teach Scottish teens a thing or two about real life. Covering problems like underage drinking and sex, they use humour and irony to provoke debate around sensitive subjects.
Creative Directors	Martin Cross	
	Iain Finlay	
Copywriter	Martin Cross	
Art Director	Mark Williams	
Illustrator	Alan McGowan	
Client	National Health Service, Glasgow, "Be Books"	

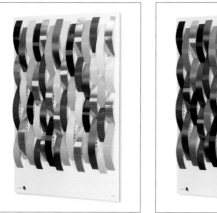

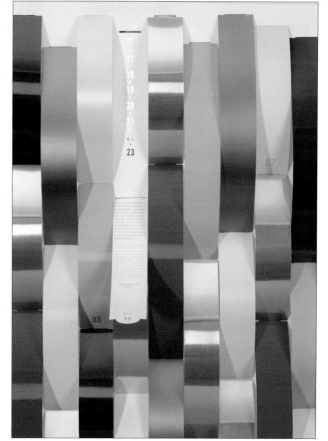

Agency	Heimat, Berlin	Entitled "Every Second Counts", this
Creative Directors	Myles Lord	brochure highlights recent international
	Alexander Weber-Gruen	events that were covered live on CNN
Copywriter	Nikolai Diepenbrock	as the news broke.
Art Director	Matthias Walter	
Client	CNN	

Agency	Zinnobergruen, Düsseldorf	A three-dimensional wall sculpture created exclusively from the Chromolux paper range.
Creative Directors	Bärbel Muhlack	Each page of the 2008 calendar is a single
	Tobias Schwarzer	strip of paper. At the end of the week, the
Client	Chromolux	paper strip is folded back into its original

position and the next week opened. This turns the calendar into an ever-changing object. Congratulatory messages are printed on the reverse sides of the 53 Chromolux strips to mark the 50th anniversary of the brand. The calendar is accompanied by a CD composed by Thomas Taxus Beck, who took its colours as his inspiration.

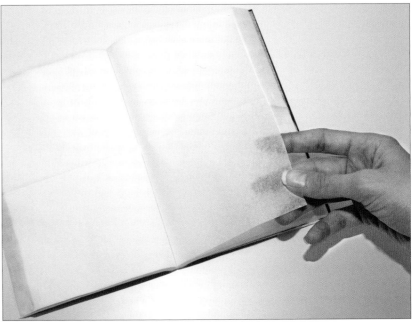

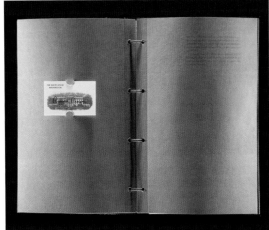

Agency	TBWA\Raad, Dubai
Creative Director	Milos Ilic
Copywriters	Bassam Doss
	Sandeep Fernandes
Art Director	Sakib Afridi
Photographer	Fouad Abdel Malak
Client	Trillion for Lebanon

Trillion for Lebanon is a non-profit organization set up to support rebuilding efforts by eventually raising a trillion Lebanese pounds (about US$ 700 million). The charity needed a mailer to invite wealthy individuals to a fundraising dinner. To avoid using pictures of injured children, a tourist guidebook called Treasures of Lebanon was mailed. The reader expected to see beautiful pictures of Lebanon inside. Instead, the pages were made of tissue paper. After 34 days of relentless bombing in 2006, the tears of the victims were all that remain.

Agency	Garbergs Reklambyrå,
	Stockholm
Copywriter	David Orlic
Art Director	Johan Wilde
Photographer	Martin Runeborg
Client	Södra

Södra manufactures paper pulp; it already has a substantial customer base, so this publication is primarily designed to maintain a dialogue with existing clients on the subject of their end-product, paper and its various uses. The theme of this mailing is business cards. In Water Valley, Mississippi, Södra located the world's finest collection of business cards; the Jack Gurner collection. The mailing reproduces a selection of cards from Gurner's collection, with anecdotes, tips on etiquette and the dos and don'ts of good business card design.

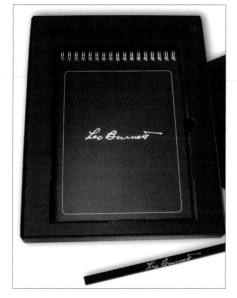

Agency	Bilić_Muller, Zagreb	This catalogue was created for Danijel Srdarev, a young Croatian artist, to promote his exhibition, "Theatre of Drawings". The content is purely visual, the textual component is relegated to the end of the catalogue on translucent paper that also serves as a jacket.
Creative Directors	Dora Bilić	
	Tina Müller	
Client	Danijel Srdarev	
	"Theatre of Drawings"	

Agency	Leo Burnett Frankfurt	At an advertising agency, even the best ideas begin with a blank piece of paper and a pencil. So rather than making a normal brochure, Leo Burnett created an ordinary spiral-bound notebook with its logo on the cover. Inside, facts about the agency were scrawled in pencil and crayon. Award-winning ads and ideas were either pasted on as photos or secured by paper clips. The brochure cuts out slick design and focuses on what matters: ideas.
Creative Director	Andreas Pauli	
Copywriter	Nicola Wassner	
Art Director	Matthias Fickinger	
Illustrator	Philipp Haffner	
Client	Leo Burnett Frankfurt,	
	"Idea Notepad"	

Agency	Depot WPF Brand & Identity, Moscow	The packaging in the form of a voyager's trunk evokes an independent, courageous woman from the Golden Age of Travel. The outer box is made from exclusive paper with tactile golden fibres. Inside are four compartments reflecting four different cultures: Byzantine, Egyptian, Arabic and Greek.
Creative Director	Alexey Fadeyev	
Art Director	Vadim Bryksin	
Illustrator	Vadim Bryksin	
Client	Comilfo Chocolates	

Agency	Pemberton & Whiteford, London	Packaging for an extensive range of cooking ingredients incorporated a recipe card on each pack, with suggestions of how the product might be used.	
Creative Directors	Simon Pemberton Adrian Whiteford		
Client	Tesco Cooking Ingredients		

Agency	Stockholm Design Lab, Stockholm	Mail order service Askul is one of Japan's fastest growing companies. It offers more than 18,000 items, with nationwide delivery within 24 hours. Stockholm Design Lab was behind a comprehensive design solution embracing corporate identity, product development and packaging.	
Creative Director	Björn Kusoffsky		
Art Director	Sharon Hwang		
Designers	Fredrik Neppelberg Per Carlsson		
Client	Askul		

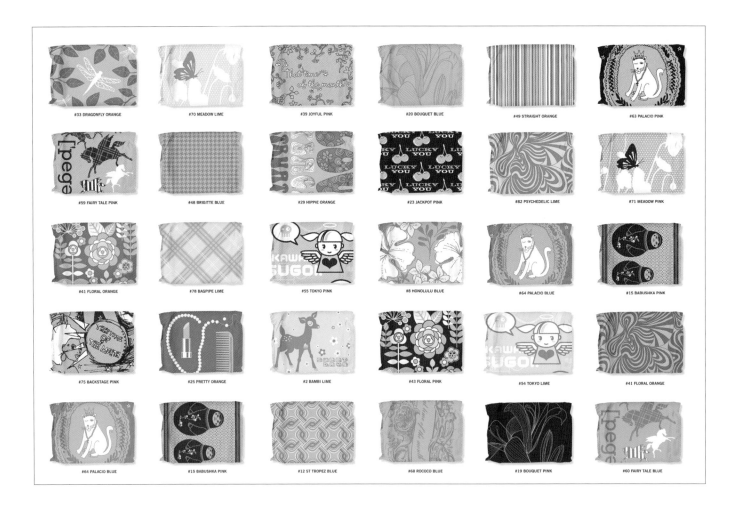

#33 DRAGONFLY ORANGE	#70 MEADOW LIME	#39 JOYFUL PINK	#20 BOUQUET BLUE	#49 STRAIGHT ORANGE	#63 PALACIO PINK
#59 FAIRY TALE PINK	#48 BRIGITTE BLUE	#29 HIPPIE ORANGE	#23 JACKPOT PINK	#82 PSYCHEDELIC LIME	#71 MEADOW PINK
#41 FLORAL ORANGE	#78 BAGPIPE LIME	#55 TOKYO PINK	#8 HONOLULU BLUE	#64 PALACIO BLUE	#15 BABUSHKA PINK
#75 BACKSTAGE PINK	#25 PRETTY ORANGE	#2 BAMBI LIME	#43 FLORAL PINK	#54 TOKYO LIME	#41 FLORAL ORANGE
#64 PALACIO BLUE	#15 BABUSHKA PINK	#12 ST TROPEZ BLUE	#68 ROCOCO BLUE	#19 BOUQUET PINK	#60 FAIRY TALE BLUE

360   **Packaging Design**

Agency	Trigger Momentum, Gothenburg	The idea behind these designs was that sanitary protection should be something that women should want to keep in their handbags. Wraps around the sanitary towels became a medium for 84 different designs.
Creative Director	Markus Naslund	
Copywriter	Markus Naslund	
Art Director	Linda Pabst	
Client	Libresse	

Agency	Blidholm Vagnemark Design, Stockholm	Blidholm Vagnemark Design has designed the packaging for a special edition of Blossa Glögg (Swedish mulled wine) for five years running. Every Christmas brings a new taste, a new bottle and a new typographic solution. The 2007 design is dark brown with a copper-coloured 07. The colours represent flavours: brown for cinnamon and copper for sea buckthorn. Sea buckthorn is an energy-rich berry that grows along the Scandinavian coastline. It's also called "the passion fruit of the north".
Creative Director	Catrin Vagnemark	
Art Director	Susanna Nygren Barrett	
Client	Blossa Glögg	

Agency	Turner Duckworth, London & San Francisco	A simple typographic design plays with the E in "honey" to create the stripy body of a bee while also resembling a traditional wooden twizzler stick.
Creative Directors	David Turner Bruce Duckworth	
Art Director	Christian Eager	
Illustrator	John Geary	
Artworker	Reuben James	
Client	Waitrose Honey	

Agency	Pemberton & Whitefoord, London	Loseley makes quintessentially British ice cream. Now it's under new ownership and the brief was to express the brand's values without seeming too pompous. The solution was to commission five subtly humorous portraits, each by a different artist. The pack copy expands the theme as the characters sing the praises of their chosen flavour in an eccentric manner.
Creative Directors	Simon Pemberton Adrian Whitefoord	
Client	Loseley Ice Cream	

Agency	Kolle Rebbe, Hamburg	The task was to persuade Munich's number one luxury food retailer, Dallmayer, to stock liqueurs from the basic-sounding Anthony's Garage Winery. The designers came up with the Anthony's Super range. In keeping with their "garage" origin, the liqueurs come in handy schnapps canisters. The packaging concept included designing and naming Anthony's Super P (plum liqueur), Super C (cherry schnapps) and Super W (Williams Christ peach liqueur).
Creative Director	Katrin Oeding	
Copywriters	Sabine Manecke	
	Alexander Baron	
Art Directors	Reginald Wagner	
	Banjamin Pabst	
Graphics	Sonja Kliem	
Client	Anthony's Mini Garage	
	Winery, Super Schnapps	

Agency	AGH & Friends, 's-Hertogenbosch	This is not a house wine, but a "no house" wine. The proceeds from sales of the wine go to The Dutch Homeplan foundation, a charity providing housing for AIDS orphans in South Africa.
Creative Director	Patrick van der Heijden	
Copywriter	Jeroen Tebbe	
Art Directors	Patrick van der Heijden	
	Edwin Vollebergh	
	Studio Boot	
Client	No House Wine	

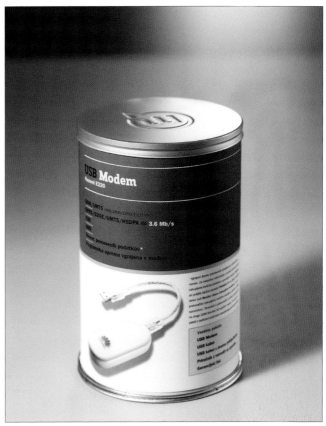

Agencies	Publicis, Ljubljana, Ajax Studio, Ljubljana	Mobile operator Mobitel launched a mobile internet service that was highly affordable and very easy to install and use. To communicate this, the packaging design recalls instant food products.
Creative Director	Gal Erbežnik	
Copywriter	Miha Bevc	
Art Director	Gsus Ajax	
Client	Mobitel Instant Internet	

Agency	Pemberton & Whiteford, London	Liberation is a new fair trade company selling snack nuts. It is part-owned by the farm workers themselves, who share in the profits. The logo substitutes the "i" in "Liberation" for an exclamation mark. The brand spokesmen are nut characters waving banners to get their message across. The bright colours against a black background create maximum shelf standout.
Creative Directors	Simon Pemberton Adrian Whiteford	
Client	Liberation Nuts	

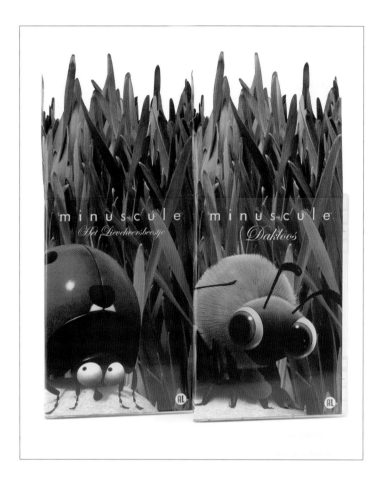

Agency	McCann Advertising, Amstelveen	The TV series Minuscule explores the tiny world of insects. Their natural habitat is evoked by grass sticking out of the packaging, which grabs attention on the cluttered shelves of DVD stores.
Creative Director	Martijn van Sonsbeek	
Copywriter	Niels van Lith	
Art Director	Roel Verhoeven	
Client	Miniscule DVD	

Agency	Tank/Y&R, Stockholm	The design of this wine box means that the viewer always sees a panoramic landscape, no matter how it is placed on the shelf. This provides an obvious competitive advantage in a retail environment.
Creative Director	Hans Ahlgren	
Art Director	Hans Ahlgren	
Final Art	Ulrika Ekman	
Client	Vino Rosso	

Agency	Taxi Studio, Bristol	The Knobbly-Carrot Organic Food
Creative Director	Spencer Buck	Company was an award-winning
Art Director	Ryan Wills	organic soup manufacturer with two
Illustrator	Stuart Williams	major problems: declining sales and the
Designer	Spencer Buck	assumption that carrots were present
Client	Knobbly-Carrot Soups	in all its products. The challenge was to

The Knobbly-Carrot Organic Food Company was an award-winning organic soup manufacturer with two major problems: declining sales and the assumption that carrots were present in all its products. The challenge was to radically re-design the packaging while keeping the name intact. The solution: meet the Knobbly-Carrot family, Masters of Organic Foods.

Agency	Turner Duckworth,
	London & San Francisco
Creative Directors	David Turner
	Bruce Duckworth
Art Directors	David Turner
	Shawn Rosenberger
	Chris Garvey
	Brittany Hull
	Rachel Shaw
Illustrator	John Geary
Client	Fat Bastard Wine

The name of this wine refers to the wine maker's description of its flavour. The label was re-designed to communicate the high quality of the wine while celebrating its whimsical personality. A hippo had been a symbol for the brand since its inception. The designers brought him to life by re-drawing him and sitting him on the label. Every detail was carefully considered, even down to the wording of the product descriptions.

← BACK TO STREAM   11:30 Posted by Heidie 1

Dear hotel manager, we are sincerely sorry

Day 1   Day 2   Day 3   Tomorrow ??

Blog: Jan 24   RSS

11:52 Posted by Heidie 1   [0] Comments

TIME FOR OUR OWN FASHION SHOOT!_

What should we wear to become famous?

A) Wigs   33%
B) Orange Jumpsuits   18%
C) Fluffy Animal Suits   50%

11:30 Posted by Heidie 1   [1] Comment

Making a messy backdrop

Here are some pictures of us making a backdrop for the upcoming photoshoot.

10:35 Posted by Heidie 1   [0] Comments

DIESEL HAS RESPONDED. WE ARE NOT GETTING A PHOTOGRAPHER!

We demanded that Diesel should get us a proper fashion photographer. Well, we are not getting one. We'll have to do it our way. Hang in there this is going to be great

10:29 Posted by Heidie 1

I need to work, but I cant go awa

CHOOSE CAMERA   LIVE

This is so good!

Cam: Main

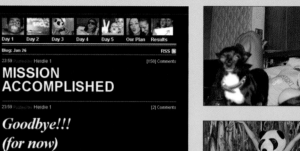

Day 1   Day 2   Day 3   Day 4   Day 5   Our Plan   Results

Blog: Jan 26   RSS

23:59 Posted by Heidie 1   [158] Comments

MISSION ACCOMPLISHED

23:59 Posted by Heidie 1   [2] Comments

Goodbye!!! (for now)

Our final message to you...

23:55 Posted by Heidie 1   [1] Comment

STEFANO ROSSO SHOWED UP!

Stefano Rosso, Son of Diesel founder Renzo Rosso came to collect the underwear collection (and Juan to our disappointment), but we made him get into his underwear before we would give it back.

22:22 Posted by Heidie 1   [0] Comments

Your name with the Heidies

We asked you to post your names so we could pose with them. Are you one of the lucky ones who got a personal picture?

21:28 Posted by Heidie 2   [0] Comments

Renzo, we are waiting for your son!

Our reply to Renzo: ◆Make sure your son is here by midnight. We expect to get an offer we can't refuse. But be ready, we might have a surprise.: Tune in at 24:00◆ :)

CHOOSE CAMERA   Jan 25

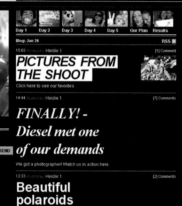

Day 1   Day 2   Day 3   Day 4   Day 5   Our Plan   Results

Blog: Jan 26   RSS

15:03 Posted by Heidie 1   [1] Comment

PICTURES FROM THE SHOOT

Click here to see our favorites.

14:44 Posted by Heidie 1   [7] Comments

FINALLY! - Diesel met one of our demands

We got a photographer! Watch us in action here.

12:33 Posted by Heidie 1   [2] Comments

Beautiful polaroids

A short film with some nice polaroids.

11:52 Posted by Heidie 2   [22] Comments

WILL TODAY BE THE LAST DAY???

We can sense Diesel knocking on the door.

Say something: Your name: SEND

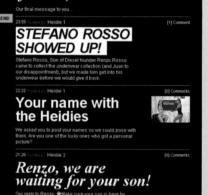

Agency	Farfar, Stockholm
Production	Hobbyfilm
Client	Diesel Underwear, "The Heidies"

Reality TV went online to promote Diesel's new range of lingerie. Six video cameras, 24 hours a day, live for five days on diesel.com. Two gorgeous and crazy girls – who were both named Heidi – "stole" the new Diesel Intimate collection, "kidnapped" the salesman, and then locked themselves (and him) in a hotel room. The results were broadcast to the world – or at least to the millions who logged on to the site. Clad in Diesel underwear from start to finish, the Heidies got their 15 megabytes of fame.

Agency	Valve Branding, Helsinki	UPM specializes in turning forests into paper. Wood is UPM's most important raw material. This natural, renewable and recyclable resource comes from sustainable forests. Over the years UPM has shaped the opinion of thousands of paper buyers and other stakeholders by taking them to Finnish commercial forests. This website does the same job, showing every aspect of modern forestry in a highly realistic way. During the journey, the visitor is shown cut as well as preserved areas and a wealth of detailed information on forest life and fauna.
Creative Director	Jarkko Könönen	
Copywriter	Jarkko Könönen	
Art Director	Jussi Niemi	
Photographers	Pertti Puranen	
	Mete Ufacik	
Illustrators	Simo Santavirta	
	Mika Onnela	
Project Manager	Toni Laturi	
Designers	Simo Santavirta	
	Niko Helle	
	Mika Onnela	
	Pekka Meskanen	
Client	UPM, "Forest Life"	

Websites (Durables)   367

Agency	Tribal DDB, London	The Volkswagen Passat easily competes with premium marques in terms of quality, but without the flashiness that goes with them. Passat drivers are middle-class men in their 40s and 50s. Feeling marginalised by youth culture, they're just the kind of guys who might succumb to a mid-life crisis – and the temptation to buy a flashy car. The site shows how the Passat is the very antithesis of the superficiality that can lead to manifestations of mid-life crisis.
Creative Director	Ben Clapp	
Copywriters	Al Brown	
	Algy Sharman	
	Ben Clapp	
Art Directors	Al Brown	
	Algy Sharman	
	Ben Clapp	
Designers	Paul Robinson	
Client	Volkswagen Passat, "Mid-Life Crisis"	

Agency	DDB Stockholm	A different type of person needs a different type of Golf. This slice of online entertainment introduces the viewer to a number of peculiar characters waiting for an audition. Click on each one and watch them present their favourite Golf – in a highly individual manner.
Creative Director	Johan Holmström	
Copywriter	Magnus Jakobsson	
Art Directors	Fredrik Simonsson	
	Viktor Arve	
	Erik Winn	
Production	Acne Film	
Director	Jakob Marky	
Interactive Director	Markus Forsberg	
Client	Volkswagen Golf, "Golf Auditions"	

Agency	LBi, London
Creative Directors	Jeremy Garner
	Paul Knott
	Tim Vance
Photographers	Mark Johnson
	Paul Knott
Designers	Simon Gill
	Robin Bates
	Andy Garnett
	Rufus Kahler
	Sam Gilbey
	Pero Gouwerok
	Mireia Cortinas
Flash Developers	Joe Rufian
	Liam O'Donnall
	Jim Hall
	David Terranova
Producer	Esther Cunliffe
Motion Director	Motioncult
Technical Director	Simon Gill
Client	PlayStation, "This is Living"

PlayStation3 is a living, evolving games console. Therefore the campaign launch micro site was also a piece of living, evolving entertainment. The website was based on the same characters and hotel featured in the PS3 "Grenade" commercial (see page 136). Visitors could check in to the hotel, explore the guests' rooms and uncover their lifestyles. The experience changed depending on the time of day: no two journeys through the site were the same.

Agency	King, Stockholm
Creative Director	Frank Hollingworth
Production	Magoo
	Web Development, From Stockholm With Love
Client	Åhléns, "Cosy Living Room"

Visitors to the site of department store Åhléns are invited to decorate a virtual room with the store's products to make it as cosy as possible. A resident couple judges the ambience and general "cosiness level". Having won their approval, visitors can share their dream room with others or print a shopping list of the products they've chosen – to make their dream a reality.

Agency	Framfab, Copenhagen
Creative Director	Rasmus Frandsen
Copywriter	Andrew Smart
Art Directors	Eduardo Marques
	Toke Kristensen
Producer	Paul Maingot
Technical Directors	Jesper Arvidson
	Martin Ludvigsen
	Philip Heyde
Video Editor	Rune Milton
Digital Director	Danny Tawiah
Client	Nike T90 Laser, "The Perfect Kick"

Nike's most technically advanced football boot, the T90 Laser, required an ambitious online presentation that would score with media-savvy, football-crazy teens. Deploying a colour palate of aggressive yellow and contrasting black and white, the agency created a unique product experience. Using six digital video cameras shooting at 950 frames per second, the site allowed users to discover the skill that goes into every strike. Product features were displayed in detail.

Agency	Farfar, Stockholm
Client	Nokia N95, "Great Pockets"

Tailors Henry Needle & Sons create an incredible invention, the Great Pockets. These capacious receptacles allow people to carry all their multimedia devices with them. Visitors to the site could interact with Henry Needle and enjoy the surreal and ridiculous nature of his invention before finding their way behind the scenes. There they discovered a better solution to their ergonomic woes: the Nokia N95.

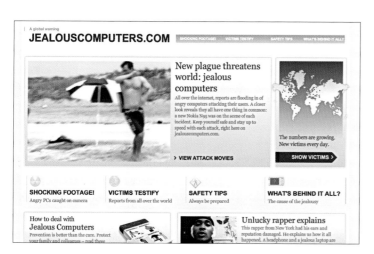

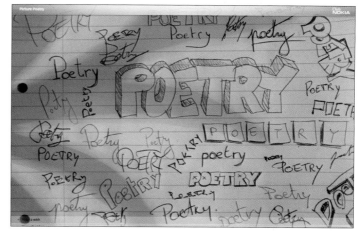

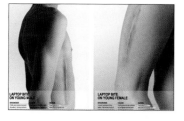   

Agency	These Days, Antwerp
Creative Director	Sam De Volder
Copywriter	Paul Van Oevelen
Art Director	Gerdien Stevense
Illustrator	Bert Beckers
Designers	Valentijn Destoop
	Bert Beckers
	Gilles Deketelaere
Multimedia	Pascal Van Hecke
Project Manager	Liesbeth Stevense
Client	Nokia N95, "Jealous Computers"

The computers strike back! The idea behind this campaign was that the launch of the new Nokia N95 – a mini computer – provoked jealous rage among old-school computers and hardware. Online films showed witnesses describing violent attacks by laptops, along with other absurd yet oddly realistic reports of vengeful hardware.

Agency	These Days, Antwerp
Creative Director	Sam De Volder
Copywriters	Tim Borremans
	Luk Cattrysse
Art Director	Philip Tregunna
Project Manager	Liesbeth Stevense
Designers	Valentijn Destoop
Multimedia	Kris Meeusen
	Raf Vervink
	Nicolas Lierman
Client	Nokia Corporate, "Picture Poetry"

Nokia wanted to offer a digital alternative to Christmas cards. The objective was to bring ordinary people's wishes to life in an unconventional way. As visitors typed in their wish, their words were translated into pictures: each wish generated a photo stream. They could even choose the theme and mood of their wish. The database contained more than 6,430 pictures shot specifically for the project. Almost any given wish could be translated into a visual poem. Visitors lacking ideas were forwarded an inspirational message from a VIP.

370   Websites (Non-Durables)

Agencies	Lowe Brindfors, Stockholm	**Photographer**	John Wallin	Stella Artois beer can trace its roots back to
	Lowe Worldwide	**Graphic Design**	Tim Scheibel	1366 and the Den Hoorn Brewery in the city
Creative Director	Matthew Bull		Noel Pretorius	of Leuven, Belgium. The "Le Courage" site
Copywriters	Mats Brun	**Producer**	Espen Bekkebråten	brings the challenges of the 14th century to
	Håkan Engler	**Motion Design**	Daniel Isaksson	life. It shows how the brave people of Leuven
	Johan Holmström		Linus Niklasson	confronted terrible dangers in order to brew the
Art Directors	Tim Scheibel	**Client**	Stella Artois,	perfect beer. Help the brew master collect the
	Johan Tesch,		"Le Courage"	finest ingredients, while facing horrors unheard
	Rickard Villard			of today: vengeful gods, blazing comets – and
	Kalle dos Santos			the possibility of falling off the edge of the earth.
				A print, billboard and online campaign led
				visitors to the site.

Agency	Saatchi & Saatchi, Frankfurt
Executive CD	Burkhart von Scheven
Creative Directors	Sebastian Schier
	Peter Huschka
	Florian Pagel
Copywriter	William John
Art Directors	Patrick Ackmann
	Christian Bartsch
Programmers	Markus Fischer
	Erik Neugebohrn
	Martin Nawrath
Designers	Martin Anderle
	Chan-Young Ramert
Client	Main Taxi Frankfurt, "The Piss Screen"

The website describes an initiative launched by this Frankfurt taxi firm to reduce accidents related to drink-driving and to generate more business at night. Pressure-sensitive inlays were installed inside the urinals of bars across Frankfurt, with a video screen at eye-level. Using their pee, visitors could take control of a car and steer it through the city streets. The game ended when the guest crashed the car, (or when their pee ran out – whichever happened first). A message then appeared on the screen: "Too pissed to drive? Take a taxi instead".

Agency	Great Works, Stockholm
Creative Director	Ted Persson
Copywriter	Kristoffer Triumf
Art Director	Mathias Päres
Photographer	Stefan Wendin
Illustrator	Kongotec Animations
Production	Perfect Fools
Producers	Jocke Wissing
	Sofie Vestergren
Project Manager	Charlotta Rydholm
Client	Absolut Vodka, "Absolut Disco"

How to transfer the concept of Absolut Disco to the internet? The answer: a webcam and some willing hands. The site was inspired by John Travolta's iconic pose in Saturday Night Fever. Use your hands to "dance" in front of the camera and add disco effects. The webcam senses movement, allowing users to make their hands glow, sparkle or multiply.

Agency	Great Works, Stockholm
Creative Directors	Ted Persson
	Joakim Karlsson
Art Director	Mathias Päres
Production	Proportio, Colony
	JMW Kommunikation
Producer	Mårten Ekenberg
Project Manager	Kaj Bouic
Programmer	Jocke Wissing
Designer	Jimmy Poopuu
Client	Absolut Vodka, "Absolut Design"

At the time of its launch in 1979, the design of the Absolut bottle was groundbreaking. This site takes visitors back in time to the moment the design team was briefed to create the bottle. Sitting at a virtual table with the other designers, the visitor is encouraged to design their own bottle shape and show it to the team. The designers then start to imagine how it might look in the future. An online movie tells the story of the bottle from 1979 to today, with the visitor's design now included in the saga.

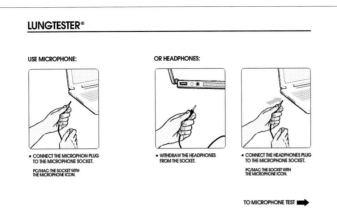

LUNGTESTER®

USE MICROPHONE: **OR HEADPHONES:**

Agency	McCann, Oslo
Copywriters	Daniel Wahlgren
	Jakob Nielsen
Art Directors	Daniel Wahlgren
	Jakob Nielsen
Project Managers	Anniken Schjött
	Marius Zachariasen
	Anne Gro Carlsson
Designers	Jan Cafourek
	Kathrine Helene
	Slapgård
Production	From Stockholm
	With Love
Client	Dent Breath Pastilles,
	"Lungtester"

This operation was "disguised" as an online lung test that gave users a chance to measure their lung capacity. But when people blew into their microphones, the exercise was interrupted by a message from Dent fresh breath pastilles, warning them of their foul breath.

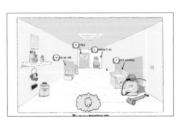

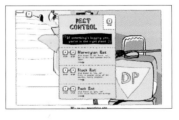

372 **Websites (Non-Durables)**

Agency	Scholz & Friends, Stockholm
Creative Directors	Zeke Tastas
	Leo Dahlin
Art Directors	Fredrik Wallgren
	Erik Olsson
Illustrators	Mikael Eriksson
Designers	Daniel Domermark
	Johan Lindqvist
	Morgan Kane
Client	Castillo de Gredos Wine

Welcome to Castillo de Gredos, a village that is a mixture of all the things that make Spain great. The sun, the fiesta and the "olé!" attitude attract millions of tourists every year. On the site, visitors meet Conde Francisco de Gredos, a man who is really making an effort to promote his village. For instance, there's the village party with its special attractions – including Castillo de Gredos wine.

Agency	Vitruvio Leo Burnett. Madrid
Creative Director	Rafa Antón
Copywriter	Francisco Cassis
Client	DPSL Pest Control, "Mouseless Site"

This "mouseless" site for a pest control company forces visitors to use their keyboard to navigate to the different features. Those who try and click on a button with their mouse find that the arrow is trapped in a mousetrap. No mice allowed here!

Agency	Pilot 1/0, Hamburg
Creative Director	Damian Rodgett
Designers	Jörg Pasternak
	Daniela Algieri
	Robert Stoklossa
Programmers	Steffen Konczak
	Chris Roehing
	Jens Hinrichs
	Stefan Grüllenbeck
Client	Wicked,
	"The Magical Land
	of Oz"

Wicked is a hit Broadway musical – based on the life of the wicked witch from The Wizard of Oz – that was relatively unknown outside the United States and the United Kingdom. A multimedia presentation on the web introduced the show to Germans. Wickedwelt.de featured numerous elements from the musical. It included a trailer and clips, the ability to upload pictures and some wickedly fun games.

Agencies	In2media, Copenhagen
	&Co., Copenhagen
Art Director	Pelle Martin
Designer	Pelle Martin
Flash	Kim Lynge
Client	Café Noir

Welcome to the virtual Café Noir hotel, where anything can happen and where the laws of physics don't apply. The site expresses the many different facets of the Café Noir universe, executed in the same sinister style as the brand's TV campaign (see page 50).

Agency	BETC Euro RSCG,
	Paris
Creative Directors	Christophe Clapier
	Vincent Malone
Copywriters	Benjamin Le Breton
	Arnaud Assouline
Art Director	Christophe Clapier
Client	Canal+, "Vote More"

This website was active during the run-up to the French presidential election. Canal+ used puppets from its satirical news show to encourage a disinterested French public to vote. The puppet version of a famous news presenter asks voters a number of impertinent questions in order to determine the most suitable candidate for them. The result is usually a bizarre hybrid of all the candidates. The user can then embark on an election campaign by picking an election poster and sending it to friends.

Agency: Farfar, Stockholm
Client   Nokia N800, "The Internet Walk"

The Nokia N800 Internet Tablet allows you to take the internet to new places. What better way of expressing that notion than by putting visitors in the shoes of a person using the machine? Visitors found themselves staring at the hands and feet of a virtual person. They could steer this character around town and through the countryside for various adventures, occasionally clicking on the Nokia tablet to seek internet advice.

Agency	Scholz & Volkmer, Wiesbaden
Creative Director	Heike Brockmann
Copywriter	Tim Sobczak
Art Director	Tobias Kreutzer
Project Manager	Pia Tannenberger
Designer	Christoph Noe
Technical Direction	Peter Reichard
Programmers	Kerem Gülensoy
	Timm Kreuder
	Wolf Rauch
	Florian Hermann
	Manfred Kraft
Client	Nastuh Visual Effects, "Nastuh Abootalebi"

This is a website for visual effects artist Nastuh Abootalebi, presenting his portfolio in an unusual way. Users can move their mouse over a film clip that was processed by Nastuh to find out what it looked like before he added his visual magic.

Agency	Dubois Meets Fugger, Antwerp
Creative Director	Peter Foubert
Copywriter	Ben Van Asbroeck
Art Director	Caroline Vermaerken
Illustrators	Eugene and Louise
Design	Studio Plum
Client	Dubois Meets Fugger, "Benny the Brave"

The animated website introduces the offbeat world of advertising agency Dubois Meets Fugger. Join your guide Benny the Brave as he travels around the agency's universe. Benny and 27 guests accompany you on an unpredictable journey that leads to hidden secrets, downloadable desktop wallpapers, a screensaver and a set of Benny the Brave icons.

Agency	Garbergs Reklambyrå, Stockholm
Copywriters	Henning Wijkmark
	Stefan Pagréus
Art Directors	Sebastian Smedberg
	Malin von Werder
Design	B-Reel
Web Director	Bjarne Melin
Producer	Anna Adamson
Client	Telenor One, "The Definitive End to Office Phones"

With its corporate cell phone service, Telenor wants to rid the world of office phones. The site gives users a chance to destroy office phones by playing an online game, while introducing them to Telenor and its services. Find out how you can combine a T-Rex, a candle, a banana skin and a couple of sticks of dynamite to get rid of your office phone.

Agencies	In2media Copenhagen
	&Co., Copenhagen
Art Director	Pelle Martin
Photographer	Pelle Martin
Design	Pelle Martin
Flash Design	Felix Nielsen
Client	&Co.

The challenge was to create a website for the Danish advertising agency, & Co. that would give the user the impression of a highly creative agency that delivered anything but common solutions. To do this it created a dynamic Flash website with emphasis on the agency's work, which covers both print and film. The site's background is a series of surreal video sequences.

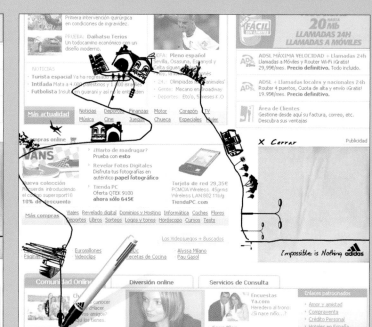
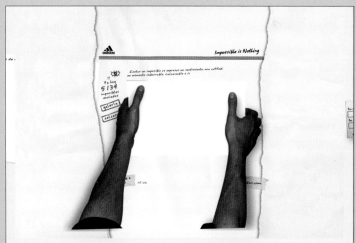

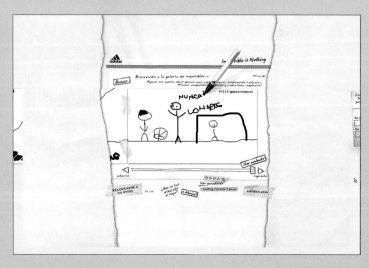
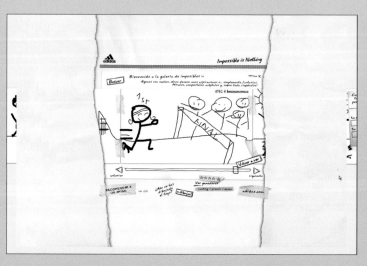

Agency	Netthink, Madrid
Creative Director	Mario Sánchez del Real
Copywriter	Jesús Henares
Art Director	Mario Sánchez del Real
Flash Designer	Iván Gajate
Client	Adidas, "Impossible is Nothing"

A viral teaser film shows the "Impossible is Nothing" team drawing a huge mural that expresses their dreams, wishes and challenges. By clicking on an icon of a felt tip pen, users then activate a micro-site. Here they are confronted by a blank sheet of digital paper. They are invited to draw their own "impossible wish". They submit it with a click, where it will join the dreams of other users to form an online collection of wishes and ambitions.

Agency	Ogilvy, Frankfurt
Creative Directors	Christian Mommertz
	Dr. Stephan Vogel
Copywriter	Dr. Stephan Vogel
Art Director	Christian Mommertz
Photographer	Jo Bacherl
Sound Design	Toni Maniscalco
Motion Graphics	Dirk Neugebauer
Creative Consultants	Dr. Ulf Schmidt
	Uwe Jakob
Client	Malteser
	Ambulance Service,
	"Malteser Typo
	Crash Banner"

Many road accidents are caused by teenage drivers under the influence of alcohol. To evoke public awareness, cut down on drink-driving and direct users to a website about the issue, the agency developed this banner. In the typographic language of popular alcoholic drinks, scrambled letters spin like a slot-machine to confront young people with the physical risks of drinking and driving. The banner was placed on sites for nightclubs, bars and music events.

Agency	Elephant Seven,
	Hamburg
Creative Directors	Oliver Viets
	Daniel Richau
Copywriter	Benjamin Bruno
Art Directors	Kai Becker
	Till Hinrichs
	Oliver Baus
Project Manager	Matthias Krause
	Jost Thedens
Designers	Mirko Gluschke
	Christian Koop
Client	Mercedes-Benz

Using some extraordinary ideas rather than relying on text, these viral emails promoting the Mercedes Benz Off-Road website hooked the recipients. Once they'd entered the site, users saw a Mercedes Benz in rugged terrain. By clicking various points on the screen, they could read about off-road tours and see short videos of impressive off-road action.

Agency	Elephant Seven,
	Hamburg
Creative Directors	Dirk Ollmann
	Daniel Richau
Copywriters	Samir Hamami
	Stefan Roest
Art Director	Oliver Baus
Project Manager	Jost Thedens
Designers	Mirko Gluschke
Flash Designer	Arne Otto
Client	Jeep Grand Cherokee,
	"Bernhard" &
	"Ritsch-Ratsch"

Jeep claims the Grand Cherokee is the original SUV – and that it still has the most traction power. The banners demonstrate in a fun way that the Cherokee is virtually unstoppable. In the first version, users can move a pneumatic drill around with their mouse and use it to drill chunks out of the banner. The Grand Cherokee then effortlessly negotiates the potholes. In the second execution, users can tear off a strip of the banner as if it's a piece of paper. The Cherokee then drives effortlessly along the rough edge.

Agency	Netthink, Madrid
Creative Director	Mario Sánchez del Real
Copywriter	Jesús Henares
Art Director	Mario Sánchez del Real
Flash Designer	Iván Gajate
Client	Mini, "Incredibly Mini"

After clicking on the banner, users can use their mouse to drive a highly responsive Mini through a cornfield. The images inter-cut with scenes from the TV ad, giving you the impression you're controlling the characters and their car. Once your Mini has exited the cornfield, the door opens and a pile of popcorn spills out. It's lot of fun – and very Mini.

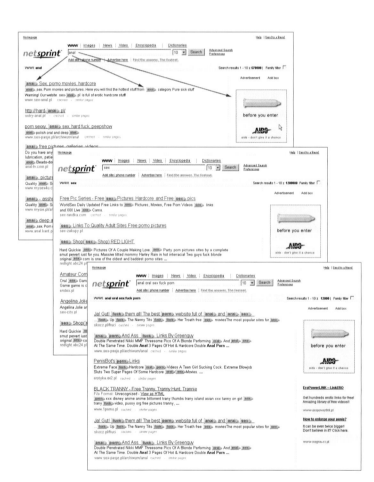

378   Online Ads

Agency	Arc Worldwide Polska, Warsaw
Creative Director	Rafal Gorski
Copywriter	Rafal Gorski
Art Director	Rafal Gorski
Designers	Adam Smereczynski Konrad Grzegorzewicz
Client	Krajowe Centrum Anti-AIDS, "Before You Enter" (Wear Condoms)

This AIDS awareness campaign was developed in association with the Polish Centre against AIDS and the search engine NetSprint.pl. The campaign "protected" erotic sites: when a user searched for terms such as "sex", "anal" or "porn", the words on the results page were wrapped in small condoms. A banner then appeared next to the results, showing a condom, a logo of the Centre Against AIDS and the punning headline "Before you enter".

Agency	Jung von Matt, Stuttgart
Creative Directors	Michael Zoelch Holger Oehrlich
Copywriter	Matthias Kubitz
Programmers	Oliver Mueller Stefanie Hezinger
Client	Kabel Deutschland - RedX Club, "Kama Sutra"

RedX Club is a 24-hour adult movie channel showing hardcore flicks on demand. The goal was to develop an interactive banner, advertising RedX Club's "Kama Sutra" show, without being too explicit. The agency created a highly flexible banner that users could play with, offering an endless number of positions.

Agency Farfar, Stockholm
Client SJ Prio,
"Labyrinth" & "Pinball"

With the new bonus system introduced by Swedish state railways (SJ) users earn points each time they travel. These online ads demonstrated the idea of gaining points when you travel by depicting the journey as a game. Users could negotiate a labyrinth or play pinball using the mouse.

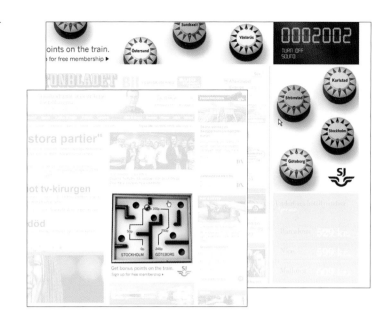

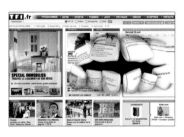

Agency DDB Paris
Creative Directors Alexandre Hervé
Sylvain Thirache
Copywriter Julien Kosowski
Art Director Stéphane Soussan
Client AGF insurance,
"Ball", "Golf",
"Flame", "Engine" &
"Dental"

These ads manipulate various websites to demonstrate different types of insurance. For example, on a sports-related site a soccer player runs across the screen and kicks a ball through a window. On another, flames appear to incinerate a page. Property, fire, car and even dental insurance are all depicted in imaginative ways.

Agency DDB Paris
Creative Directors Alexandre Hervé
Sylvain Thirache
Copywriter Julien Kosowski
Art Director Stéphane Soussan
Client Club Internet,
"The Duel"

This ad promotes an online movie service. In what appears to be a movie trailer, we see two 19th century swordsmen in the middle of a duel. But suddenly they leave the small frame of the trailer and begin rampaging all over the web page. They exchange their swords for increasingly modern weaponry: machine-guns, bazookas, and finally a laser device. The slogan says: "Be ahead of your time, with Club Internet."

Agency	Saatchi & Saatchi Interactive, Frankfurt	This ad uses Google Map technology to promote the destinations served by Emirates Airline. With a click of the mouse, the little plane on the screen can be flown to 90 different locations. By "flying" over the destination concerned, users can experience it in advance. Emirates: keep discovering.
Creative Directors	Sebastian Schier Peter Huschka	
Copywriter	Peter Huschka	
Art Director	Martin Anderle	
Project Managers	Ines Horn Stefanie Wildner	
Designers	Martin Anderle	
Client	Emirates Airline, "Keep Discovering"	

Agency	Scholz & Friends, Berlin	To increase awareness and brand likeability for refuse collection vehicles built by Mercedes-Benz, the agency designed a small computer application. Every time the user empties the recycle bin on his computer desktop, a Mercedes-Benz refuse truck trundles onto the screen and empties the trash.
Creative Directors	Constantin Kaloff Julia Schmidt	
Copywriter	Felix John	
Art Director	Maja Mack	
Programmer	Elmar Braun	
Client	Mercedes-Benz Refuse Collection Vehicles, "Desktop Refuse Collection"	

Agency	Jung von Matt, Stockholm	All Gore-Tex products are inspired by animals. For instance, these gloves were inspired by the gecko's feet, which seem capable of gripping even the smoothest surface. The ad demonstrates the strength of a gecko's grip. When users move their cursor over the ad, it appears to get stuck. The cursor of each user is "collected", until pretty soon the gecko is bristling with arrows. A very sticky website indeed.
Copywriter	Magnus Andersson	
Art Director	Max Larsson von Reybiekiel	
Production	Ben Trovato	
Client	Gore-Tex, "Sticky Banner"	

Agency	Shimoni Finkelstein DraftFCB, Tel Aviv
Creative Director	Kobi Barki
Copywriters	Kobi Barki
	Noam Shamir
Art Directors	Kobi Barki
	Keren Nissim
Web Developer	Elad Ziv
Client	Meir Panim
	Soup Kitchen,
	"SMS for Lunch"

Charity Meir Panim delivers lunches to 10,000 needy children every day. The brief was to encourage people to donate at least one meal. The online ad shows a girl facing an empty plate, clearly wondering if she's ever going to eat. The copy invites users to make a donation via SMS. The moment the system receives the SMS, the banner changes immediately: the plate fills and the girl smiles.

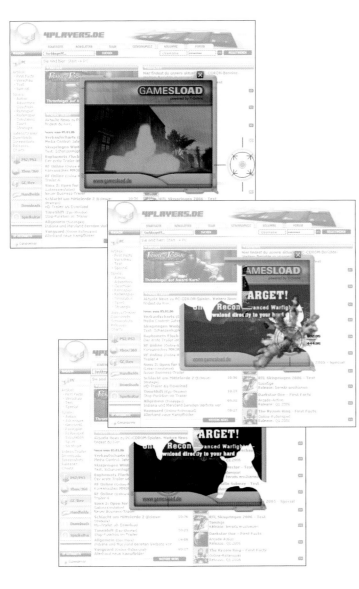

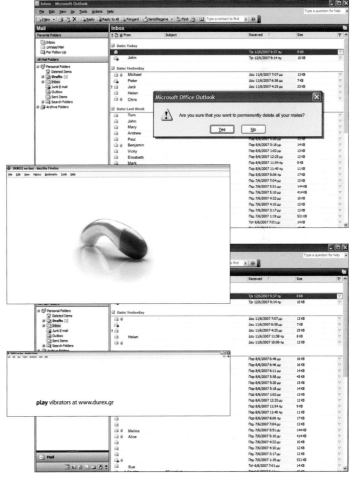

Agency	Serviceplan Munich/ Hamburg
Creative Director	Michael Frank
Copywriter	Cosima Hoellt
Art Directors	Michael Reill
	Axinja Werner
Programmer	Michael Reill
Graphic Design	Michael Reill
	Axinja Werner
Client	Gamesload, Online
	PC Game Provider,
	"First Play, Then Pay"

Gamesload.de invites customers to test its video games before buying. This ad dramatises the idea: "First play, then pay." The pop-up format is adapted in an entertaining way for once, plunging a user directly into one of the brand's top-selling games and encouraging them to play until they're utterly hooked and determined to buy the full version.

Agency	McCann Erickson Athens
Creative Director	Anna Stilianaki
Copywriter	Maria Alexiou
Art Director	Sonia Haritidi
Designer	Yannis Ioannides
Client	Durex Play Range,
	"Delete Males"

Durex Play is a new series of vibrators created by Durex. A viral email was sent to women with subject heading: "For pleasure out of the box, open attachment!" The attachment contained an .exe file with the appropriate title "Delete Males". Resembling an Outlook Inbox, it selectively deleted all the male names. The message was clear: the Durex Play vibrator has made men redundant!

Agency	Far From Hollywood, Copenhagen	This fake TV news item recounts an unlikely project by the Danish police to reduce speeding in urban areas. As the
Creative Directors	Charlie Fisher Morten Hoffmann Larsen	newscaster explains, a number of attractive "Bikini Bandits" – in fact, topless young
Copywriter	Charlie Fisher	blondes – were placed at strategic points along the roadside with signs indicating the
Production	Far From Hollywood	speed limit. At the sight of blonde hair and
Director	Peter Harton	jiggling breasts, men instinctively slammed
Producer	Morten Hoffmann Larsen	on their brakes. Quite a few traffic jams
Client	Danish Road Safety Council, "Speed Bandits"	were caused. In reality, it's a humorous way of encouraging debate over speeding.

Agency	Abbott Mead Vickers BBDO, London
Creative Director	Paul Brazier
Copywriters	Selda Enver
	Shaheed Peera
Art Directors	Shaheed Peera
	Selda Enver
Production	Gorgeous Enterprises, London
Director	Tom Carty
Producers	Ciska Faulkner
	Paul Goodwin
Client	ABC
	Against Breast Cancer, "Anyone"

A pole dancer goes through her teasing routine, finally removing her top. That's when we see that she's had a mastectomy. Anyone can get breast cancer, warns this public awareness spot.

Agency	Saatchi & Saatchi, Copenhagen
Creative Director	Simon Wooller
Copywriters	Lasse Bækbo Hinke
	Rasmus Petersen
Art Directors	Lasse Bækbo Hinke
	Rasmus Petersen
Production	Saatchi & Saatchi Film
Director	Jonas Arnby
Producer	Anna-Marie Elkjær
VFX/Flame	Jan Tvilling
Client	Quiksilver, "Dynamite Surfing"

"Urban surfers" approach a river in the centre of a city. As one of the team paddles into the middle of the river on his surfboard, another lobs a hissing stick of dynamite from a nearby bridge. The resulting explosion causes a wave that enables the surfer to jump on his board and pull a few fancy moves before the boiling waters subside. The grainy quality of the film captures the brand values of hip surf, skate and snowboard brand Quiksilver.

Agency	& Co., Copenhagen
Creative Director	Thomas Hoffmann
Art Directors	Thomas Hoffmann
	Martin Storegaard
Director	Joachim Nielsen
Client	JBS Underwear, "Naked Men"

How do you promote men's underwear when men clearly don't want to look at images of naked men? Simple: you get a beautiful girl, dress her in a pristine pair of JBS men's pants – and nothing else – and then get her to do guy stuff. Sashaying around her apartment, the girl belches, scratches her arse, puts beer on her cereal and farts joyfully. Her manners aren't pretty, but for the male of the species, it's a lot more fun than watching a guy do the same thing.

Agencies — Lowe Brindfors, Stockholm, Lowe London
Copywriter — Henrik Haeger
Art Directors — Tim Scheibel
Johan Tesch
Noel Pretorius
Production — Alphabetical Order
Producer — Espen Bekkebråten
Motion Design — Dread
Programmer — Alex Kerber
Client — Artois, "Le Passage"

A UK campaign for Stella Artois developed the theme "Pass on something good", referring to the heritage and tradition behind the beer. An animated film dramatized this idea by bringing to life "The Brewmaster": a cartoon figure apparently inspired by 1920s French poster genius Cassandre. Throughout the film "Le Passage", the Brewmaster passes on something good – the beer – from one scene to the next. And each scene links to different parts of the Stella Artois website, including campaign micro-sites and commercials.

Agency — Nordpol+ Hamburg
Creative Director — Lars Ruehmann
Copywriters — Ingmar Bartels
Sebastian Behrendt
Art Directors — Dominik Anweiler
Bertrand Kirschenhofer
Tim Schierwater
Production — Bigfish, Berlin
Director — Marc R. Wilkins
Producer — Andrea Roman
Client — Meinestadt.de
Internet Directory,
"Open Cities"

This compelling viral film depicts cities around the world with all the walls removed. We get to see what a city would look like if everything was "open" to our curious gaze. The viral ad is for an internet directory that makes cities, their businesses and their inhabitants accessible to everyone.

Agency — Leo Burnett, Milan
Creative Directors — Sergio Rodriguez
Enrico Dorizza
Copywriter — Sofia Ambrosini
Art Director — Stefano Volpi
Production — The Family, Milan
Miracle Production, Milan
Director — Kathryn Bigelow
Producers — Stefano Quaglia
Antonello Filosa
Client — Pirelli P Zero,
"Mission Zero"

Like BMW before it, Pirelli is positioning itself as a provider of "advertainment" with a series of expensive online films. In the latest version, Pirelli ups the ante as action director Kathryn Bigelow puts superstar Uma Thurman through her paces in a yellow Lamborghini. The car is kitted out with Pirelli P Zero tyres, naturally. The action is relentless and both the star and the car look suitably gorgeous.

Agency	Tribal DDB Germany, Hamburg
Creative Directors	Amir Kassaei
	Stefan Schulte
	Friedrich v. Zitzewitz
	Bert Peulecke
Copywriters	Ludwig Berndl
	Jan Hertel
	Catharina Hauernherm
	Philip Bolland
	Christian Fries
	Angela Gillmann
Art Directors	Kristoffer Heilemann
	Thomas Bober
	Torben Cording
	Alexandra Sievers
	Tim Schmitt
Producers	Boris Schepker
	Michael Blendow
Programmers	Marc Hitzmann
	Sascha Hertel
	Gregory Jacob
	André Wischnewski
Client	Volkswagen Golf, "Schlämmer's Quest"

To promote the VW Golf as "the people's car", the agency created a "typical German" named Horst Schlämmer. After promoting this amusing character in the mainstream press, the agency gave Schlämmer his own video blog. The plot? The inept Horst tries to get his driving licence in order to have more success with women. For eight weeks, visitors to the blog could follow their hero's misadventures in a series of hilarious films. Tales of his deeds spread online and captivated the media. Finally, the website revealed that it was all a promotion for the Golf. But nobody minded, as they'd been well entertained along the way.

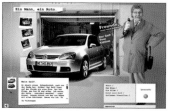 

Agency	JWT, Paris
Creative Directors	Vincent Pedrocchi
	Xavier Beauregard
Copywriter	Vincent Pedrocchi
Art Director	Xavier Beauregard
Production	Wanda, Paris
Director	Claude Fayolle
Producer	Elisabeth Boitte
Client	Wilkinson Quattro Titanium, "Fight for Kisses"

This animated film – a trailer for an online game – features a man who has been deprived of his wife's affectionate kisses ever since their baby boy was born. It's because the baby has far softer skin than the man's stubbly cheeks can offer. That's until the new Quattro Titanium razor from Wilkinson comes along. Now the man's jaw is silky again, he wins back his wife's kisses. But there's one problem: his jealous baby wants revenge...

Agency	Redurban, Amsterdam
Creative Directors	Jelle Kolleman
	Robert Hagendoorn
Copywriter	Robert Hagendoorn
Art Director	Guido de Ridder
Production	25FPS
Director	Tim Oliehoek
Producers	Bas Pinkse
	Hanneke Kramer
	Patrick Nelemans
Web Director	Kees van Dorp
Client	De Lotto, "Millionaire – The Film"

Dutch lotto is known for its campaign about "the risk" of becoming a millionaire. So could you handle the millionaire lifestyle? The agency teamed up with director Tim Oliehoek for a short film in which users could decide the outcome of the narrative. It was described as "more interactive than YouTube and more accessible than conventional gaming".

Poster

an advertising or information bill with visually laid-out design of text and illustrations.
The earliest examples of posters were produced
in the late 14th century, when paper printing
was introduced in Europe. Small editions of
leaflets, illustrated with woodcuts, were used
by booksellers and theatrical companies, and
also for political propaganda. Until the 1790s,
both single-sheet printing and posters were
used. During the French Revolution etching
techniques were rationalized and posters were
used to a greater extent for propaganda and
information purposes.
(Source: NE/National Encyclopedia)

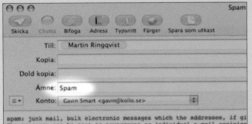

spam: junk mail, bulk electronic messages which the addressee, if gi
The messages can be sent to newsgroups or individual e-mail recipien
controversial and organizations and individuals have started to figh
compared to advertising via telephone, but with the difference that
than the receiver.

On April 1, 2004 a law was introduced in Sweden to obstruct spam wit
included). The receiver (private individuals or private firms) must
Furthermore, e-mail advertising must include a valid address of the
that no e-mail advertising is wanted. However, the requirement that
person has already purchased goods or services from a company and, i
Sweden follows an EU directive concerning a common European legislat
and other legal entities.

The word spam may possibly derive from a sketch by the comic group M

Business card

a small card made of thin carton with the owner's name
and, usually, address. In Europe, business cards were introduced in the 16th century. Similar objects, large and
made of silk, existed earlier in old China. Visiting cards
became common in the France of Louis XIV since they
simplified the very complicated visiting system among
the aristocracy. *(Source: NE/National Encyclopedia)*

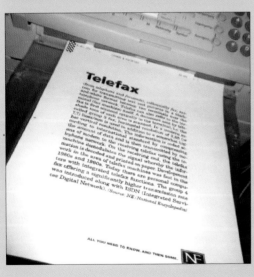

Agency   Forsman & Bodenfors, Gothenburg
Client   NE, The Swedish National Encyclopedia

What if the whole world became an encyclopedia,
with objects troubling to describe themselves to
onlookers? That was the idea behind this highly
integrated but cost-effective operation for The
Swedish National Encyclopedia. More than 50
different media were used, including posters,
balloons, press ads, toilet paper, flags, stickers,
TV spots, screensavers and viral films. The slogan
was: "All you need to know. And then some."

Cheese

a fresh or matured milk product made from whey after coagulation or other treatment of milk or milk product. Milk from cows, sheep or goats is used for cheese production. Cheese contains most of milk's fat, protein and calcium in a sustainable, concentrated form.
(Source: NE/National Encyclopedia)

ALL YOU NEED TO KNOW. AND THEN SOME. NE

Toilet paper

(soft) sanitary paper used for drying or cleaning after relieving oneself: *a roll of toilet paper.*
(Source: NE/National Encyclopedia)

ALL YOU NEED TO KNOW. AND THEN SOME. NE

Toilet paper
(soft ...

Balloon

from French *ballon* 'air' meaning 'air balloon', 'large ball', 'football' from north Italian *ballone*, compare Italian *pallone* for 'air balloon', 'football') a light and gasproof case filled with hot air or a gas lighter than air, such as hydrogen or helium.
(Source: NE/National Encyclopedia)

ALL YOU NEED TO KNOW. AND THEN SOME. NE

Screen saver

a computer program starting up automatically when the user has been passive, for a certain period, in operating the keyboard and the mouse. The screen saver's job is to vary the picture on screens made of cathode-ray tubes as as to avoid the risk of a immobile picture burning into the tube. For LCD-type screens there is no such risk and screen savers now often serve a decorative and safety-promoting purpose. *(Source: NE/National Encyclopedia)*

ALL YOU NEED TO KNOW. AND THEN SOME. NE

Poster

an advertising or information bill with visually laid-out design of text and illustrations. The earliest examples of posters were produced in the late 14th century, when paper printing was introduced in Europe. Small editions of leaflets, illustrated with woodcuts, were used by booksellers and theatrical companies, and also for political propaganda. Until the 1790s, both single-sheet printing and posters were used. During the French Revolution etching techniques were rationalized and posters were used to a greater extent for propaganda and information purposes.
(Source: NE/Natinal Encyclopedia)

ALL YOU NEED TO KNOW. AND THEN SOME. NE

Plastic bag

a mouldable enclosing container with an opening at one end.
(Source: NE/National Encyclopedia)

ALL YOU NEED TO KNOW. AND THEN SOME. NE

Agency | .start, Munich
Creative Directors | Marco Mehrwald
| Shin Oh
| Andreas Teigeler
Copywriters | Gunnar Immisch
| Ulrike Dreyheller
| Bjoern Pfarr
| Nils Treutlein
Art Directors | Verena Janzik
| Kathrin Flake
| Michael Fuesslin
Production | Florian Seidel
Programmers | Klaus Neher
| Florian Schleuppner
| Albert Huber
| Sandra Savickyte
| Alexander Schliebner
| Hermann Schroefl
Client | Mini,
| "Safety Features"
| Campaign

As well as being fun, the Mini is equipped with extensive safety features. In order to communicate these features, an online record label called Def Mini was created. But all the bands and their songs have one thing in common: they're all about the Mini and its outstanding safety, as summarised by the slogan: "Live fast. Die old." Visitors can watch music videos: for example, The Disc Brakes performing "Save Me". All the bands have their own web pages featuring screen savers, games and other goodies. Look out for heavy-metal band Xenon or the electro-pop combo Rain Sensor.

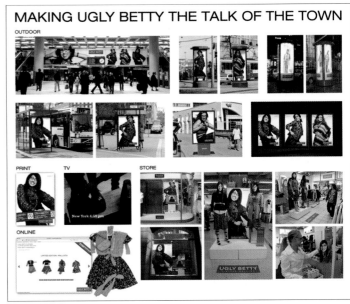

388 Integrated Campaigns

Agency | Scholz & Friends, Stockholm
Creative Directors | Zeke Tastas
| Leo Dahlin
Copywriters | Leo Dahlin
| Zeke Tastas
Art Directors | Zeke Tastas
| Leo Dahlin
| Fredrik Wallgren
| Erik Olsson
Illustrators | Mikael Eriksson
| Rithuset
Client | Castillo de Gredos

Castillo de Gredos wine wanted to revitalise its brand with a digital campaign. The agency created the imaginary village of Castillo de Gredos, a place that sums up everything that makes Spain great: the sun, the fiesta and the "Olé!" attitude. The village was represented by the count El Conde Francisco de Gredos, who suddenly cropped up across the web. He appeared on social networking sites, attended real-life parties and starred in amusing viral films. All this led users to a site about the village – and about the wine.

Agency | Hasan & Partners, Helsinki
Creative Director | Timi Petersen
Copywriter | Saku Everi
Art Director | Mikael Nemeschansky
Photographers | Peter Gehrke
| Adamsky
Graphic Desinger | Jarkko Talonpoika
Producer | Katie Rinki
Client | Channel Four Finland, "Ugly Betty" Campaign

Ugly Betty is a US TV series about a plain but big-hearted girl working in the looks-obsessed fashion industry. To promote the launch of the series on Channel Four Finland, a real clothing brand called Ugly Betty was created – and sold in selected stores. The collection was promoted on all the media platforms you might expect a real fashion brand to choose: outdoor, TV, web and point of sale.

Agency	DDB Germany, Hamburg & Berlin	The integrated tale of "ordinary German" Horst Schlämmer and his attempts to get his driving licence delighted audiences across the country. As well as visitors to his online video diary, Horst attracted the attention of the mainstream media and became a star in his own right.
Executive CD	Amir Kassaei	
Creative Directors	Amir Kassaei	
	Stefan Schulte	
	Friedrich v. Zitzewitz	
	Bert Peulecke	
Copywriters	Ludwig Berndl	
	Jan Hertel	
	Catharina Hauernherm	
	Philip Bolland	
	Christian Fries	
Art Directors	Kristoffer Heilemann	
	Thomas Bober	
	Torben Cording	
	Alexandra Sievers	
	Tim Schmitt	
Producers	Boris Schepker	
	Michael Blendow	
Programmers	Marc Hitzmann	
	Sacha Hertel	
Photographers	Markus Bachmann	
	Sven Schrader	
Client	Volkswagen Golf, "Horst Schlämmer" Campaign	

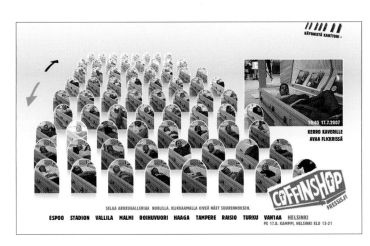

Agency	Hasan & Partners, Helsinki	The Finnish Cancer Society wanted to encourage young people to quit smoking. The first move was to open and promote a real "Coffin Shop", in which teenage smokers could be photographed laying in pink coffins. The photos were posted on a website. At the same time, muzak that served as "hymns" in the shop was released as a disc and downloads. In return for giving up smoking, teens were given a subscription to a mobile service with built-in blogging capability. Now their peer group is in their back pocket – where their cigarettes used to be.
Copywriters	Timo Livari	
	Saku Knopp	
Art Directors	Ale Lauraeus	
	Antero Nuutinen	
	Maria Kämäri	
Producer	Antti Zetterbrg	
Dev. Manager	Virve Laivisto	
Photographer	Pekka Mustonen	
Client	Cancer Society of Finland, "Coffin Shop" Campaign	

Agency	Selmore, Amsterdam	Which Dutch company is next in line to be snapped up by a foreign corporation? This question drove a campaign promoting the investigative nature of the newspaper De Volkskrant. First of all, a guerrilla advertising campaign involved placing two question marks next to the signs outside leading Dutch firms – from KLM to Heineken. The stunt was covered by the media, but nobody knew who was behind it. Finally, De Volkskrant revealed itself with a TV spot that resembled a short news report about the future of Dutch industry. Need to know? De Volkskrant.
Creative Directors	Poppe van Pelt	
	Diederick Hillenius	
Copywriters	Poppe van Pelt	
	Peter van der Wijk	
Art Director	Diederick Hillenius	
Client	De Volkskrant Newspaper, "Question Marks" Campaign	

Agencies	Nitro, London
	Framfab, Copenhagen
Creative Directors	Paul Shearer
	Rasmus Frandsen
Copywriters	Paul Shearer
	Dave Jennings
	Andrew Smart
Art Directors	Paul Shearer
	Dave Jennings
	Eduardo Marques
	Toke Kristensen
Illustrator	Stevie Laux
Producers	Paul Maingot
	G. Civitillo
Tech. Director	Jesper Arvidson
Project Manager	Martin Ludvigsen
Digital Director	Danny Tawiah
Flash	Philip Heyde
Video Editors	Rune Milton
	Ron Gelfer
Client	Nike T90 Football Boot
	"The 'Put it Where You
	Want it' Tour"

When you claim to have designed the world's most accurate football boot, you have to prove it. Nike challenged the world's most accurate footballers to try out the T90. The resulting films appeared on nikefootball.com. On the same site, amateur sharpshooters were encouraged to download T90 targets and demonstrate their pinpoint accuracy. They filmed themselves and uploaded the clips to the site. The films appeared alongside those of the soccer superstars. Footballers of all levels revelled in the opportunity to show off and sharpen their skills.

Agency	Forsman & Bodenfors,
	Gothenburg
Production	B-Reel
Client	Ving Travel,
	"How Many Countries?"
	Campaign

Ving is Sweden's largest travel company, offering trips to a mind-boggling array of destinations. To help customers tailor their ideal trip, Ving introduced an online service called the Travel Finder. On its website, an array of sliders allows users to fine-tune aspects of their vacation: price of hotel, number of nearby beaches, shopping facilities versus cultural attractions. And once they've found the trip that best matches their search, they can book. The service was promoted via TV, print, web and viral advertising.

Agencies	Forsman & Bodenfors,
	Gothenburg
	Starcom, Stockholm
Production	Frost
Client	Tele2,
	"Champion" Campaign

The task was the launch of Tele2 Champion: the cheapest phone service in Sweden. But how much can one person talk on the phone in a single day? Six celebrities – each one representing a popular topic of conversation – competed to see who could talk the most on the phone. On the campaign site, users could send their telephone number to the celebrity they had always dreamed of getting a phone call from. The resulting phone calls where broadcast live over the web.

Agencies	Lowe Brindfors, Stockholm	Postcards, posters, an online trailer
	Lowe London	and a website all formed part of the
Creative Director	Ed Morris	"Pass on something good" campaign
Copywriters	Henrik Haeger	for Stella Artois beer in the UK. The
	Patrick McClelland	link between them was a cartoon
Art Directors	Tim Scheibel	figure called "The Brewmaster",
	Johan Tesch	apparently inspired by the work of
	Noel Pretorius	1920s French illustrator Cassandre.
	Simon Morris	
Illustrator	David Lawrence	
Designer	Noel Pretorius	
Production	Alphabetical Order	
Producers	Espen Bekkebråten	
	Gary Wallis	
Flash	Dread	
Client	Artois	

Agency	CHI & Partners,	When the Carphone Warehouse sponsored
	London	The X Factor – a TV show that selects future
Creative Directors	Warren Moore	pop stars from the public – it decided to let
	Thiago De Moraes	ordinary people star in its ads. Contestants
Copywriter	Tom Skinner	could call a free number and sing into
Art Director	Rick Standley	their mobile phones. The recording was
Production	Unit 9	then uploaded to the TV show's site,
Producer	Kingsley Pang	where it was rated by the judges. Every
Client	Carphone	week, the best (and worst!) auditions
	Warehouse,	were transformed into ads, which played
	"The X Factor	during the show. In the first few weeks
	Challenge"	the operation attracted more than 1,800
		auditions and over 115,000 votes.

Agency	Nitro, London	When Nike wanted to increase its presence
Creative Directors	Paul Shearer	in Russia, it devised an initiative to connect
	Tom Evans	with Russian kids and encourage them
Copywriters & ADs	Olly Farrington	to play sport. Having found that young
	Neil Richardson	Russians felt restricted in their daily lives,
	Paul Shearer	Nike showed them that sport was a way
Photographer	Rick Guest	to break free. Using the theme "Don't
Director	Paul Shearer	Let Anything Stop You", it challenged
Producer	Amy Sherwin	and motivated kids through traditional
Client	Nike Russia,	media, while helping them to "play" with
	"Don't Let Anything	a co-ordinated campaign of live events,
	Stop You"	competitions and promotions. All these
	Campaign	initiatives were linked to a central website.